Situation Red, The UFO Siege!

Situation Red,
The UFO Siege!

by
Leonard H. Stringfield

WITH A FOREWORD BY
MAJOR DONALD E. KEYHOE,
USMC (Ret.)

DOUBLEDAY & COMPANY, INC.
GARDEN CITY, NEW YORK
1977

The author and publisher express their appreciation to the following for permission to include the material indicated:

Letters for publication from John Acuff, Director of NICAP; Walter Andrus, MUFON Director; Thomas Eichkoff; Robert C. Gardner; Senator Barry Goldwater; Horacio Gonzales G.; Dennis Hauck, Director of International UFO Registry; Major Donald E. Keyhoe, USMC (Ret.); John B. Musgrave; William Spaulding, Director, Ground Saucer Watch; Ray Stanford, Director, Project Starlight International; Major Richard E. Stevenson, USAF; Dr. Clyde Tombaugh.

Unpublished material for use in this book from Ted Bloecher; David Branch; Gordon Cooper; Charles Crecos; Mrs. Idabel Epperson; Richard Lee Hoffman; Dr. J. Allen Hynek; Bob Klinn; Edward F. O'Herin; Dr. Leo Sprinkle, PR Director of MUFON; Ray Stanford, Director, Project Starlight International.

American Institute of Aeronautics and Astronautics—Los Angeles Section, publisher of *Thesis/Antithesis* and joint sponsor with World Futures Society—Los Angeles Chapter, of the symposium at which the following papers were presented and from which excerpts used in this book were taken:

Dr. J. Allen Hynek, "On the Problem of UFO Hypothesis"; Dr. Jacques Vallee, "The Psycho-Physical Nature of UFO Reality"; Stanton T. Friedman, "A Scientific Approach to Flying Saucer Behavior."

Center for UFO Studies (Dr. J. Allen Hynek, Director) for material from the *Proceedings of the 1976 CUFOS Conference*, Chicago, May 2, 1976: Dr. David Jacobs, "UFO Research and the ETH . . ."; Wido Hoville, "UFOs & Parapsychology." Copyright © 1976 by Center for UFO Studies, Evanston, Illinois.

Raymond Fowler for material from UFOs: INTERPLANETARY VISITORS, Copyright © 1974 by Raymond E. Fowler. Appeared in *Official UFO* (April, 1976); Copyright © 1976 by Countrywide Publications, Inc.

MUFON (Walter Andrus, Director) for use of *Symposium Proceedings* of 1973 and 1974.

Skylook (Dwight Connelly, Editor) and Ann Druffel for the article. "The Mystery Helicopters" (February, 1976); and the magazine for the article "Aircraft" (August, 1975). Copyright © 1975, 1976 by Skylook, the UFO Monthly, 26 Edgewood Drive, Quincy, Illinois.

Library of Congress Cataloging in Publication Data

Stringfield, Leonard H
Situation red.

1. Flying saucers. I. Title.
TL789.S83   001.9′42
ISBN 0-385-12316-7
Library of Congress Catalog Card Number 76–42403

To my wife, Dell; daughters, Colette, Denise and Camille; grandchildren, Erich and Beau; and my mother; for their abiding faith in me. May they in their time know the truth about a stubborn mystery: the UFO.

Contents

Acknowledgment

There is little of the idyllic in writing nonfiction and even less when the subject is the UFO. Every author dealing with the controversial UFO knows, as I do, that he may be leading with his vulnerable chin.

One, then, must be "moved" or compelled by some great urgency to want to write a book about ufology. I have felt this urgency, a feeling that is shared by many of my colleagues. But ufology holds many theoretical views that command respect. Many who espouse differing views have been generous contributors to my research and my book.

To those lending me the encouragement to write a book, I am especially indebted to Bill Whitaker, Major Donald E. Keyhoe, Patricia McGowan, and George Quigley, whose optimism triggered my typewriter into action.

Also, my sincerest gratitude goes to Richard Hall and my English cousin, Raymond Eckersley, visiting from London, for their editorial advice; to William Spaulding, Joseph Brill, and Mrs. Idabel Epperson for their generous contributions of material including photographs.

Names of contributors are as endless as the vast number of uncelebrated field investigators who deserve recognition. But I want especially to thank Tom Adams, Raymond Fowler, Ted Bloecher, Dr. David Saunders, Dr. Leo Sprinkle, David Webb, Dr. David Jacobs, Sherman Larsen, Dr. Berthold Schwarz, Ted Phillips, Stan Gordon, Edward O'Herin, Jim Kibel, Dr. Bruce Maccabee, and Charles Bowen, editor of the British *Flying Saucer Review*. In addition, I should like to thank Senator Barry Goldwater and Astronaut Gordon Cooper for their cooperation.

And of the Ohio group I am indebted to Charles and Geri

Wilhelm, Richard Hoffman, Larry Moyers, Jerry Black, Jim Miller, Thomas Stegmaier, Jim Carnes, David Dobbs, Mrs. Janet Tubbs, Earl Neff, Jim Miceli, and Pat Kaforey.

A special tribute, of course, to the directors of the major research groups for their invaluable assistance. Here I must single out Walter Andrus, director of the Mutual UFO Network; Dr. J. Allen Hynek, director of the Center for UFO Studies, and his former secretary, Miss Margo Metegrano; Dr. Dennis Hauck, director of the International UFO Registry; Ray Stanford, director of Project Starlight International; James and Coral Lorenzen, directors of the Aerial Phenomena Research Organization; and John Acuff, director of the National Investigation Committee on Aerial Phenomena.

Foreword

In *Situation Red, The UFO Siege!* Len Stringfield makes a valuable contribution toward ending the long Air Force censorship. Covering his twenty-six years of investigations, he presents irrefutable evidence of UFO reality and proof of the cover-up.

Having known Len since 1953, I can confirm his detailed knowledge of the UFO problem. One surprising—and enlightening—experience occurred in the early fifties, when Len, publishing a nationally distributed UFO research bulletin, was selected by the Air Force for an off-the-record role in the official reporting system. Assigned a telephone code number, he was instructed to screen and transmit important area sightings immediately from all sources—the police, the media and the Ground Observer Corps—to the Air Filter Center of the Air Defense Command in Columbus, Ohio. Significantly, more than once, his special phone was connected with interceptors through Air Force base radio so he could help guide the pilots to nearby low-flying UFOs. Through his hidden operation, Stringfield learned of the serious Air Force concern over UFOs and its secret attempts to capture one of these mysterious objects.

Then, suddenly, the GOC reporting system was ended, as Air Force Headquarters tightened the cover-up. Some early investigators became discouraged when the Air Force thwarted their efforts to get the truth about UFOs. But Len only increased his attempts to secure verified evidence. In 1957 he became Public Relations Advisor and field investigator for the National Investigations Committee on Aerial Phenomena, serving through the thirteen-year period when I was the NICAP director.

In recent years, Len has concentrated on the puzzling and at times frightening effects caused by UFOs. Some writers have seized on this disturbing phase and—without careful research—have rushed out books or articles warning that we are in grave danger. In contrast, Len has carefully evaluated hundreds of U.S. and foreign "scare" reports, weeding out hoaxes and dubious claims before considering cases involving competent and reliable observers.

The strange UFO effects and UFO-linked incidents fall into four general classes:

I. Interference with plane communications and instruments, home appliances, television, car ignition and lights, and extensive power failures causing blackouts in cities.

II. Physical effects on humans during close UFO approaches to cars or people on the ground, including burns (mostly minor), confused thinking and in some cases memory blackouts.

III. Aircraft crashes and lesser accidents following close UFO encounters, and the disappearance of military planes pursuing these seemingly controlled objects.

IV. Reported abductions of humans who claim to have been taken aboard alien spacecraft, examined and returned to Earth unharmed.

In Class I, the effect has been proved by solid evidence. In II, there is enough evidence from responsible witnesses to support at least some of the claims. The recorded cases in III, thought relatively few in number, indicate that UFOs caused the disasters, accidentally or deliberately. This is not necessarily proof of hostility; the UFOs' actions could have been reactions to Air Force pursuits and occasional firing, possibly warnings for us to cease capture attempts. The abduction claims in IV, if true, could be frightening even though no harm has been reported. However, most of such stories have been apparent hoaxes. But the few reports that come from reputable witnesses have kept the question open. As Len points out, even if only one such claim is true, it could reveal a sobering situation.

As his book makes plain, something very strange, possibly serious, is going on. In 1962 the Space Science Board of the National Academy of Sciences made this powerful statement:

"If life does indeed exist on another planet . . . that discovery will have an enormous and lasting impact on people of every race and culture the world over. . . ."

If an advanced alien race is observing our world, we should be told the truth—even if the Air Force does not have all the answers. The cover-up must be ended. The public should be sensibly prepared—for whatever may develop.

Major Donald E. Keyhoe
USMC (Ret.)

Introduction

Since the advent of the UFO, dating back officially to the "foo fighter" of World War II, Earth's civilization has been the obvious target of an alien surveillance.

Close encounters with the UFO on the ground and in the air have been frightening experiences for thousands of human beings worldwide—some sent into a state of shock. This alone is disconcerting, but my greatest concern goes to the victim suffering physical effects: flesh burns, eye damage, paralysis or the traumatic experience of a time lapse, and, beyond that, the indignities of an alleged abduction. Also of concern is the effect on man's necessities—power outages in his city, his automobile, his home appliances—and to military aircraft that dared to challenge the interloper.

Encounters affecting man tell a sobering story. Their supporting evidence has been too long silenced—facts the public should know. In *Situation Red, The UFO Siege!* I bring these facts into present-day focus. My purpose is *not* to scare, sensationalize or paint a picture of doom, nor is it an attempt to enlighten the ufologist, who is already conversant with the complex problems. Basically, my book is a narrative history, much of it personalized, of UFO events, with special emphasis put on a collection of incredible UFO reports made by credible people—some so bizarre they stagger the imagination.

For too long the general public has been misled by official denials claiming that a real UFO—a "nut and bolt" alien craft—does not exist. UFO research today is too busy *researching* to continue the fight against secrecy. In its ranks are serious, dedicated professionals and a growing number of scientists who give freely of their own time. To this end I serve a number of major research groups: the Mutual UFO Network as a board member and director of public relations, the Center for UFO Studies as an associate in field investigation, the International UFO Registry as a board member, and the Ground Saucer Watch as an investigator for Ohio.

While ufology today has certainly gained respectability, there still remain a stack of unresolved issues as research's methodology reaches for the final answer. It seems the more that is learned the greater is the problem of fitting man's square peg of thinking into a round hole of the UFO's abstract dimensions. Thus, ufology is at a crossroad. While it knows incontrovertibly that the UFO exists and is intelligently controlled, it remains disturbing to *not know* its source, its nature, and the purpose in keeping Earth under constant surveillance.

Since the great siege of 1973, there are increasing rumors, hints and leaks that suggest that soon there may be an official lifting of the lid that conceals the truth about the UFO. Once we know the truth, from whatever source, perhaps the world will find cause to unite. The answer may even bear a cornucopia of goodness for man, a sharing of scientific and cultural knowledge—or it may spell man's ultimate doom.

What is important is knowing the truth so that man can rediscover himself.

Leonard H. Stringfield

PART I

The UFO Status Quo

I

The Buildup

Serious UFO research groups, who tirelessly sift, sort, and systematize reports, will never forget 1973.

Autumn of that year staged the biggest UFO flap since bush pilot Ken Arnold captured headlines in 1947 with his sighting of nine "saucer-like things" over Mt. Rainier, Washington.

The tornadic effect of 1973's flap was to stun a nation already troubled by Watergate and a Middle East crisis. At its peak, October 17—in one 24-hour period—there were more than fifty cities and towns reporting concentrated UFO activity. Switchboards of the news media and police were jammed by calls from frightened citizens. Many reported extraordinary lighted objects at low levels; others claimed closer encounters.

The Air Force was cool to the UFO's incursive action. Publicly they said nothing. Since the termination of their UFO investigative agency known as Project Bluebook, in 1969, they were no longer charged with the responsibility of investigating UFO reports. The demise of Project Bluebook was a direct result of a government-funded three-year study headed by the late Dr. Edward U. Condon and headquartered at the University of Colorado. In his summary report, Condon dismissed the UFO as a problem unworthy of further scientific research.

I knew the inside story of the Condon project, its design to cover up the facts about UFOs, and I knew about its internal fiasco triggered by the project's fellow scientists who heatedly disagreed with Condon's summary. Dissidents were fired; others resigned.

Despite the project's questionable tactics, I still glimpsed a hope that the Air Force, the defender of the nation's skies, would come up with a new, realistic "line"—especially for facing up to a crisis.

At the flap's peak, hoping to get word of an official shift in policy, or at least a clue of emotional reaction, I called the Air Force press desk in Washington. I reached Major John Duemmel, Air Force information officer. No change!

Duemmel emphatically reminded me that the Air Force since 1969 was no longer in the UFO business. He also restated the Air Force's "canned" position claiming that the UFOs, past or present, posed no threat to the security of the United States. Duemmel was careful and terse with his comments, but I also knew, after twenty-three years of dealing with Air Force techniques in hiding the facts about UFOs, that the current siege was being monitored by the North American Aerospace Defense Command.

In the estimation of research, the UFOs—from whatever source —touching down on hundreds of cities posed a possible threat from the skies. Inability to grasp the events in their entirety and thus to make predictions quickly brought to mind a military term to describe the fluid conditions: *SITUATION RED!*

It all began spottily in July and August. High in the night skies, strange, glowing lights—bigger than stars and unlike aircraft— cavorted over the Carolinas and Georgia. By September, the flap had picked up momentum, lashing out across the Deep South. Quickly it swerved up the Mississippi Valley, fanned out broadly over the eastern United States, and touched down like twisters in the West. Although it was not generally publicized, parts of California were hard hit.

Common targets for this new, low-level phase of reconnaissance, mostly over sparsely populated areas, were a solitary house, a barn, a watercourse, a lone car or tractor-trailer on a lightly traveled road, or, for some inexplicable reason, as evidenced in so many reports, a schoolhouse.

A typical night during the early siege is described in the UPI news-wire release datelined Griffin, Georgia, September 10:

019A
UFO 9–10
DAY LD

Griffin, Ga. (UPI)—New reports of strange hovering objects with brightly-colored lights were received Sunday night by local authorities as part of a rash of recent sightings of unidentified flying objects in the Southeast.

For nearly two weeks, reports of UFOs have flooded authorities in Central and South Georgia, Alabama, Tennessee and Florida. The reports have come from civilians, military policemen, local law enforcement officers and state troopers.

Sunday night, a Spalding County deputy answered a call reporting an object hovering over a house. The deputy radioed his office that he saw "two red lights descending slowly to Earth," and then the lights disappeared.

Mrs. Hugh D. Beall told local police an "upside down cup and saucer-shaped object" hovered over her house. She said the object had gold, red and green lights on the bottom.

Mrs. Beall said the object, which she said made a "funny" noise, was too low for an airplane and was just above tree-top level. She said the lights changed colors.

There were at least two other reports in Griffin and other sightings in Newnan, Ga., 30 miles to the west.

In other weekend sightings, two military policemen at Hunter Air Force Base near Savannah reported something dived at their car as they were on routine patrol and then pursued them as they raced back to the base.

A Georgia highway patrolman in Manchester said he saw a UFO hovering at tree-top level Saturday night.

"It went over the unit (patrol car), and was going so fast there was no way he could even get close enough to identify it," said a Patrol spokesman.

Unidentified flying objects were also reported in five East Central Alabama cities early Sunday. Officer Keith

Broach of Auburn, Ala., said he saw something the size
of an airplane, which appeared red and white, changed
to green and then to white before flying away.
        UPI 09–10 01:00 AED

Discs, cones, spheres and spindle-shaped things, coming in
close, revealed metallic surfaces, domes, portholes or rotating
lights. Eleven policemen in Georgia and Alabama, in the thick of
one night's rash of sightings, agreed on the general description of
the UFO: fast-moving, noiseless, basketball-size, brightly lit with
red, green, orange, or all-white lights, blinking and revolving. Said
Georgia State Trooper Sam Taylor, interviewed by the *National
Enquirer,* who made his sighting in Manchester, "It was oblong
but not quite thin enough to make it cigar-shaped. It seemed solid
and when I saw it, it gave off a gentle white glow." Taylor, a Vietnam flying veteran, added, "I was absolutely mystified. What I
saw was certainly no airplane or natural phenomenon."

During the same wave, Patrolman Dave Maddux, of Lanett, Alabama, told the *National Enquirer,* "At first I thought I saw a star
maybe distorted by a heat haze. But then it started to move, first
toward the ground, then up again and went over a hill."

The case of the two military policemen cited in the UPI release
took place at Hunter Air Force Base, near Savannah, Georgia,
during the same wave. The two MPs, Randy Shade and Burt
Burns, were on a routine security patrol of the base, which was
scheduled for a shutdown soon. Burns, a former helicopter crew
chief, said he first spotted a cluster of lights in the sky about two
thousand feet up. The lights, he said, tracked across the sky
flashing red and orange and blue and white. The UFO then disappeared behind some trees, but fifteen minutes later, at 2:45 A.M.,
it returned. After hovering at one end of the deserted runway, its
lights flashing brilliantly, it began moving toward the MP patrol
car. Said Shade, "When it got closer, we could see the lights were
clustered underneath a metallic-looking, saucer-shaped body. I
thought it was going to hit us, at least smash the blue light on top
of our car."

Shade, who kept his foot on the gas, pushing near 100 mph
with the UFO in close pursuit, admitted that he had difficulty
keeping the car on the road at this speed and that he could hardly

see through the windshield because of the red and white flashes of the UFO's lights, which he described as "just a few feet above us."

Said MP Burt Burns, his partner, "I was terrified when the saucer chased us. I was crouched under the dashboard just waiting for it to hit our roof lights. The saucer itself wasn't lit, but we could see its outline clearly in the glow from the flashing, pulsing lights underneath it. It couldn't have been more than a couple feet above us. I reckon the saucer's size at 50 to 75 feet across."

For nearly a mile the patrol car was paced by the UFO. Shade, seized with fear, swerved off the roadway at a right-angle turn and screeched to a stop in the grass. He later reported that the UFO backed off at tree-top level and shot off into the sky and vanished.

A base spokesman, Lieutenant David Anderson, said, "There is no official explanation as to what it was. Nothing showed on radar."

Stories of the tallest kind were now making the small-town newspapers; only a few, treated tongue-in-cheek, were carried by the news wires. Nationally, Watergate had top billing; UFOs were "old hat," their credibility snuffed out by the Air Force long before.

Stories, fantasies, rumors: needed was proof, a piece of hardware, a good photograph of a UFO. A newspaperman tried to get that proof.

In Camilla, Georgia, on September 1, 1973, Chester Tatum, publisher of the *Sowega Free Press,* responding to calls from people seeing UFOs, went outdoors with his Polaroid camera and shot two photos of night lights he could not identify. The Tatum photos, showing a large blob of light—hardly proof that UFOs exist, as night photos seldom do—were scooped up by the UPI news services, but they failed to get national press coverage.

Far away from Camilla, Georgia, on the same date, September 1, in the village of Mariemont, east of Cincinnati, Ohio, there was no hint of an impending UFO crisis. My daughter's wedding was at hand, and after twenty-three years of UFO research at the highest levels, the lack of UFO activity offered a welcome diversion. To me, there were no UFOs brewing into a thunderhead in the Deep South, no Chester Tatum trying to get photographic proof, and no "saucer" chasing two MPs in a patrol car at Hunter Air Force Base.

As a matter of fact, what little UFO news that had trickled my way in recent months—reports of a light in the night sky—was shrugged off. Lights in the sky were common, and top researchers had long since declared them useless in their studies. Good sightings, the low-level, close-encounter kind causing electromagnetic effects, leaving evidence for scientific evaluation, were just not happening—or not, at least, to my knowledge.

During the early-1973 hiatus, I was already immersed in a new challenge. This was my newly built conservatory. I found in its exotic domain the opportunity to experiment ecologically with live plants—rare foliage, fernery and orchids—in a controlled atmosphere to be shared with free bird life, lizards, toads, and a pond with tropical fish. Overhead, instead of sunlight, I had carefully installed rows of Gro-Lux fluorescent lamps and a large turbulator fan to maintain even temperature and humidity. The room also provided a commercial experiment for my employer, for whom I bench-tested a new soil-buffering agent. It was a serious horticultural effort—a lot of work, but it was rewarding.

I was in the midst of photographing the comparative growth of plant-root systems as a result of extensive bench tests when Larry Moyers called me from Akron, Ohio. Moyers was the Ohio state director for Mutual UFO Network, one of the nation's prime UFO research groups, with more than 750 field investigators. I had served MUFON since its inception, in 1969, as state section director for southwestern Ohio.

Moyers, with more than fifteen years in research, voiced concern: "What's going on down there?" he asked.

I recall my response: "I'm getting a few nocturnal lights in the sky, not much else."

Moyers sounded surprised, almost disappointed. "Anything low-level?" he asked.

"Nothing," was my reply.

Moyers then rattled off a number of low-level UFO incidents occurring throughout Ohio, mostly in the north. I promised him I would check locally with my usual sources: the local media and the police.

I learned of nothing unusual, again only reports of lights in the sky. Nothing to follow up. From my early research I had learned that time is wasted checking on a light in the sky. It deserved only a note in my log just in the event I might later hear of a close encounter on that same date. Then research would benefit from its added evidence.

When September slipped into October, locally the tempo changed. UFOs were bolder, more aggressive. Calls were coming in nightly; others reached me at my office the following day. During the day at home, my wife, Dell, familiar with flap situations since 1952, took calls and made notes.

Many calls came from the growing network of reliable informants I had developed from my earliest saucer-sleuth years: old, faithful buffs who wanted to "stay in touch"; people who were well informed on military matters but preferred anonymity and scores of compatriots in serious research who knew fact from fiction in ufology.

For the reader to understand fully my historical profile in ufology, my re-emergence to "active duty" during the great UFO siege of 1973, and my present association with the major research groups, I must digress and retreat back in time. . . .

My great awakening to the seriousness of the UFO began sometime in 1950. Two unusual, low-level saucer sightings, which I got firsthand from genuinely sincere people, leaped into real significance. These brought into sharp focus a personal experience dating back to World War II—an incident of near disaster that I had wanted to forget. It occurred on August 28, 1945, during the delicate period of Japanese surrender. I was one of twelve 5th Air Force specialists—mine an intelligence assignment—aboard a C46 flying from Ie Shima to Iwo Jima for a stop-off, then on to Atsugi Airdrome, near Tokyo. Our flight was scheduled to land in Japan three days prior to the major occupation forces.

Approaching Iwo Jima at about ten thousand feet in a sunlit sky, I was shocked to see three teardrop-shaped objects from my starboard-side window. They were brilliantly white, like burning magnesium, and closing in on a parallel course to our C46. Suddenly our left engine feathered, and I was later to learn that the magnetic navigation-instrument needles went wild. As the C46 lost altitude, with oil spurting from the troubled engine, the pilot sounded an alert; crew and passengers were told to prepare for a ditch! I do not recall my thoughts or actions during the next, horrifying moments, but my last glimpse of the three bogies placed them about 20 degrees above the level of our transport. Flying in the same, tight formation, they faded into a cloud bank. Instantly our craft's engine revved up, and we picked up altitude and flew a steady course to land safely on Iwo Jima.

This one experience near Iwo Jima was proof enough to me in 1950 that the "foo fighter" of World War II—sometimes dubbed "kraut fireball" in the European Theater—and the flying saucer were one and the same kind of machine and from the same source: outer space! Major Donald E. Keyhoe had proclaimed the "outer space" theory as far back as 1949 in a bombshell article in *True Magazine,* and came up with even more convincing evidence in a book he published in 1953, *Flying Saucers from Outer Space.*

As the evidence piled in from the great 1952 flap, I felt uneasy about the continuing saucer probes. I pondered the disturbing facts: the rumored loss of Air Force interceptors chasing UFOs, the low-level green fireballs over Sweden and the southwestern United States, and my incident near Iwo Jima. I could not help feeling concern about the meaning behind the probes—the *intent.*

By 1953 I had had the opportunity to know Major Keyhoe on a personal basis. When we talked by phone or exchanged letters, I felt that he was honestly convinced that the Air Force was hiding the true saucer facts. With my own evidence at hand, I believed him. What were the hidden facts? *Were saucers from space hostile?*

In March 1954, certain that saucers were not U.S. or Russian secret weapons, I activated Civilian Research, Interplanetary Flying Objects (CRIFO), and published my first monthly newsletter. It was a limited run, and I charged two dollars a year for a subscription, to cover printing and mailing costs. It was the simplest way to keep my growing list of correspondents informed of the latest sightings. Response was instantaneous. In May I got national recognition when Frank Edwards, a popular radio newscaster for the Mutual Broadcasting System in Washington, D.C.—long a champion of saucers—chanced upon a copy of my newsletter. He liked it, called me for permission to announce it over the air, and advised me to get a post-office box. On May 18 Edwards urged his 10 million listeners to write for a copy. Within a week Box 1855 received 6,000 letters!

Overnight, I was put "dead center" in the UFO business. Within a few months CRIFO snowballed beyond belief. Newspapers and radio stations from coast to coast called, wanting saucer news. During this period my incoming mail maintained a steady flow of more than 100 letters a day, and with the oil burning past midnight, I made it a goal to answer at least twenty-five. Sighting reports poured in from everywhere. *Also taking note of CRIFO was the Air Force.*

On September 9, 1955, Captain Hugh McKenzie of the Air Defense Command in Columbus, Ohio, phoned me at home. He seemed keenly knowledgeable of CRIFO and its methodology. He was impressed, as I recall, by its pulling power to get firsthand sighting reports. Wanted, as he put it politely, was my cooperation, a means to get up-to-the-minute sighting reports from my vast network of sources. Then, surprisingly, he informed me that the Ground Observer Corps in southwestern Ohio was to be instructed to report UFO activity to me for screening. Screened data, weeding out a good report from a misperception such as a star or aircraft running lights, were then to be called in to the filter center of the Air Defense Command by using a telephone code number. My code was FOX TROT KILO 3-0 BLUE. I could use any phone at any time to report to the center, and all expenses were to be paid by the Air Force.

I agreed to cooperate. And I thought I knew the Air Force's reasons for concern. Again I thought of my incident at Iwo Jima and the rumored losses of our interceptors to the aggressive—or was it defensive—saucer. But the official *cooperation* was soon spelled out. Said McKenzie, "My only request is that you *not ask any questions.*"

I was later to learn from Frank Whitecotton, coordinator of the Ground Observer Corps of the Ohio Valley Civil Defense Authority, that once my screened report was processed by the 4717th Ground Observer Squadron of the Air Defense Command in Columbus, Ohio, and the UFO was confirmed by radar, jet interceptors were to be scrambled. In short, when a UFO became confirmed, all matters pertinent to that case became classified information.

As UFO sightings piled in from all sources, I kept the Air Defense Command filter center's switchboard busy with "screened" reports. Commented Captain Edward Ruppelt, the initial head of

Project Bluebook at Wright-Patterson Air Force Base, in a letter dated February 21, 1955, in which he requested information about CRIFO for a book he was writing, "I must say that you have a very effective report-collecting net established." Despite secrecy, during the course of my screening operations I learned by circuitous channels that a number of my reports ended in radar confirmation and that jets were scrambled.

On August 23, 1955, during a local flap, a bewildering incident occurred. About midnight, residents throughout the city were jarred by the roar of jets. From S.A.C. at Lockbourne AFB, south of Columbus, Ohio, the Air National Guard jets were alerted, scrambled, and were aloft over Cincinnati. The alert began when three UFOs were sighted and confirmed by radar somewhere between Columbus and Cincinnati. In the meantime, Walter Paner, superintendent of Hamilton County GOC (major, Air Force Reserve), on duty at the Mt. Healthy post, phoned me of the existent alert and relayed the word that jet interceptors were due over the area. He said the UFOs had been active over Mt. Healthy and could be seen clearly by observers from the tower.

In twelve minutes the jets, at approximately twenty thousand feet, were overhead, but poor visibility prevented me and a visiting friend from Toronto, Canada, from seeing the UFOs, which had deployed over a wide area. According to radar, the interlopers had extended thirty-seven miles south into Kentucky, as far as 234 miles north, and ten miles to the west of Cincinnati. A later call from Paner disclosed that a UFO was seen hovering in pendulum-like motions directly over the tower. At about 12:10 A.M. the interceptors made contact, and, swooping in, chased the UFO—which disappeared at incredible speed. In the meantime, the Forestville and Loveland GOC posts reported the erratic flights of UFOs to the filter center, describing them as round, brilliant white spheres and discs.

I remained on watch from my home with binoculars until 1:00 A.M., but heavy clouds prevailed, obscuring the activity. Overhead, however, the continuous din of low-flying jets reminded me of combat conditions in the Pacific campaigns, a mixed feeling of awe and anxiety while waiting for the inevitable contact with the enemy, a burst of action and its toll. Incongruously, the public, asleep or perhaps wondering about the noisy jets, did not suspect the truth.

The following morning, jet aircraft were still aloft over Greater Cincinnati, but it was not until nightfall that a UFO again was spotted by the GOC in Forestville.

Confirming reports of UFO activity also came from the GOC in Loveland and as far west as Vevay, Indiana. From a "researcher's" standpoint, the incident was extraordinary! Here, like the dawn of day, was evidence, according to radar confirmation, of a solid body, or machine; evidence, according to GOC observers, of its control and maneuverability; evidence of the Air Force's policy to scramble and intercept the UFO; and evidence of our government's concern over the UFOs invading American skies.

Equally extraordinary, I thought, was the fact that the entire incident was "cleared" for publication in my newsletter, *Orbit*. And this, too, had come about uniquely. Having written up the report as I knew it had happened, I phoned Paner at his home, asking for his advice about publishing it. He said he wasn't sure but would check with the authorities, and suggested that I call back. When I did so, minutes later, Paner told me it was perfectly acceptable as I had written it. Then, to my surprise, he volunteered additional information regarding the radar tracking, which included the distances traveled by the UFOs. For further confirmation of the UFOs' activity, I phoned the control tower of the Greater Cincinnati Airport, in Boone County, Kentucky. They, too, admitted that unidentified blips were tracked on their radar screen.

Stunned, my only rationalization was that the Air Force had suddenly changed from their program of silence, or that I was being taken under their wing for special duty, or possibly that somebody was talking out of turn. Indeed, before me was startling evidence and a startling story that Cincinnati and the world had awaited. *But the Cincinnati newspapers weren't interested!* When I phoned the *Enquirer,* they shrugged it off. A *Post* reporter took notes, but the story never appeared in print. The *Times Star,* however, stumbling with promises to send a reporter out to get all the facts, finally, after a conference between reporter and city editor, decided against it.

The following day, I learned from a Cincinnati *Times Star* reporter, Ed Chapin, that he had called Wright-Patterson to get confirmation of the incident. It was officially denied. To add to my disbelief, he said the spokesman claimed that he knew nothing of my "duties" with the Air Defense Command.

I continued my "cooperation" with the Air Force through 1956. But with the introduction of new, sophisticated sky-watch methods the GOC was disbanded and my screening duties ceased. Contrary to official UFO debunkers Captains Charles Hardin and George Gregory, successors to Ruppelt at Project Bluebook, my work for the Air Defense Command was not overlooked. Major General John A. Samford, director of Air Force Intelligence in Washington, D.C., wrote to me on March 16, 1956, "The Air Force greatly appreciates the interest which you and your organization, as well as others, have taken in the Unidentified Flying Object program. The success of this program has been, in part, due to the excellent cooperation of such individuals and groups in submitting UFO reports for consideration either directly or through various publications. These reports have become an important part of the UFO picture. A continuation of this assistance is indeed welcome. . . . In conclusion, please accept our thanks for your interest in this matter and be assured that we are always glad to receive contributions such as yours. . . ."

In 1957, CRIFO and its monthly publication, *Orbit,* bowed out of research. It was a soul-searching decision for me to deliberately knock down the blocks I had so painstakingly built up. Perhaps an apt summary of my early UFO experience is best expressed in my editorials excerpted from the final issues of *Orbit:*

"So much to say in this 36th and last issue of *Orbit.* Might say I'm relieved knowing that I will no longer thread copy through a needle, or that I must meet deadlines. Or, I might say, reaffirming my beliefs, that flying saucers are from outer space; that the Air Force is sitting atop a powder keg of information, or, that all 'contact' stories seem more fictitious than factual—but, the hardest thing to say, or admit, is that *Orbit* is now finished. To me, *Orbit* was more like a member of the family—it breathed triumph and despair, it had complexes, it joined in at the dinner table, and it was a brief sleeper. What others thought is best told in the recent deluge of letters and phone calls from readers and prominent researchers—even critics. . . .

". . . With the passing of *Orbit,* rumors will be rife in saucerdom. Dark ones will tell of mysterious men dressed in black threatening Stringfield into silence. Others will have the Air Force at work with pins-under-the-nails—and, of course, there will be the one claiming that Stringfield left for Mexico in a Cadillac with lots of loot. But the truth of the matter is that bowing out is not a goodbye from CRIFO's director."

CRIFO was to become a springboard to new ventures. When the National Investigations Committee on Aerial Phenomena (NICAP) was formed, in 1957, under the direction of Major Keyhoe, I served as public relations adviser. I held that post until 1972, at which time NICAP, on the brink of financial disaster, changed its policies and command to a new, business-oriented director, John L. Acuff. In 1969, following a two-year stint of "duty" with Dr. Condon's Colorado Project as Early Warning Coordinator, I chose to teach an evening class in UFOlogy at Mariemont High School.

In this scholastic endeavor, I tried to be objective in reviewing the UFO's historical struggle for recognition. With equal objectivity, I stressed the need for critical analysis of all UFO reports, even the classical cases, as it was my belief then, as it is now, that possibly three out of four UFO reports received have conventional explanations.

Since 1969, despite official silence, the UFO has persisted. The past and the present have not changed. There are national flaps, mini flaps in one small geographical area, and there are lulls and some long droughts when UFOs seem to have gone forever. During these cat and mouse performances, there are hundreds of incredible cases reported by credible people. Some are close encounters with multiple witnesses, some leave trace evidence in the soil. At any time, on the other end of any *one* phone call, there might be that *one* incident to break it all open!

Many spectacular calls during October 1973 seemed earmarked to be that *one* incident. During the crisis of day-by-day events, I got a call from Mrs. Geri Wilhelm. She and her husband, Charles, directors of the Ohio UFO Investigators League, with headquarters in their home in Fairfield, Ohio, were being deluged with phone calls following Geri's appearance on WLW-TV. Geri, relatively new in UFO research, was appalled by the frantic calls from people reporting UFOs up close. Some saw them land. Some even claimed they saw creatures.

The Wilhelms and I agreed to coordinate our incoming UFO raw data, but our endless phone calls from an aroused public and the demands by the local media pressing in for statements and guest appearances, allowed little time for a meaningful exchange.

Then came the big bomb! UPI news broke the story to the nation, October 15, of the two fishermen in Pascagoula, Mississippi, who claimed they were abducted into a UFO. Their captors: three grotesque creatures with crab-like hands. Promptly on the scene to investigate was Dr. J. Allen Hynek, author of *The UFO Experience: a Scientific Inquiry,* and former scientific consultant for the Air Force's Project Bluebook, and Dr. James Harder, from the University of California, Berkeley.

The fishermen, Charles Hickson and Calvin Parker, were interrogated separately, hypnotized by Harder, and even subjected to trickery to get to the truth—resorting to a hidden tape recorder when they were left alone in a room—but their "other world" tale stood up under every test.

Said Hynek, "These men have had what was to them a very real and frightening experience."

This one case, just like the many other bizarre cases making hot news during October, was the spark to bring Dr. Hynek and me together after twenty-one years of working on the UFO problem from opposite ends.

I called Hynek at Northwestern University (then chairman of the Department of Astronomy) praised him for his bold stand on the Pascagoula affair, related a case of analogous characteristics, and found myself inexorably arranging a meeting at the Marriott Inn in Columbus, Ohio. On October 27, I met him in his room amid stacks of computerized UFO print-outs, and we agreed, without rehash of our past roles, to tackle the immediate crisis head on.

It was in Columbus that I learned of Hynek's great ambition to set up the Center for UFO Studies. The base of its methodology was to be scientific!

II

Scientific Ufology

Flap situations spawn UFO incidents rich in raw data. Scientific ufology, however, will not wholly accept raw data as it usually surfaces, in anecdotal form. An anecdote may be thrilling to read, but for the ufologist—a new kind of scientist—to prove a point, it is deficient in vital technical details, statistics of every kind, knowledge about the witness, analyses of trace evidence, and many other factors that can come only after thorough investigation. Raw data is simply that, raw data; it is a preliminary necessity. In fact, it commands a high priority in research, for in its nebulous mass can be the ultimate case—that one case which may tell us that the real UFO is a vehicle from planet X. Thus, flaps are closely watched, especially the earliest-reported incidents, by witnesses who have not been swept up by the storm of hysteria.

No doubt, in the great 1973 flap in southwestern Ohio and the nation, some of the more dramatic reports were simply misperceptions of familiar objects and perhaps a few exaggerations. Many other 1973 reports, no longer "raw," with time allowed to investigate in depth, analyze, and compute, have rallied strong scientific interest. Some cases, according to Dr. Hynek's grading scale,[1] rate *significantly high* in categories of "strangeness" and "probability."

Southwestern Ohio has had sporadic, short, but intense flaps since 1973. Following is a brief preliminary report covering a con-

[1] Grading scale described in detail in *The UFO Experience, a Scientific Inquiry,* by Dr. J. Allen Hynek, director of the Center for UFO Studies.

centrated flap, rich in raw data, which I sent to the Mutual UFO Network and the Center for UFO Studies for evaluation and to serve as a quick reference for correlation with other incidents in the same time frame, October 22 to November 20, 1975:

October 22: After dark, engineer observed UFO hovering over Covington, Kentucky, Municipal Building (across the river from Cincinnati) from 14th-floor window. The UFO moved close to his window at low level. Through binoculars he could see rotating lights around the disc-shaped object's catwalk. The UFO had a peculiar set of "wings" protruding from the body. He got camera, went outdoors, and watched UFO go around his building at low level, making no sound. Before he could adjust his camera the UFO shot away.

October 22: About 11:00 P.M., the night the Cincinnati Reds won the final game of the World Series, Mr. and Mrs. Jeffrey Sparks saw a bright red glow in their house window. They went outdoors expecting to see "victory" fireworks. Instead, they were surprised to see their neighbor's house, yard, and trees, and the street bathed in a red glow. Both saw a round, red ball in the sky moving low and soundlessly across the sky in a horizontal flight pattern.

October 23: About 9:00 P.M., S.C. and girl friend and another female passenger in car in Fairfield, Ohio, were pursued by a low-level UFO. The UFO passed over the car and, while they were driving up a grade in the road, the UFO's cigar shape was caught in the car's headlights. UFO sent out a rod device with four small orange balls at the tip. Girls became hysterical.

October 26: About 1:20 P.M., an instrument-rated pilot in Cherokee aircraft, flying near New Baltimore, Ohio, called the control tower of the Greater Cincinnati Airport to report observation of an unidentified large glowing silver object, hovering at 8,000 ft., in clear weather, visibility 12 miles. The UFO shot off and out of view.

October 26: S.R., a boy 15 years of age, saw a disc-shaped UFO come in low over his house in Mt. Healthy. "The bottom," he said, "was dull reddish black and was divided into squares like graph paper." (See October 29 for his next experience with a UFO.)

October 27: At 8:30 A.M., two artists for a publishing company in eastern Cincinnati saw a brilliantly lighted disc from their second-story office window. The UFO hovered and occasionally vacillated jerkily over electric power line about a half mile away. After about 30 to 40 seconds, the UFO shot off at 30-degree angle with incredible speed, of a "flashlight beam."

October 27: About 11:00 P.M., Cincinnati police officers reported seeing a UFO in eastern Cincinnati. They described it as a large bright light with little red lights on both ends. The sergeant on duty drove to Ault Park, at a higher altitude, to view the light. He confirmed the unidentified light. "I've never seen anything like it," he said.

October 27: About 10:45 P.M., J.H., of Westwood, in western Cincinnati, saw two UFOs for about 10 minutes. He said they were about 1,000 ft. high and flying back and forth about 100 feet apart.

October 28: About 2:30 A.M., police patrolman R.P., of Campbell County, Kentucky, saw two UFOs while driving on a highway. He said one of the objects was on his left, the other to his right and that he was driving between them "very close!" The UFOs made no sound, he said.

October 29: In evening, S.R. was walking home after selling candy for a school benefit. Suddenly a UFO shaped like a "beer can" appeared about 25 ft. overhead. On top was a white light with rotating red lights on the bottom. The UFO made no sound and, after hovering for about 20 seconds, it shot straight up into the sky.

S.R. came home frightened, tried to relate his sighting to unsympathetic parents. He called the police, who gave the boy my phone number. I was not available. The next day, S.R. left a "runaway" note on the kitchen table in which he expressed great agonizing fears of the UFO and said that he knew that the UFO was after him. He signed his note with love and promised to call when he was safe. The father, J.R., who had been in touch with the police, called me in his confusion over his son's behavior and the UFO. He said his son withdrew $500 from his bank account and is missing.

The next day, the boy was apprehended by security police at the Atlanta Airport. He was brought home and before retiring from fatigue asked to call me. He was incoherent and still frightened. He admitted that he was still shaking in fear of the UFO.

I have since had several talks with S.R., and he has related the root of his fears. One year ago, in October 1974, he witnessed a UFO, with portholes, in his high school yard at tree-top level. This frightened the boy, and while in bed that same night he said he experienced a dream of, or in a trance-like state saw, a non-human, oval-shaped head with oval eyes and wrinkled skin that had no nose, and a slit for a mouth, before him. The "creature" related telepathically that he would take him away and not to be afraid.

November 4: About 6:45 P.M., in Ross, Ohio, six witnesses in a car spotted a UFO hovering at tree-top level. It was cylinder-shaped, about 75 feet in diameter, with blue and green rotating lights. Square windows were observed. While the UFO hovered over a wooded area it started into a spinning motion, and a small glowing red ball of light about three feet in diameter was ejected out of the bottom. The car's engine and lights went out.

After red ball disappeared, the witnesses were shocked to see "landing gear," glowing blue, come out of the bottom of the UFO, which appeared to land in a wooded area. When the object vanished from sight, the car's engine started, as did all the "woodsy insect" sounds, which had stopped into absolute silence, according to witnesses.

November 10: About 6:30 P.M., two gas station attendants in Ross, Ohio, saw a large steady glowing white light in the sky about five times larger than the brightest star. The UFO moved toward the station and "blinked out." When the UFO disappeared, both attendants smelled the strong odor of sulphur. Also, a motorist driving in for gas remarked about the strong, offensive odor.

November 19: At 11:30 P.M., a design engineer for Bausch & Lomb was flying a Beechcraft single-engine Sundowner 180 from Portland, Indiana, to Cincinnati. He spotted a large brilliant object descending in his flight path as he approached Lunken Airport from 7,000 feet. The pilot said that a moderate shock wave buffeted his aircraft twice. Received other UFO reports same evening from northern Kentucky.

November 20: Five hours following the aircraft incident, L.B., driving home in his pickup truck in the Cincinnati suburb of Cherry Grove from night-shift work, was followed by a low-level

UFO. The white light was blinding, said the witness. The shape was like a cigar, about 15 feet long.

L.B. tried evasive action on the road, but the UFO, making a humming sound, stayed close to the top of the truck. "It was about 30 feet above my windshield," said the alarmed witness.

When L.B. reached home, he awakened his wife and three teen-age children. They all witnessed the UFO, now disc-shaped, hovering above their house, then ascend to a higher position in the sky, still making a humming sound. The police were called. Two patrolmen confirmed the UFO. One officer put his spotlight on object and it moved in close to the cruiser. L.B.'s dog barked violently while the UFO hovered over the house. Received excellent cooperation from police chief.

The flap ended as fast as it started. After November 20, southwestern Ohio went into a lull. I checked repeatedly with the Wilhelms; they had no reports through December except some questionable nocturnal lights.

It was a short, intense flap, one of the several reported in various parts of the United States. According to William Spaulding, director of Ground Saucer Watch in Phoenix, Arizona, UFO activity in his area was inordinately heavy. "I need more investigators," he told me by phone. Checking by phone with other researchers from coast to coast, I found either extreme activity or none. Except for southwestern Ohio, western Pennsylvania, and isolated regions in the Midwest, the main UFO incursions were in the West, concurrent with continuing reports of cattle mutilations.

Understandably, flaps of livestock mutilations have baffled ranchers throughout the western states since 1973. Many have often been reported coincidentally with UFOs in the vicinity. Being perpetrated mysteriously and with no sure culprit except in rare instances, the mutilations have been blamed on UFOs. Hundreds of investigated cases show a macabre pattern: animals found dead far afield from their pasture, surgically dismembered of their sex organs, eyes, tongue, rectum. Generally, UFO researchers have opted to treat this new intrusive ogre with low-key caution. Some have backed off completely in the belief that a widespread but well-organized Satanist cult is responsible. While federal agencies have been working with local police investigating mutilation flaps—with some states on an emergency status—the heads of UFO research remained bewildered as unexplainable cases continued to be reported into the summer of 1976.

Why flaps? Why Arizona, Colorado, Pennsylvania, Ohio, in October and November 1975? What in the name of "exobio" logic, triggers a UFO strike?

Just before the big '73 flap, Dr. Hynek, while doing his spadework for CUFOS, was the featured speaker at the MUFON annual symposium, held in Akron, Ohio, on June 16, 1973. Keenly knowledgeable of UFO flaps and the superabundance of UFO reports, and kept up to date by Dr. David Saunders and his computer bank called UFOCAT,[2] Hynek's chosen title for his talk was "The Embarrassment of Riches." We quote from it, in part, as follows:

> A paradoxical situation exists in the whole UFO problem area: we have too many sightings, not too few; yet we are far from a solution. We are, frankly, embarrassed by our riches.
>
> Are they really riches? Those of us actively engaged in UFO research are fully aware that UFO reports continue to be made in ample quantity. Yet, how many of us would be willing to play "UFO Russian Roulette"? Let us dip into Dr. Saunders' impressive UFOCAT readout of cases for 1972, and let our finger come to rest at random on some particular case. Would you stake your life on that particular case? Of course not. Yet all of us are most certain, from our accumulated experience, that a great many of the cases in the Saunders UFOCAT and others are bona fide, "real" UFOs.
>
> In 1972 we have 737 UFO reports, relatively few of which ever hit the public press. And this number, 737, is just the tip of the iceberg. Not only is the listing of cases that were reported in one way or another incomplete, but we have no way of knowing how large the 1972 reservoir of *unreported* cases is. And this reservoir most certainly exists! Any serious investigator is well aware of the phe-

[2] UFOCAT is an acronym for the random-access, disc-packed catalog of entries compiled from UFO sighting reports. This project was initiated by Dr. David Saunders, who formerly served as co-principal co-ordinator of the Condon Project.

nomenon of reports "crawling out of the woodwork" when he or she is engaged on a specific case. I have never gone out on a case but that at least one other event, often quite unrelated, was reported to me, unsolicited. These often represented a temptation to leave the case I was working on and follow the new lead, or leads. That such a reservoir of unreported cases exists is further attested by my experience, and that of others, notably Stan Friedman; when we ask an audience for a show of hands of those having had a UFO experience, we get from ten to twenty per cent response; but when we next ask how many of those persons reported the case officially, either to the Air Force or to the police, we get very few hands indeed. The existence of this reservoir is further supported by persons—especially pilots—who have told me, "If I ever see anything like that, I sure won't report it." People are well aware of the ridicule that awaits them should they make a UFO report. Those who do report, I have found, do it mainly because of a sense of duty or of overwhelming curiosity to try to find out from some "experts" just what it was they saw.

So, then, if we apply fairly conservative guesswork about the total number of *sightings* (not *reports*) over the world in 1972, I believe we must count them in the thousands, rather than the hundreds. Make whatever logical estimates you will about geographical distribution, report sources, probable ratio of reporters to witnesses, etc., and you can hardly escape the conclusion that 737 actual reports for 1972 represents the well-known drop in the bucket. Our answer must lie in the thousands; and even if we then make ample allowance for the fact that some of the already screened-out reports may not really be "good" reports, we still come up with an impressive number. Much too large, indeed, for comfort.

What does such a large number mean to us? What are its implications? First off, of course, such a large number spells frustration for the serious investigator. Secondly, it means, even though incomplete, there are still too many

cases to investigate properly, and thus one has the sinking feeling that he is up against a situation with which he
cannot fully cope—valuable data just going down the
drain. We are, in short, in a situation in which the very
riches of our original, raw, unprocessed, uninvestigated
data blocks us from presenting a good, thoroughly convincing case to the world, particularly to the scientific
world.

There is an even deeper and more sinister embarrassment of our riches, and that is what they imply about
the origin of UFOs. While I, at least, do not feel quite
ready to theorize about the ultimate origins of UFOs, the
implication of the great number of reports per year is
quite clear, and any theory of UFOs will have to explain
their abundance. To our earthbound minds, one or two
Apollo missions per year is something we can understand; two or three Apollo missions *per day* would be
quite another thing! Consider, too, that the nearest star
to us is more than one hundred million times farther
than the moon—well, I hardly need explain further!

A few good sightings a year, over the world, would
bolster the extraterrestrial hypothesis—but many thousands every year? From remote regions of space? And to
what purpose? To scare us by stopping cars and disturbing animals, and puzzling us with their seemingly pointless antics? It really becomes embarrassing when we try
to present this aspect of our riches to the public, to science, and, if we are really honest, to ourselves also. Of
course, we can get around much of this embarrassment
on an ad hoc basis. We can say that UFOs come from
bases elsewhere in the solar system, or even here on
Earth, and not from far-off places. In this way, not every
one of the, perhaps, thousands of sightings a year represents a round trip from some distant place, at least one
hundred million times farther away than the moon. Or,
as long as we are "blue-skying," we can say that UFOs
can travel much faster than light, thus throwing away
without a shred of laboratory evidence a foundation
stone of modern science: Einstein's theory of relativity.

We can always say that UFOs have transcended our known physical laws. We can say that, and perhaps feel justified in saying it, by thinking of a chap crossing the western plains a century or so ago in a covered wagon. He was limited in his thinking, too. When he thought of greater speed, he probably thought of faster horses and more efficient wagons—it wouldn't have occurred to him to think of automobiles or 747's! Perhaps we are caught up in that kind of limited thinking, too—but I would be ruled out of any society of physicists should I even so much as suggest the possibility of speeds greater than that of light and some entirely new laws of physics.

Astronomer Hynek had become puzzled by the superabundance of the UFO reports. For this reason, plus being knowledgeable of other paranormal aspects associated with the phenomenon, he continues to hedge in committing himself to a strong hypothesis that tries to pinpoint their origin or nature. He has been especially cautious about espousing the popular belief that UFOs are extraterrestrial. Publicly and privately he cannot readily accept the logistics of an endless task force of *"nut and bolt"* spaceships that simply cross many light-years of void to visit Earth and return to their own planet in a distant solar system. On the other hand, Hynek indicated during our private dinner in Evanston, on February 1, 1975, a willingness to talk about UFOs being a "thing" or "thought form" from another realm or dimension—and seemed more amenable to the extraterrestrial hypothesis as he linked the UFOs' behavior to the principles of psychokinesis.

In this provocative domain, Hynek could see the armadas of spaceships probing Earth. We agreed, with a chuckle, that an alien intelligence with teleportative powers and cybernetic controls need only "pull a switch" to be on Earth in an instant, do its surveillance and, in the next, return. Hynek, since our speculative chat, remains noncommittal. In fact, as more and more anomalous data reaches the hands of research, shaping into patterns that defy every physical law of science, the greater is his concern about finding a straight and simple answer that would satisfy his querulous fellow scientists and convince a totally benighted public.

Hynek tells of his continuing dilemma in a paper he presented

to a Joint Symposium of the American Institute of Aeronautics &
Astronautics in Los Angeles, September 27, 1975:

> We come to UFO hypotheses. We are in the sad state
> of not even being sure of the facts we want an hypothesis
> to explain. . . . It is almost impossible to verify UFO
> facts—the phenomenon is strangely isolated in space and
> time.
>
> If you object, I ask you to explain—quantitatively, not
> qualitatively—the reported phenomena of materiali-
> zation and dematerialization, of shape changes, of the
> noiseless hovering in the earth's gravitational field, accel-
> erations that—for an appreciable mass—require energy
> sources far beyond present capabilities—even theoreti-
> cal capabilities—the well-known and often reported
> E-M effects, the psychic effects on percipients, including
> purported telepathic communications, the preferential
> occurrence of UFO experiences to the "repeaters"—those
> who are reported to have so many more UFO sightings
> that it outrages the noble art of statistics. I think of one
> recent case in which the person was able to go out and
> photograph a daylight disc, on several occasions, after
> experiencing a severe headache."

For another broad overview of the UFO, we refer to Dr.
Jacques Vallée, author of several popular UFO books, the latest
The Invisible College, and long associated in the study of UFOs
with Dr. Hynek. We find in Vallée, an astrophysicist, a careful
and trenchant examination of the data on hand, and, again, a cautious search before grasping a random hypothesis as a possible
single answer to all the UFO anomalies.

Vallée also presented a paper before the A.I.A.A. symposium
in Los Angeles, entitled "The Psycho-Physical Nature of the
UFO: a Speculative Framework," from which we quote in part:

> Let us consider the characteristics of the sightings that
> are not explained by trivial natural causes; we can recog-
> nize six major "dimensions" in terms of our perceptions
> of these characteristics.
>
> First is the *physical* dimension. Most witnesses de-
> scribe an object that occupies a position in space; moves

as time passes; interacts with its environment through thermal effects as well as light absorption and emission; produces turbulence; and, when landed, leaves indentations and burns from which approximate mass and energy figures can be derived. Furthermore, it gives rise to photographic images and magnetic disturbances.

The second dimension is *anti-physical*. The variables are the same as those in the previous category but they form patterns that conflict with those predicted by physics—an object that is described as physical and material is also described as a) sinking into the ground, b) becoming fuzzy and transparent on the spot, c) merging with an identical object at slow speed, d) disappearing at one point while appearing elsewhere instantaneously, and e) remaining observable visually while not detected on radar.

The third dimension is the psychology of the witnesses and the *social* conditions that surround them. Human observers tend to see UFOs while in their normal environment and in normal social groupings. They perceive the objects as non-conventional but they try to explain them away as common occurrences, until faced with the inescapable conclusion that the object is truly unknown.

Physiological reactions are another significant dimension. The phenomenon is reported to cause burns, "beeping" sounds, vibrations, partial paralysis, heat sensation, pricklings. Some witnesses have become temporarily blind when exposed to the objects' light. Others have described nausea, difficulty in breathing, loss of volition. The most frequent reported symptom in the days following a close-range encounter is drowsiness.

The fifth category of effects is labeled *psychic*, because it involves a class of phenomena commonly found in the literature of parapsychology, such as a) impressions of communication without direct sensory channel, b) levitation of the witness or of objects and animals in the vicinity, c) poltergeist phenomena: motions and sounds without a specific cause, outside of the observed presence of a UFO, d) maneuvers of a UFO appearing to anticipate the witness' thoughts, e) premonitory dreams or "visions," f) personality changes promoting unusual abilities in the witness (as in the case of Uri Geller and others), and g) healing.

The sixth category could be called *"cultural."* It is concerned with society's reactions to the reports, the way in which secondary effects (hoaxes, science-fiction imagery, scientific theories, cover-up or exposure, censorship or publicity, sensationalism, etc.) become generated, and the attitude of members of a given culture towards the concepts that UFO observations appear to challenge. The greatest impact of the phenomenon has been on general acceptance of the idea of life in space and a more limited, but potentially very significant, change in popular concept of nonhuman intelligence.

A framework for scientific speculation on the UFO phenomenon can be built on the identification of the six major dimensions of UFO effects as follows:

a) The phenomenon is the product of a technology. During the observation, the UFO is a real, physical, material object. However, it uses either very clever deception or very advanced physical principles, resulting in the effects I have called "anti-physical," which must eventually be reconciled with the laws of physics.

b) The technology triggers psychic effects either purposely or as a side effect of the presence of a UFO. These psychic phenomena are now too common to be ignored or relegated to the category of exaggerated or ill-observed facts. All of us who have investigated close-range sightings have become familiar with these effects.

c) The purpose of the technology is cultural manipulation—possibly but not necessarily under control of a form of non-human intelligence—and the physiological and psychological effects are a means to that end.

Researchers and so-called researchers of every stripe and of every shade of gray are quick to express their opinion about what the UFO is or where it is from. I have heard of every conceivable theory ever spoken or written: UFOs are angelic manifestations, UFOs are devices of the devil, UFOs are tropospheric animals, UFOs are from inside Earth and have entrances at each pole, the

UFO's occupants are disciples of Christ ready to return Him to Earth from the moon, where he had ascended on Easter in a UFO, and UFOs are Russian or U.S. secret weapons. I have often said that these opinionators use putty to fit into the round holes of the UFO puzzle.

For many researchers, writers, and lecturers, the extraterrestrial answer for the UFO is less difficult to digest than for Hynek or Vallée. For this school there is little fuss about astronomical space-time problems and no concern or embarrassment for the *riches* of UFO reports on a monthly or annual scale. For them— at the risk of being tagged conservative—the round peg of over-whelming evidence that UFOs are controlled vehicles from outer space fits into a round hole. The only great questions left are: From where? And why?

Stanton Friedman, professional ufologist and former space sci-entist, also lectured before the A.I.A.A. symposium in Los An-geles. As in all past public appearances, Friedman took a strong stand on the UFOs' outer-space connection. Excerpts of his views follow:

> Eighteen years of study and investigation have con-vinced me that the evidence is overwhelming that Earth is being visited by intelligently controlled extraterrestrial vehicles. . . .
>
> One objection to the Extraterrestrial Hypothesis raised by Hynek is that there are simply far too many visits for UFOs to be extraterrestrial nuts and bolts vehicles. He would be satisfied with visits at the rate of perhaps one a year or several every decade, in the manner of our Apollo missions. The logic behind this objection seems to be non-existent. One underlying assumption is that anybody else venturing out in space got started when we did, less than 20 years ago.
>
> Does Hynek or anyone else have any information about how many visitors there are to us? Too many? Compared to what? Nobody has the faintest idea of how to judge how many interstellar jaunts there have been to produce the number of unexplained sightings or even how many different interstellar space lines there are with trips our way or how many different planets with life or

different galactic federations are represented by our visitors.

Are there only occasional visits by space craft equivalent to an aircraft carrier *Enterprise* carrying 50 Earth Excursion Modules each of which makes five 1,000-mile jaunts per day for two weeks before returning to the back side of the moon? Or does each landing represent an individual galactic Charles Lindbergh flying non-stop on his own? We really don't know. This question is, of course, badly obscured by the exobiologists, who, with no data at all, try to compute the number of civilizations and the average distance between them on a galactic basis rather than on a galactic-neighborhood basis. Dealing with 200 billion stars is very impressive *if* one is impressed easily with large numbers and ignores the absence of data.

Why so many landings these last 25 years? Obviously, again, we can only speculate. First we can presume that a Galactic Federation would pay attention to any planets known to be suitable for life and to have potentially technologically advanced civilizations. Periodic monitoring would be expected, with occasional trips and with more frequent instrumented flybys looking for signs of technological development such as the emission of radio waves and of bursts of nuclear radiation. This would not be out of idle curiosity but, rather, from recognizing that it takes a very short time on a cosmic scale to go from being the Genghis Khan of a local planet to the Genghis Khan of the galactic neighborhood. Probably there would be a Standard Operating Procedure as soon as certain signals were detected: pick up powerful radio waves or high pollution levels, then send remote devices to make a more detailed evaluation. Certainly the brief period from 1939–1945 would have provided enough information to know that Earthlings would soon be able to travel to the stars. Combining the facts that we had exploded nuclear weapons, launched rockets and developed sophisticated radar systems and the beginnings of computers and the electronics revolution, it would certainly be necessary to send out a bulletin indicating that a hostile society—us—would soon be venturing forth in its galactic neighborhood.

Of the same strong conviction but taking a different track in his research to prove that UFOs are interplanetary is Major Donald E. Keyhoe, USMC (Ret.) and former director of NICAP. One of the first to proclaim that UFOs are from outer space, Keyhoe is convinced that the Air Force has this *proof* and has deliberately concealed the facts from the public. In five best-selling books, he has castigated the Air Force for their cover-up operations, and in his recent book, *Aliens from Space* (1974), charges that the CIA was part of the conspiracy. He now believes that high-level Pentagon officials are embroiled in a bitter fight on how to treat the extraterrestrial proof that they hide, fearing that revelation would expose all their past mismanagement.

The position taken by Dr. David M. Jacobs, Department of History, Temple University, and author of *The UFO Controversy in America* (1975) is quoted from a paper presented before the Chicago conference sponsored by CUFOS, April 30–May 2, 1976, as follows:

> I have seen no substantial evidence to suggest that the old-fashioned extraterrestrial hypothesis is untenable. It still seems to explain the vast majority of data we have encountered. The new theories about the origins, purposes, and psychic components of UFOs have tended to place the extraterrestrial theory in disfavor without really offering a shred of evidence to disprove or discount it. I believe that it would be a fundamental mistake to abandon the nuts and bolts hypothesis without first proving it to be unfeasible.

Despite all the simplistic views by researchers about outer space and theoretical interstellar travel, the bastion of astronomy must play a key role in establishing the final proof that the UFO—in a thought-projected, materialized form or as nuts and bolts—comes from a habitable planet from somewhere in the Milky Way.

Astronomers disagree among themselves on many scientific issues in their field. Certainly, a debate on UFOs will not appease their differences, unless, of course, they were all allowed to peek at the bodies of "little men" rumored to be preserved in the vaults of the Pentagon. Most astronomers, too busy with quasars, pulsars and black holes, have little time for UFOs and have never seriously reviewed the evidence on hand.

In the August 1975 issue of *Griffith Observer,* a director of a major planetarium, commenting on Dr. Hynek's book *The UFO Experience,* asked, "Why doesn't a good UFO sighting happen over a meeting of the American Astronomical Society?"

In the very book that drew the director's comment, it was stated by Hynek that during an astronomers' conference he attended in Victoria, British Columbia, in 1968, an evening session was interrupted by a report that strange lights—UFOs—were being observed outside. According to Hynek, several hundred scientists responded with embarrassed giggles, *but not one astronomer ventured outside to see for himself!*

Astronomer Dr. Clyde Tombaugh, renowned for his discovery of the planet Pluto, in our solar system, in 1930, also stirred the scientific community with the news of his own UFO sightings. Dr. Tombaugh related his observations to me by letter in 1957, which follows:

> I have seen three objects within the past seven years, which defied any explanation of known phenomena, such as Venus, atmospheric optics, meteors, or planes. I am a professional, highly skilled observing astronomer. In addition, I have seen three green fire balls which were unusual in behavior from scores of normal green fire balls.
>
> There might be observations of these objects with theodolites obtaining angles for parallax, thence distance, size and speed. Unless such objects are seen under clouds, or in the tangent rays of the sun just after sunset, or with a pair of observers equipped with theodolites at the end of a measured base line, any other reported heights, sizes and speeds are mere guesses, and most people guess badly on such aerial phenomena.
>
> Most of the sightings can be traced to known phenomena, but some ten or five per cent cannot. But there are still things to learn about the atmosphere, which may whittle down the percentage even more.
>
> I think that several reputable scientists are being unscientific in refusing to entertain the possibility of extra-

terrestrial origin and nature. It is yet too early for any decision of finality.

Tombaugh's planet Pluto is 3,666,000,000 mean miles from Earth. But Pluto is not nearly so "far out" as some of the anomalous cases that have surfaced since 1973 and now rest in the confidential hands of research. Had the astronomers at the Victoria conference known of any of these highly complex cases, even those well documented, they would have probably giggled them off as sheer nonsense.

Indeed, the few who have shared in bizarre UFO experiences, which Vallée describes as *psychical,* rarely make them public domain. These are the cases, involving close encounters, that concern Hynek. Even the conservative ufologist, who would have dismissed a psychic-oriented case ten years ago, is now listening.

I have received several of this kind in just the past year, which I have entered as *confidential* in my daily UFO diary, UFOLOG. One of the strange cases comes from a lady who knew of my research for a long time, but admitted that she could not force herself to talk about her experience except to members of her own family.

On October 30, 1975, Mrs. Everett Steward (name changed by request) called me at dinnertime. She said that she had called me in 1966 about her UFO sighting; then she admitted sheepishly that she had not told me the whole story. "You would've thought I was a kook," she said. "Now I must tell you the rest, but only on one condition—" Mrs. Steward paused, then went on: "My name and even the part of Cincinnati where I live must be kept confidential."

I promised and offered to keep the trust she had in me in writing. Nine years before, on October 2, 1966, at 8:20 P.M., according to notes carefully kept hidden in a desk drawer, Mrs. Everett Steward, then forty-nine years old, was talking on the telephone with a friend when she became aware of a foul odor in the room. Instantly she was beset by dizziness and nausea. Excusing herself to her friend on the phone, she hastily retired to her bedroom upstairs. Before undressing she recalls having a "feeling of being watched," and looking out the window, to her amazement she saw a brightly colored oval-shaped object with portholes that appeared to be hovering near the ground in a wooded area several hundred feet away.

Everett Steward, a dispatcher at a large Cincinnati plant, had already retired for the night. He recalls that his wife had awakened him to see the strange object, which he at first thought might be a low-level aircraft. After a quick second look, he changed his mind. As he watched, the object began moving away from the house, then, he said, it "cut back" and hovered about one hundred feet off the ground for about ten minutes. The craft, he estimated, was about seventy-five feet in diameter, with red, green, and white lights rotating swiftly around the rim.

As the UFO began to wobble and shift its position, Mrs. Steward realized that its location was near the house of her married daughter, Mrs. Janet Emery, about a mile away. "I was feeling quite sick when I called to alert Janet," recalls Mrs. Steward. "The odor seemed stronger and I was so dizzy I had to sit down."

Janet was mopping the floor when her mother called. She quickly aroused her husband, Ken, and they sighted the UFO about two hundred yards from their upstairs window. Both agreed the object was large, metallic, and with a row of yellowish lights. Ken, overwhelmed by the UFO, "being right before my very eyes," hastened to get his neighbor, David Stites. A Naval Reserve officer, Stites grabbed his binoculars and with Ken joined Janet at the upstairs window. The binoculars were high-powered, and Stites, being familiar with celestial navigation, quickly resolved the object in his view. Unquestionably, the disc had *square windows,* and from each came a yellow glow.

As the three watched, the UFO's lights brightened, and the body wobbled and began a slow, horizontal shift. "About this time, all the dogs in the neighborhood began barking," said Ken. "Obviously something unusual was happening."

Convinced that an aircraft was not the cause, Ken and David went outdoors for a better view. "To my surprise," said Ken, "my pet cat, Nightcap, darted up to my side from a bush. It was hunched and its hair stood straight up. Then it squealed and jumped up into the screen door and got hung up in the mesh. I had to almost declaw the cat to free it."

The UFO in the meantime had shifted again. Recalled Ken, "It seemed as though it was about ready to take off, so I urged Dave to join me in my car to get a closer look." As they drove toward Mt. Airy, the UFO streaked overhead and they lost it.

Janet, left alone, continued to watch the wobbling UFO. She

wanted to go outside to look but was frightened. Then, when the UFO started to move, her curiosity won out. "I was scared, but went out anyway," she said.

At the Stewards' residence it was panic. Mrs. Steward, after alerting her daughter, called the Greater Cincinnati Airport, which admitted that "something unidentified passed over Cincinnati." Then she called the police. She recalls the chief's response: "Lady, you're the forty-fifth person to call tonight." Later, said Mrs. Steward, while the craft was close to the ground, the airport called back and asked, "Where is it?"

The strong "chemical" odor had now filled every room in the Steward house. "It was an ill-smelling chemical odor," said Mrs. Steward, "a smell that made me lose my equilibrium." Later in the evening, her younger daughter, Debbie, who had been at the theater with her date, arrived. Debbie, who had also witnessed the UFO, was immediately taken aback by the foul smell and asked, "Mom, what did you spray in the house?" Completely unnerved, Mrs. Steward collapsed in a chair. She was given an aspirin and escorted to her daughter's bedroom. In there was a spare bed, in which she hoped to get a good night's rest. . . .

No sooner had Ken and David departed than Janet wished she had stayed in the house. The UFO had shifted, then returned to its original position. With its yellow lights turning faster, suddenly from its side a smaller object was ejected. "It looked like a red ball," said Janet.

Janet stood petrified as she watched the antics of the red ball. "It wobbled and bounced, it made erratic movements from side to side and it was able to turn on a dime," she said. "Then it took a positive course and came toward my house in sort of a gliding motion. All this time, it made no sound." During the red-ball maneuvers, Janet said she saw the large craft with yellow lights "take off fast to the south and disappear."

In the next instant, Janet said, the red ball shot a white ray of light over her house and then it passed about seventy-five to one hundred feet directly overhead. "It was oval-shaped when it went over," she said, "and its underside was like aluminum foil, smooth and shiny. I couldn't believe its actual size, but it was bigger than my cottage and yard combined. It seemed so close that I thought I could touch it—and I even tried by putting my arms up."

In answer to my questions about physiological effects from her close encounter, she said that she suffered no illness, felt no sensations like numbing or tingling, nor recalled a body-temperature change.

"The only thing strange, and I mean strange," she said, "when the thing passed over me, I suddenly felt no fear. It was the eeriest feeling I've ever had." Janet was also aware of the strange, "disagreeable" odor in the air. When asked to associate it with a familiar smell, she answered, "Yes, bad garbage!"

Finally, Everett Steward, exhausted, retired, and was asleep despite a lingering odor in the house. Debbie was also fitfully asleep, but her mother, in the adjoining bed, was wide awake. As she lay there, she tried to dismiss the UFO from her mind and the odor that made her ill.

As time ticked away, there suddenly was a split second when the darkness vanished and the room was filled with a brilliant white light. Mrs. Steward sat up in shock. She was too stunned to scream. The room, wall to wall and from floor to ceiling, was bathed in light so bright that all the furniture stood out. There were no shadows! In the next instant, the light flicked out, and in the middle of the void of darkness appeared a globe of the same intensity of light at the foot of her bed. Inside the globe, which Mrs. Steward recalls was the size of a 21-inch TV screen, were five non-human, hairless heads with oval eyes "sunken like skulls' eyes." She added, "All the heads were the same. Instead of noses there were slits, and they had no mouths—and there were no necks, bodies or arms." The mouthless heads did not speak, but Mrs. Steward received their message: *"We have made contact."* The message, telepathically, was repeated several times. Mrs. Steward screamed! Debbie, dazed, leaped from her bed, and Mr. Steward came running from his bedroom. His wife was in hysterics. Incoherently she tried to explain what she saw. The globe with heads had gone. For the Stewards, it was a terrible night and for many nights thereafter.

Mrs. Steward consulted a doctor the next day, who treated her for nervous disorder. But, as her nightly dreams became nightmares, she was referred to a psychiatrist. For two years she was under special medical care, including shock treatment.

Scientific Ufology is now seriously studying these paranormal cases.

III

Macrocosmic Thinking

"This one is *not* elementary," Sherlock Holmes would have told Watson if he had been commissioned to investigate the "Case of the Invisible Ray." In fact, Holmes, Hercule Poirot, and Lord Peter Wimsey together could not have solved it. The answer lies somewhere hidden in the unknown . . . and finding it may require *macrocosmic thinking*.

John Warner (name changed by request) was not talking science fiction when he claimed he witnessed the effects of the invisible ray. Warner is a spry man in his seventies with alert eyes. It was October 20, 1975, when he came to my office and sat stiffly in a chair next to mine at my desk. "I was directed to your office by the Defense Department," he said tensely.

I offered him a cup of coffee, lit my perennial pipe. In a way, I was stalling to get a grip on myself for whatever was to come, especially with Defense Department involvement.

Warner told his story almost impatiently. It was the last week in February 1975, when he and his wife, Elizabeth, were watching a soap opera on TV about 3:00 P.M. Suddenly the picture flickered and went black. At the same moment, they both heard a loud, shrill, piercing sound "like glass being cut." Said Warner, trying to be accurately onomatopoetic, "It went zzzzzzzzzzz and lasted for about five minutes."

Frightened, the Warners got up and looked out the front window. They saw nothing unusual. Mrs. Warner then checked the kitchen and bathroom, found nothing amiss, and entered the dining room. Instantly her eyes caught a strange glow inside the china cabinet, which faced the window. Edging closer, she observed that the glow—multicolored, like a rainbow—radiated from a pair of silver salt and pepper shakers that stood amid a display of upended china plates.

"Elizabeth yelled and I came running," said Warner. "I couldn't believe my eyes. There they were, the shakers all lit up in reds, purples and blues . . . all colors. Maybe it was my imagination, but the lights seemed to shimmer like they were vibrating from that sound."

Warner paused, his alert eyes watching mine for the slightest trace of disbelief. "You'll never believe this," he said, even though my eyes gave him no reason to doubt his word. "Both pieces of silver were burned, yes, sir, burned. About halfway down, they were singed with a black powder—but the top part was still glowing."

Warner said that he and his wife watched the phenomenon for a full minute, too puzzled to move. Then Mrs. Warner impulsively opened the door of the cabinet, grabbed the pieces of silver, still aglow, and held them, arms outstretched in each hand. In the next instant she scurried across the room and put them in the kitchen sink. Said Warner, *the moment she crossed in front of the window,* the glow around the top of the silver vanished, the piercing noise stopped, and the TV picture returned to normal.

"I was convinced that a ray of some kind had come through that window," he said, demonstratively pointing at my office window. "It was an invisible ray and it came from somewhere outside, and it was powerful enough to knock out my TV. But, when I went outside, I didn't see a thing."

Taking notes as Warner talked volubly about the puzzling halo and sound, I finally pushed aside my papers and assured him that I believed his story completely. I noticed instantly that he was less tense, and I think he smiled intentionally to show his relief.

Knowing that he felt more at ease, I proceeded to ask questions about the weather conditions, the layout of his house, his yard, then I homed in on the silverware, which seemed to be the primary target.

"They were a Christmas gift, just two months before, from my daughter," said Warner. "We had used them several times before this incident, and I know they were on the shelf in good, clean condition."

I next asked if he found traces of burns or residual powder on the chinaware in the cabinet or on the glass of the cabinet. Said Warner, "The glass door, the crystal and china had no marks— only the silver set."

"What about physical effects, which your wife may have felt at that time or later?" This was my main question, knowing that she had "blocked" the window to cut off the halo, the sound and the interference to the TV. Also in mind was the fact that she had handled the silverware while it was glowing.

"No ill effects," replied Warner. "When she touched the silver, it wasn't even warm."

Finally I asked Warner why he had not called the police following the incident. "I didn't say anything to anybody about it," he replied. "Who in the world would believe me?"

"Then, why did you go to the Defense Department today, at this late date?" I asked, which had puzzled me from the beginning.

Said Warner, matter-of-factly, "Because recently there have been some mysterious power outages and fires in our neighborhood and I thought that maybe an *enemy* might be causing these strange things—maybe using a destructive ray from a satellite."

When Warner stood up to leave, he said, "Please don't use my name. I don't want anybody to know what happened."

As he stood at the door, I asked what he thought about the UFO, inasmuch as he had not mentioned the subject during our talk.

"I have no opinion," he said. "I've never seen one."

"Maybe there was one over your house last February," I said kiddingly.

"I didn't look up," he replied. "Maybe I should have."

My evaluation of Warner: a concerned solid citizen and as American as apple pie!

Shortly after my visitor departed, Pat McGowan came into my office. Pat, who has helped in my research for many years, was usually the first to know when I got a *good* UFO case. When I mentioned Warner's invisible ray from an invisible UFO, she said,

"No wonder your beard is turning white, with the cases you're getting lately."

True, many cases reaching me locally and from researchers coast to coast were mind bogglers. From one source alone, Joe Brill, of Quincy, Illinois, came a steady flow. Brill, as a MUFON investigator, always had gone to the source for facts when he heard of a good case.

Another steady source was Ted Bloecher of New York. His specialty, researching humanoid encounters, provided at least one "non-fittable" case a week. Often, in the quiet of night, I wonder about the growing stack of misfit cases, the abstracts that do not fit into man's tidy physical order or, for that matter, into the order of ufology.

Macrocosmically, every abstract fits. The UFO, an abstract to man, fits. Whatever the UFO's nature or its source, it is just one phenomenon of many that have a place in the macrocosmic scheme.

Thinking macrocosmically, the "nut and bolt" UFO is valid from anywhere in space, because man himself has produced a nut and bolt spaceship for his purposes. And just as valid is the UFO that appears to be material to the human eye and in the next instant dematerializes, or the UFO that eyes can see but radar cannot pick up or a camera cannot photograph, or the UFO that can erase time from a man's mind, heal a man's injury, rejuvenate, or give the "magic" to bend a spoon by thought, or banish aircraft from the skies. Macrocosmically, there is probably an answer for everything strange—*even Warner's rainbowed salt and pepper shakers!*

"My UFO philosophy past and present is a little *to the left* of the nut and bolt conservative," I announced as guest speaker to the Tau Beta Pi Engineering Honor Society at their winter initiation banquet, February 21, 1976. "I must add that I am intrigued by cases that don't fit into my rhyme or reason. Perhaps, if I think macrocosmically, they all fit."

Another abstract case, occurring in a village near Cincinnati, is also, like the Warners', without an observed UFO, but it fits into the familiar UFO pattern.

June Putnam was sitting alone reading in her living room, her drapes drawn, feeling snug and secure amid the reds and greens of

Christmas décor. It was 1:00 A.M., January 4, 1975. Her husband, Ray, had retired early, as he has been accustomed to do for the past year. He is a heart patient and is equipped with a pacemaker. The excitement of the holidays was wearing on him. Cliff, their son, had driven to the neighborhood all-night delicatessen for a quart of milk.

Suddenly the sound of high-pitched choral voices, like a chant, broke the deep silence. June dropped her book, listened intently. Carolers, she thought. Carolers? January 4? That couldn't be— and, besides, there was something different about the chant: it was too shrill, too monotonous, almost mechanical.

June was tempted to draw back the drapes, but something urged her not to get near the window. Suddenly she felt a chill—the chill of panic. "I think I would have screamed if it hadn't been for Ray's condition," said June. "He's a terribly deep sleeper, and to have awakened him in a state of panic could've been fatal."

But to June's surprise, and relief, Ray was awake. She could hear him puttering briskly in the hallway at the top of the stairs. In that instant the chanting stopped. A minute later, she saw Ray peering out the hallway window.

"What in the world's going on?" Ray shouted as he rushed down the stairway. Without further ado, he grabbed the phone and called the police.

The police responded quickly, checked the house and the entire yard, and found nothing. Also, they knew of no caroling groups in the neighborhood that night. A check with the neighbors, about three hundred feet across two level lawns, also confirmed that carolers were not seen—or *heard*. When Cliff arrived from his errand, shortly after the police departed, he also checked the yard and found nothing. Uneasily, the Putnams retired.

Early the next morning, June, not satisfied, investigated outside the window that faced the front lawn. Aghast, she instantly found a half-circle depression in the turf about six feet away from the window. The arc, about twenty-five feet long, ended at the outer branches of a large oak tree that stood about six feet from the driveway. Something moderately heavy, about three inches wide, had pressed down the wintered grass evenly about two inches deep from end to end of the arc. As there were no marks leaving the driveway or leaving the main street into the larger portion of the lawn, it appeared to both Mrs. Putnam and her son that whatever had made the semicircle had come from above. Left with this mystery, she decided never to discuss it with her husband, or anyone else.

It was not until April 1975 that my wife, Dell, got the story from June, whom she met at a luncheon. When Dell told me about the case and mentioned June's concern, I called her home at once to arrange to interview her and observe the "landing" site.

Checking the lawn, I found the semicircle to be still pronounced. Instead of a depression, the affected turf had risen above the lawn level, and, to my surprise, the warming weather had produced a robust belt of grass *much more luxuriant* than the remainder of the lawn. Curious, I called Ted Phillips, in Sedalia, Missouri, a specialist in trace cases, for his advice on obtaining soil samples. "Too late," said Phillips. "Whatever may have caused a molecular change in the root system would have been washed away by rains or snow by now."

During July and again in the fall, Thomas Stegmaier, MUFON investigator in the Greater Cincinnati area, checked and photographed the Putnam lawn. The arc remained! It was clearly visible from every point of observation.

"Close-up examination in the fall was most interesting," said Stegmaier. "Even the clover and crabgrass in the semicircle belt was a deeper shade of green than the rest of the lawn's growth."

Whatever caused the chanting and the semicircle also affected Ray Putnam's pacemaker, arousing him from his habit of normal deep sleep. Stegmaier tried to guess what happened on that fourth night of the 1975 new year. "If it came from the sky," he said, "it certainly had a clear shot from above, knowing it would miss the house, the large oak tree, and the shrubbery around the open lawn."

Perhaps relative to the lush vegetative growth in the Putnam semicircle is newly published data concerning the famous Tungus crater in Siberia, which scientists believed, since its occurrence, in 1908, was caused by a meteorite. According to *UFOs from Behind the Iron Curtain,* by Ion Hobana and Julien Weverbergh (1972), two Russian scientists now contend that the crater may have been caused by a thermonuclear explosive device from an extraterrestrial source. The two scientists, on a flora-research expedition, stated in part, ". . . larches and birches aged between 40 and 50 years (which had germinated after the explosion), which should normally have been seven to eight meters high, were in fact 17–22 meters in height; that is, they had reached a size which 'normal' trees of this type would attain only after 200 years. *Thus their genetic structure had been radically altered* in 1908, a phenomenon which could have been caused by radioactivity."

Researchers receive many such extraordinary UFO cases. Often there is only one percipient. These cases, usually involving an uncelebrated citizen, are always suspect, weakened by the lack of witnesses. While they may get the highest rating in strangeness, they usually get the lowest in credibility.

One case I investigated fits totally into the macrocosmic scheme. It shares the highest level of strangeness, and, despite its single witness, the credibility rating stands unusually high.

The one witness, Chuck Doyle, with an IQ of 172, looks and acts older than his age of fifteen. He likes sports, excels in swimming, plays football in high school, and is keenly conversant with scientific matters. As a pastime he plays Star Trek, a game of mathematical skill, using a sophisticated computer system installed in his home.

When Tom Stegmaier and I visited the Doyle residence for an on-the-spot investigation and photographs following a dozen phone calls I made getting basic information, we found Chuck tutoring his older brother at the computer console, showing him how to "beat the enemy." Said Chuck, "My dad's a computer technician and I sort of grew up with computers."

"Did you have the terminal installed during your UFO encounter?" I asked.

"We always have one in the house," he replied. "It's connected to the university by a phone relay. My dad conducts a lot of experiments."

Initially, I received a brief account of the incident from the Wilhelms as a result of their prompt follow-up of Chuck Doyle's phone call to a radio "rap" show, May 25, 1975. Mrs. Wilhelm talked to Chuck, took notes highlighting the incident, and referred the case to me the following day.

When I first phoned Chuck, on May 27, and presented my credentials, he seemed eager to relate his experience. His encounter was on May 10, 1975, and it took place in a sparsely populated residential area in Florence, Kentucky, between 9:00 and 10:00 P.M. (he didn't wear a watch, so does not know the exact time). Chuck went outside, with the porch light on, to bring in his eight-year-old gelding, Duke, which was out of view, in the far end of the three-acre pasture.

The first indication that something alien was in the immediate vicinity was a buzzing sound like a swarm of bees behind him. When he turned around, he saw a stationary object, shaped like a "manta ray," about twenty feet long and ten feet wing tip to wing tip, at about twenty feet elevation. It was hovering over his neighbor's vegetable garden, about eighty feet away. I asked if there was anything unusual in the garden. He said his neighbor was growing a new strain of cauliflower, along with other vegetables. The ground had been freshly furrowed.

Chuck said the stationary UFO bobbed up and down like a cork on water, at which time he felt the ground vibrate. There were two distinct sources of light on the object. One, a green, glowing light, came from a rectangular section under the craft near the front. Its luminosity was like the "diffused glow of heated metal, or like a green traffic light." He said the rectangle was about eight feet long by four feet wide, "faceted with circular lenses in rows." Each facet, he said, stuck out slightly, but the whole rectangle glowed a steady, diffused green light. I rephrased my question about the rectangle, hoping for another description, analogous to something familiar. Chuck responded, "Well, it was like a sheet of plastic wall divider with circular impressions."

"The other light," he said, "came from the manta's tail, which came to a point like a needle. It was a pulsating light, glowing a brick red."

Chuck said the right side of the craft was facing him; the pointed tail to his left. On the top, toward the front, was a "raised portion" like a dome. It had no light source, no portholes, no other noticeable features. However, said Chuck, he did recall observing that the porch light and lights from the windows reflected on the craft's body, which made its surface appear metallic green. His comment: "It was as if you'd take a piece of steel and color it with a green crayon."

"For the first two minutes or so," said Chuck, "I was so

stunned I just froze. . . . I couldn't move. I can't say I was frightened, as I don't scare easily, but I just stood in awe, I guess." I asked if he felt any physical reaction from the craft. "Not at the time," he answered. "I just couldn't believe what I saw."

I tried to steer Chuck to relate his experience in the sequence of events. "Next," he said, "a light beam came out of the green-lighted rectangle. The beam was a darker green, maybe olive green, and it poked around the bushes in the neighbor's yard." I asked him to describe the beam.

"It was a straight shaft of light that didn't get wider at the bottom, like a laser," he said. Inside this beam he could detect dust swirling as though it were being suctioned up. Also, he noticed that the branches of a nearby tree were swaying. Chuck related that the green beam then proceeded to make wider probes around the gardens and the yard. "Then it struck the water of our swimming pool and stopped. There were vapors rising from the water's surface, which is normal, but it looked like the beam was watching the vapors." During this probe of the swimming pool, Chuck remembers watching another phenomenon, which he wasn't sure was related to the UFO. He said that the light poles and the wiring that leads to the lines under the deck of the pool became aglow with a bluish light. "This I had seen before," he said. "Probably it was St. Elmo's fire."

We discussed the behavior of electrostatic phenomena and agreed that it was a stretch of coincidence for such an occurrence during the presence of the UFO. "I guess so," said Chuck. "It was specially odd because the lighting unit was not even plugged in."

"Then the beam came at me," he said. "When it hit me, it was like being hit by a bucket of ice water. I felt suddenly frozen. I couldn't move."

He said that the beam that emanated from the center of the rectangle was about four or five inches in diameter when he first saw it; then it slowly spread in diameter to about four or five feet, when it came toward him.

Chuck affirms that he was completely conscious through this "frozen" state. He remembers trying to run and that his body and limbs were poised in a forward motion but that he was "powerless" to move a muscle. He said he couldn't even blink his eyes. "It was as though I were molded in plaster," he said. During this period Chuck had no idea how much time elapsed. "I didn't blank out," he said, "but in my mind were some strange thoughts. They were thoughts being put there. It's hard to explain." Chuck stopped briefly. I encouraged him to continue and said that I found his experience believable, knowing of other, similar cases.

"Mr. Stringfield," he said, "you'll never believe this, but I could see mathematical equations that made no sense, and I remember seeing the omega symbol."

Chuck paused again, then said, "My next vision was a picture of myself looking over a hill into a red ocean. The sky above was green, the ground below me, blue." Chuck repeated, "Something was putting these thoughts in my mind."

He also recalled another vision, in which he could feel himself "floating in space with nothing touching me." He said he could see all around him, but the stars were all different colors on a black background. He said, "The colors were colors I've never seen before; they were all the in-between colors in the spectrum."

"Then," said Chuck, *"the beam went out and I fell flat on my face."* Chuck attributed his fall to his awkward and imbalanced lunging position when the beam engulfed him as he tried to escape. Lying dazed on the ground, Chuck said the terrible coldness suddenly left his body, and he realized that he had bumped his nose and forehead.

I asked if he had called for help. He had not. "The neighbors were gone, their lights were out, and my family was away. They didn't get home until after eleven o'clock," he said.

Getting up from the ground, Chuck observed that the UFO was still in view, never changing from its original position. The green beam had vanished, but the green rectangle and the red pointed tail were still aglow.

"Probably it was only a minute after getting on my feet that the buzzing sound got louder," he said. "It became a high-pitched metallic sound, and I could hear another sound, a constant drum, drum, drum."

Said Chuck, "The craft then suddenly swung around until it pointed vertically, its tail down. It held this position for about four or five seconds, then the tail's brightness increased, and next it just changed into a blur."

Chuck recalls that, following the blur, there occurred a sudden purple soundless flash, a three- or four-second lapse, then a loud thunderclap. The UFO was gone. It had become a diminishing red light in the night sky. He said it shot straight up, then appeared to curve and level off, then another flash, this one white, about the size and brilliance of a first-magnitude star.

When it had all ended, Chuck stumbled into the house, sat down, trembled, then lay down feeling highly nervous. "I was shook up," he said. He did not call the police, or even a neighbor or friend. "No one would believe me," he said.

When his parents came home, he, still trembling and apprehensive, went out to get Duke, and gave him water and grain. I asked if he noticed anything unusual about the horse. Chuck said that Duke's hair was wet from sweating, which indicated that he had been running. Chuck said Duke frequently runs during the day, but thought it was unusual that he would be sweating at that late hour.

The next day, Chuck said, he checked his yard and his neighbor's garden, looking for trace evidence. He found nothing unusual, nothing disturbed. The dried furrows in his neighbor's garden showed no evidence of disturbance: no tree limbs were broken and no foliage burns to the vegetables were apparent.

I asked about physiological effects: nausea, vomiting, numbness, temperature change? He replied, nothing that he could attribute to the UFO. However, the next day, his nose and forehead hurt from falling the night before, but showed no bruises. One other physical factor Chuck remembered. Before the incident he had felt the miseries of a head cold. The next day, there was no trace of a cold. About a week after the incident, Chuck consulted his family doctor for a routine physical. He was given a clean bill of health. He did not tell the doctor about his UFO encounter.

Never once did Chuck falter in his answers to my questions concerning his admittedly "unbelievable" experience. During my dozen phone interviews with Chuck, using the stratagem of rephrased questions concerning sequence of events, description of observed details or mental reaction, his responses were quick and seemingly an attempt to make an honest appraisal of the incident and of himself. He was honest in revealing some past daydreaming experiences, during classes in school two years before, which concerned his parents. "For this reason," Chuck admitted, "I never told my parents about my experience. They would think I was daydreaming and wouldn't believe me."

Then Chuck asked, "Mr. Stringfield, do you believe me? Do you think I was hallucinating?"

Chuck and I discussed the "anatomy" of a hallucination. Although rationalizing this psychiatric disorder is well beyond my expertise, I was inclined to believe that a number of Chuck's observations, such as dust being suctioned up inside the green shaft of light from the neighbor's garden, and the swaying of the tree branches, were more symptomatic of physical "cause and effect" than of fantasy. Also, his observation of vapors rising from the surface of the swimming pool seems more a fact of atmospherics and less a symptom of aberrant imagination.

I checked with the Center of UFO Studies, MUFON, and all local researchers for correlative UFO activity in this area for the date of the incident, May 10. None. The closest, according to an item sent to me by Ted Bloecher, was a daytime sighting over Maysville, Kentucky, for May 11.

I also checked with the FAA for radar confirmation. Their log at the control tower of the Greater Cincinnati Airport showed no UFO activity.

Chuck did not at any time refer to special interest in the UFO or the parasciences. He had no awareness of certain popularly known UFO events in the past that could have influenced his ability to describe certain aspects of his encounter.

Another factor not overlooked in my interview concerned his use of psychedelic or prescriptive drugs prior to or during his experience. His answer: "None! Not even cough medicine."

The possibility of Chuck's perpetrating a hoax is remote, as he had nothing to gain by notoriety, which he knew would cause unfavorable parental reaction. Significant perhaps is Chuck's recollection that his mother, on her returning home that night, *asked about the red marks on his nose and forehead!*

Dick Hall, MUFON international coordinator, in his extensive correspondence worldwide has received a number of paralysis reports like Doyle's. A French press release dated February 28, 1975, relates that Daniel Lorrod, while driving from Montbard to Paris, encountered a gray, metallic UFO, which ejected a "mass of rays," causing him temporary paralysis.

In Pulkinnan, Finland, December 1972, two girls in their twenties witnessed a UFO with a lighted dome shaped like an egg. Suddenly they were struck by a red light beam and both were paralyzed from head to foot; they were unable to breathe, hear or scream. Only after a great struggle did one girl manage to free herself for a few seconds. As she reached for her companion, the beam then hit her in the back, causing unbearable heat and her whole body to vibrate. In what seemed to be an eternity, they both felt completely deserted and that they had lost the sense of time. When finally free of the light beam, the girls ran into the nearest house. Their clothing was covered with mud, and one girl lost a shoe.

In the world of *Alice in Wonderland,* Alice's preposterous experiences were all a dream. The preposterous, which is experienced by real people in every stratum of worldwide society, does not simply fade away like the Cheshire cat. There is no awakening from the awful dream. . . .

Jerry Black, MUFON investigator in the southwestern Ohio area, frequently appears on radio talk shows. As a result of one of his late-hour sessions, in which he had mentioned a light-beam case, he received a letter, dated May 30, 1975, from an inmate of a penitentiary. In the letter and subsequent correspondence, the inmate describes a past experience with a green shaft of light, analogous to Doyle's, and a five-hour time lapse that had left him utterly baffled ever since it happened, in January 1968. His letter, a plea for understanding of his "nerve shattering" experience, also expresses an awareness of his social status, which may give cause to doubt his veracity. His letter, in part, which I have no reason to question, follows:

> . . . In January, 1968, during a snowstorm, I was driving a tractor trailer for a firm in Baraga, Michigan, returning from a trip on the East Coast. I checked my watch when I turned off Highway M-77 onto M-28, and it was midnight. M-28 is perfectly straight in a desolate flat stretch of the Upper Peninsula of Michigan. It was snowing heavily and clogging up my windshield wipers. About 12:15 A.M., I pulled over and got out to knock the ice off the wipers. Suddenly I was blinded by what I

can only describe as a tremendously brilliant strobe light. The area all around me lit up. My first thought was that an airplane got lost in the snowstorm. The light lasted for only a few seconds, then I seemed to be in some sort of pale green cone . . . I say cone-shaped because it seemed to get thinner as it went up. But it was huge because it covered myself and the truck. I thought I was crazy. I could see it snowing but it wasn't snowing on me or the truck. That is when I noticed the sudden warmth. That's all I remembered for a while.

The next thing I recall was standing about 20 feet away from the truck and I don't know how I got there. It was still snowing heavily and, although the snow was at least 5 to 7 inches deep, there was not one trace that showed that I had walked that distance. Also, I was completely dry and warm. Believe me, I really thought I was losing my mind. I walked back to my truck which had in the meantime stalled. This in itself is weird because I had a 335 Cummins diesel engine and a diesel just doesn't up and stall. . . . When I got back in the truck and restarted, I found the temperature of the engine was zero. To get cold it normally takes about three hours. I checked my watch thinking that I had been out of the truck for only a few minutes and I was shocked to see it was 5:00 a.m. I was baffled: I had lost nearly five hours!

After I got back in the truck, I had a severe headache and developed nausea that stayed with me for about four days. Also of interest, I noted a very unfamiliar odor during my experience which I had forgotten until 1972. At that time, I was driving a semi through Texas and had the alternator burn up. Just as I caught that smell I remembered it was the same as I smelled that night in 1968. It gave me a chill.

. . . If you should find this account a hilarious joke I would appreciate that you keep it to yourself. I am more than embarrassed by being here in prison and don't want to face ridicule when I leave. . . . Again I must remind you that I wish this kept in strictest confidence.

He was released from the penitentiary in October 1975.

The UFO that stalls a passenger car or a diesel truck shocks the unwary driver. But there are many other weird, "wonderland" happenings to motorists.

A similar case of car control by a UFO was investigated by the Tasmanian UFO Center, occurring near Bridgewater, north of Hobart, in July 1974. Said one of the witnesses, who had been driving a Valiant station wagon, in a tape-recorded interview, ". . . The object seemed to be oval with a front top light, a red one, and a larger bottom light. It hovered as we turned off the highway and it kept pace with us. It was perfectly silent. As we passed the main road near Campania, where there were a few houses, the object moved away and higher. . . . Then, when we got into open country again, it descended and resumed pacing my car. Suddenly I felt as if I was in its power, that it was taking over the controls of the car. It was hard to steer. At one time, we got near the object on the right side of the road, and to steer the car back was quite an effort. I remember after the UFO disappeared that my shoulder ached from my effort to keep the car on the road. The car wasn't in my power!"

Thinking macrocosmically, paralysis cases are no more a signal of the UFO's intent than the few known cases in which a light beam miraculously healed a wound or cured a chronic illness—or, as in Doyle's case, cured his head cold.

Healing cases on record baffle ufologists. More than a few who are looking into new realms for clues of the UFO nature and source are now seriously studying cases once dismissed as nonsense. Even more miraculous than Doyle's is a "healing" case occurring in Damon, Texas. Two deputy sheriffs, while driving, saw a UFO near the road and tried to get close. They got scared and drove back into town, the UFO pursuing them. One of them had been bitten by a pet alligator earlier in the day and had an open wound on his arm, which was resting on the edge of the car window while exposed to the light of the UFO. When he got into town, the wound was healed completely.

Stranger than healing is the *rejuvenation* case. One outstanding case, which reads like science fiction, was first published by the British *Flying Saucer Review*. Occurring in a provincial area south of Buenos Aires, Argentina, on December 30, 1972, the case was investigated by Señor Pedro Romaniuk, a person of highest credentials. He is a former commander with an international airline with more than eleven thousand flying hours to his credit and has served as technical investigator for the Argentine Air Force's Aviation Accidents Investigation Board.

The single witness, Venturo Maceiras, seventy-three years old at the time of his experience, has had only the first two years of primary schooling and is a typical Gaucho from rural Argentina. At about 10:20 P.M., Maceiras was sitting drinking the national beverage, maté, about six meters from the little shack in which he lives. By a small fire he had just finished his evening meal. At his side were his dog and a cat with her three kittens. He was listening to his transistor radio when it began to fail.

At that moment he heard a loud humming noise, "like the noise of angry bees," coming from overhead. Looking up, he saw a powerful light rapidly increasing in intensity and flooding the whole area. Within the area of light, he could clearly distinguish an enormous object. Estimated size was twenty to twenty-five meters in diameter. From tubes in the lower central portion of the object there was an emission of sparks, while around it an enormous wheel was constantly spinning.

Maceiras described the color of the object as "red-orange turning to purple." In the upper-central part, the whole of which was intensely illuminated, he could see a spherical cabin with two small windows. At one of those windows was a figure visible from the waist upward, wearing dark gray clothing made of rolls or cylinders joined together, which he described as looking like "bananas." When Maceiras sighted the occupant, a shower of sparks shot from the underpart of the object, hitting the ground in front of him. Then the object tilted slightly downward and toward him, so that he had a full view of the lighted cabin and could see a second occupant, with identical features and clothing. He described the eyes as slanted, the mouth a thin line, and he remembered no details of the nose or ears. Inside the cabin he could see a long panel with "a whole lot of instruments and clocks."

With the downward tilting movement a powerful flash of light came from the underpart, blinding the witness temporarily. The flash completely enveloped the cat and then vanished. Meanwhile the humming sound was growing louder and the color of the object was turning bluish green. It began to move forward, away from the eucalyptus trees, and descended still lower until it was no more than four to six meters above the ground. At this point, Maceiras was able to see, in the upper part of the cabin, a wheel or ring spinning fast. After that, the object moved off toward the northeast, where the main road is and where there are high-power cables. A strong smell of sulphur remained in the air. Then the object disappeared behind a tree-covered mound, its color changing to red and then greenish blue.

As soon as the flash of light ended, the cat disappeared, even though she was suckling her kittens. She did not reappear until February 16, *forty-eight days later.* Her back still showed scorch marks and burns. She refused to go near the place where she had had her unpleasant experience.

While the object was stationary in the air, Maceiras felt tingling in his legs, a sensation that lasted for twenty-eight hours. By the middle of January of 1973, Maceiras had begun to lose hair abnormally. At one pull of the fingers he would lose about two hundred strands of hair, which he performed in the presence of investigators. From the fourteenth day on, several small, red, pruriginous pustules appeared on the back of his neck, which he constantly scratched.

Another symptom was a marked difficulty in speaking, having trouble moving his tongue. This persisted for about ten to twelve days. Also, his eyes watered constantly and, besides tears, thin filaments came from the eyes.

The site where the object appeared is surrounded by eucalyptus trees about ten to twelve meters in height. Most of the tops of these trees were scorched or completely burned. Several branches were taken to the National Atomic Power Commission, which issued only an oral report stating that no traces of radioactivity were found.

A large quantity of dead catfish had been found in a small stream near the sighting. The remarkable feature is that some of the catfish were gathered up and put into a refrigerator and on the following day were found to have turned dark red. Five of the fish were sent to the Institute of Bromatology (science of foods) in La Plata. A report showing the Institute's analysis is unavailable.

Romaniuk states that Maceiras had been interrogated more

than sixty times by investigators, including doctors, engineers, police officials and the secretary to the local government office. These people have all requested that their names not be quoted regarding the case.

In a later visit to see Maceiras, February 19–21, 1973, Romaniuk discovered the following data: "Since approximately February 10, Maceiras has observed that *new teeth* have been appearing in his left upper gum. At the time of my visit, I was able to confirm that two front teeth and two cheek teeth were coming through and were approximately 2 mm to 3 mm long."

Neither science nor I may ever be able to explain the alleged emergence of new teeth or the instant cure of a flesh wound caused by an alligator any more than scores of other inexplicable human experiences attributable to the UFO. If truly the UFO is responsible for these anomalies, then we are dealing with a phenomenon so omnipotent that we as Earth's *Homo sapiens* are too low in the universe's evolutionary scale to ever understand its nature or intent.

The UFO's secrets may forever lie in the infinite mysteries of the macrocosm.

IV

Fringe Cases–ad Infinitum

Shortly after midnight, George Willis was awakened by a high-pitched sound; a bright orange glow bathed his bedroom. Looming before him were three nightmarish creatures, three to four feet in height, with rounded heads, large ears, and grayish white wrinkled skin. Their movement was unnatural, mechanical, like robots. Willis, in shock, passed out.

Willis recalls that when he awakened, on the floor, he was seized by the entities and propped upright against the wall. In the upright posture his body and limbs suddenly stiffened. Helpless, he watched the three intruders examine his entire body with a strange, small, oval object. As the device ranged down toward his leg, he dared to look. In view, through the oval instrument, was his leg bone! Instantly, he developed a severe headache and again passed out.

Willis did not awaken from his stupor until dawn. Fearfully he stared around the bedroom. The lights were still on; the bedsheets were neatly folded.

The Willis encounter occurred on October 15, 1973, in Omro, Wisconsin, four days following the Pascagoula incident in which two fishermen were abducted by similar impish creatures. But the news wires did not break the Pascagoula story until the fifteenth, leaving Willis only the barest chance of knowing about the other encounter to trigger his own grotesque experience.

The Willis incident was originally investigated by Lee Mehciz and Lois Sayon of MUFON and was later followed up for more detail by Mrs. Allen Hynek, who assiduously assists her astronomer husband in the center's UFO research. I called Mrs. Hynek in April 1976 for her updated evaluation. "George seems sincere," she said. "Whether or not his experience was a dream or a true encounter is still a question. However, there are similar details to other cases not to his awareness. . . . I must add that the witness was greatly impressed and relieved by our research interest in his case and promise that he wouldn't be ridiculed."

Following a live TV appearance during the 1973 flap in which I daringly stressed humanoid encounters, I received an anonymous call from a lady in Middletown, Ohio. Her concerned voice asked that I reach her only *after* I left the station, and she gave me her phone number.

Mrs. Quinn's (name changed) strange story was about a creature she, her two daughters, and three-month-old baby experienced while visiting her husband's parents' farm, in Rogers, Kentucky, in August 1961. After I assured her that I would treat her name confidentially, she related her story. Like the Willis case, there was no direct UFO involvement and *the encounter happened in a bedroom.*

Mrs. Quinn, with her baby, Scott, tucked in bed near her, was suddenly awakened at about 1:30 A.M. with a "terrible feeling of being pulled by some powerful force" from her bed.

"Nothing touched me," she said. "It was all in my mind and I could hardly stay in bed."

As she reached for her baby, she saw a "terrible-looking creature" standing beside her bed. "It was a big blob with a small round head with no neck, looking like a roly-poly." She explained, "Its eyes were big, real big, with wrinkles around the top and side that glowed. They looked mean, and sometimes they looked almost sad."

Mrs. Quinn explained her feeling of helplessness in resisting the creature. Unable to scream, she whimpered, "Oh, God!" With that, the ogre then moved across the room to a couch-bed where her two daughters, Brenda and Judy, were sleeping.

Judy, age fourteen at the time, related her experience: ". . . I am now twenty-six and feel a little foolish relating this. . . . It's hard to explain, but I was awakened by a sensation of being

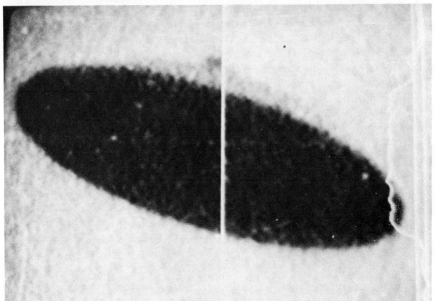

Famous McMinnville, Oregon, photo (one of two) taken by Paul Trent, May 11, 1950, from his back yard. Reportedly, Trent was at first reluctant to allow use of the two photos. "I'm afraid I'll get in trouble with our government," he said. After years of professional nit-picking over technical issues in the film, GSW computerized the two photos and confirmed the UFO as a solid vehicle. For a detailed explanation of computer testing of UFO photos, see Appendix II. Photo courtesy of GSW, Inc., and computerized enhancement courtesy of SDS.

Six adult leaders and twenty boy scouts at a summer camp in Timber Lake, Maine, on July 7, 1958, witnessed a wobbling, bronze-colored disc, making a low-pitched humming sound, appear in the sky over a wooded area. While the UFO, estimated to be thirty feet in diameter, was in view, all the normal animal noises of the forest ceased. The two photos were taken by Phil Johnson, using a box camera, just before the UFO flipped to an upright position, made a vertical climb, and disappeared at tremendous speed. Photos courtesy of Ground Search Watch, Inc. (GSW, Inc.), and computerized enhancement photographs courtesy of Spartial Data Systems (SDS) of California.

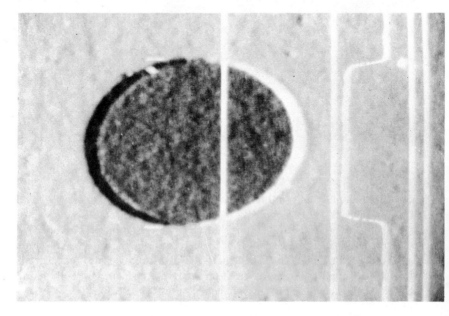

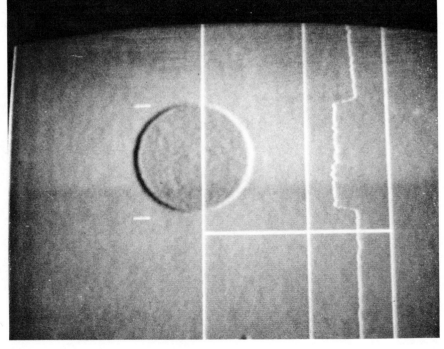

The photo above appears to be a lucky shot of a UFO. It was submitted for computer analysis to Bill Spaulding of GSW. His analysis proved that the object was a model a short distance from the camera and that it was obviously a hoax. It was suspected to be less than twelve inches in diameter, approximately ten to twenty feet from the camera. Photo courtesy of GSW, Inc., and computerized enhancement courtesy of SDS.

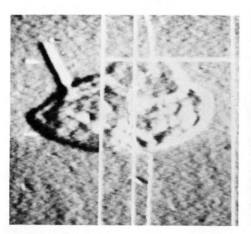
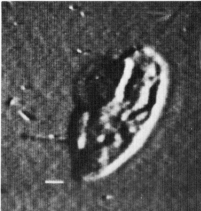

tugged out of bed. The room was dark and the thing hovering over me was darker. It actually looked like a huge tar baby with enormous eyes. They changed like a mud puddle does when you drop a large rock in the center and then drop a smaller one in. That's how it communicated. I knew it wanted me to go somewhere. When it moved closer, I felt as if I were being enveloped by some force I can't explain. It never made any sound. . . . I found myself slipping off the bed, so I grabbed my sister. She yelled, 'You crazy thing, you're pulling me off the bed.'

"Suddenly the thing released its strange force and it was gone."

When Mr. Quinn heard the commotion in the adjoining bedroom, he rushed in but saw nothing. The breast-fed baby became ill the next day, refusing to take its mother's milk. Frightened, Mrs. Quinn forced her husband to take her and her family back to Middletown, and she refused to return for another visit for more than a year. Her husband later heard that UFOs had been seen in the Rogers area during the time of the creature encounter but was unable to confirm the date.

Unlike Pascagoula, the Omro and Rogers cases lack a known UFO connection. Based on the unwritten strictures of UFO research, Omro and Rogers must be relegated to the "fringe." But it is in this unnerving, debatable fringe or vacuum that many of today's ufologists are in free float, wondering if and where the UFO and all its attendant anomalies interlace.

Said Wido Hoville, editor of *UFO Quebec,* in his paper "UFOs and Parapsychology," submitted before the Center for UFO Studies conference, April 30–May 2, 1976, "The parapsychological hypothesis rests on some observations that are so strange that they seem to belong to another realm. We should always remember the fact that any technology that is far superior to ours will appear like magic to us. . . . Even the aspects that now appear to belong to the paranormal and parapsychological field may finally prove to have a technological explanation."

Whether Willis' and the Quinns' "humanoids" were psychic phenomena or robots teleported by a push button from a spacecraft, theirs, and others just as outlandish, will eventually require scientific answers, or at least scientific cognizance. Conservative ufologists who support the extraterrestrial hypothesis with no psychic strings attached will reject Omro and Rogers and other paranormal experiences. Hoville concludes his paper on this note: "The uprise lately of more and more writers who probe into parapsychological and paranormal aspects of the UFO controversy . . . should give us all reason for concern. The direction of UFO research may very well prove to be another lure-away tactic either by the UFO intelligence or some sort of government agency."

Noticeably, and I thought significantly, many scientific confreres at the CUFOS conference who have long supported the "nut and bolt" UFO, were privately more amenable and willing to wait to see any *new* evidence for all the mystifying anomalies: the paranormal creature encounters, Bigfoot, the men in black, animal mutilation, the Bermuda Triangle, and even the neopterodactyls witnessed soaring over American skies since 1975.

On the fringes of ufology are other entities, taking a different configurative form from the bedroom intruders of the Willis home and the Quinns' "tar baby."

Stalking under the shadow of mankind, hidden and furtive in forests of the northwestern United States and western Canada is Bigfoot. This monstrous creature, sometimes known as Sasquatch, is zoologically unidentified, and like the Loch Ness Monster, Nessie, has yet no formal name. Bigfoot's historic perambulations are rich in Indian legend, and since the early 1800s the beast has been witnessed by many woodsmen and campers in the wilds. Based on descriptive reports, the Yeti, or Abominable Snowman, in the Himalayas may be Bigfoot's hominian oriental cousin. Whatever the informal name, Bigfoot's meanderings have been popularized in books such as *Sasquatch* (1973), by Don Hunter and René Dahinden, and articles by the late naturalist Ivan Sanderson. Inescapably, since its emergence into other regions of the United States in recent years, Bigfoot has been formally thrust into the fringe of UFO research.

Bigfoot is an anthropoidal creature of gargantuan size, six to ten feet in height, is covered with thick dark hair, has been seen to have large glowing eyes, has great agility, is odorous, possesses herculean strength, and can vanish suddenly as though it were a member of the spirit world. And, of course, the feet are enormously large, with three or four toes. Despite existing photos of Bigfoot and traces of footprints preserved in plaster of Paris, no specimen has yet been captured or any of its lairs found. Like the UFOs' little men, little hairy bipeds, and scary dwarfs, Bigfoot is mysteriously elusive. Professor Grover Krantz of the Anthropological Department at Washington State University, in a paper titled "Anatomy of the Sasquatch Foot," published in *Sasquatch,* concluded, "No matter how incredible it may be that the Sasquatch exists and has remained uncaught, it is even more incredible to believe in all the attributes of the hypothetical human track maker. As Sherlock Holmes put it '. . . When you have eliminated the impossible, whatever remains, however improbable, must be the truth.' Even if none of the hundreds of sightings had ever occurred, we must still be forced to conclude that a giant bipedal primate does indeed inhabit the forests of the Pacific Northwest."

Had Bigfoot as a primate remained in the Northwest, his eventual identity might have been resolved by science. But Bigfoot, or a psuedo Bigfoot, geographically shifted. As a nomad, perhaps by subterranean routes, or by other, more abstract methods, Bigfoot suddenly, in the 1970s, emerged in the wilds of numerous regions in the United States: Wyoming, Colorado, Missouri, Arkansas, Illinois, Florida's Everglades, and most formidably—as though with a vengeance—in Pennsylvania.

Stan Gordon, Pennsylvania state director for MUFON, who resides in Greensburg, is also director of the Westmoreland County UFO Study Group. In a paper presented to the MUFON symposium in Akron, in 1974, Gordon stated in part:

> . . . At first glance the creatures fit the basic physical characteristics of the typical Bigfoot. When you begin to take a closer look at the accounts, you find such statements from an eye witness as, "The animal had bright, glowing red eyes. . . ." Then you uncover the fact that distinct three-toed footprints were found in the area where the creature was sighted. In the same area, game officers are investigating animal mutilations that can't easily be explained. . . . In a number of cases, UFO activity was reported in the area about the same time that a creature was seen.
>
> Our group had investigated UFO-occupant and other

creature reports prior to 1972, but in the summer of that
year, the first indications that creatures of an unknown
nature were stalking the mountains of Western Pennsylvania became apparent. The State Police and Game
officers had reports of gorillas and baboons that were
climbing over guard rails and walking in front of cars on
busy highways. . . . By the end of July of 1973, the
most unusual events during my 14 years in the field
had taken place. . . . Until I personally became involved in the investigations of many cases during this
bizarre flap, I was quite skeptical of the reality of the
reports. What was most convincing was the fact that
numerous witnesses in a large geographic area reported
identical confrontations with various types of unexplainable phenomena. . . . The cases uncovered present
definite indications that we are dealing with an intelligence that is far superior to ours both in technology
and in the knowledge of the human mind. This data is
presented with the hope that scientific ufologists will
emerge from their shells and take a detailed look into
all aspects of UFOs, no matter how strange the facts
may be. . . .

Gordon records 118 documented creature sightings up to June
1974 from the counties of Allegheny, Beaver, Fayette, Indiana,
Somerset, Washington, and Westmoreland. One abbreviated report follows:

On the night of October 25, 1973, the first definite
case that showed a relationship between UFOs and hairy
creatures occurred. The report is thoroughly documented
and since I was a witness to what occurred after the actual sighting I have no doubt that the incident did occur.
The case was personally investigated by Dr. Berthold E.
Schwarz, an eminent psychiatrist from Montclair, New
Jersey, who came to look into the unusual events. . . .
    At 10:30 p.m., our UFO Control Center received a
call from the Uniontown Police Barracks. The trooper
who called had just returned from investigating a UFO

landing/creature sighting. The main witness was also at the barracks and was interviewed by phone.

At 9:00 p.m., the witness and 15 other people in the vicinity of his father's farm had seen a large red ball descend toward the pasture. He ran into the house and got a .30-06 rifle; then in the company of two neighbors proceeded by truck up a dirt road toward the area where the object had descended. As the object approached closer, the truck's headlights dimmed. The trio went by foot to the top of the hill and they could see the object resting on the ground. The object was bright white and appeared to be about 100 feet in diameter and made a loud sound like that of a lawn mower.

. . . From the illumination of the craft they could make out two tall, ape-like creatures with glowing eyes. The creatures were making crying sounds and the smell of "burning rubber" filled the air. One of the boys became terrified and fled. The man fired several shots over the heads of the creatures, which didn't stop them. Then he shot three more rounds, this time directly into one of the creatures. There was a whining sound, then the one that was hit raised its arm and both moved off into the woods. The UFO disappeared.

A trooper was dispatched to the alleged landing site at 9:45 p.m. He found an area about 150 feet in diameter glowing white. "It was light enough to read a newspaper," he said. The trooper also noted that the horses and cattle stayed far outside the illuminated area. As they continued their investigation, they reported they could hear a noise in the woods following them. According to the trooper, the witnesses became hysterical and they all returned to the barracks. The police then called my office.

We felt that the case warranted a field team sent to the area immediately. The team included George Lutz, former Air Force pilot and retired Major in the Air Force Reserves; Dave Smith, physics instructor and Civil Defense Radiation Officer; Dennis Smeltzer, majoring in sociology; Dave Baker, professional photographer; and myself.

It was about 1:30 a.m., when we arrived on the scene. We checked for radiation. None. The glowing ring was no longer visible, but the animals remained outside the landing area. . . . About 2:00 a.m., a bull in the nearby field seemed scared by something. The witness' dog at the same time began to track something in the same direction. . . .

George Lutz was asking the witness questions when all of a sudden he noticed him rubbing his face and shaking as if he were going to faint. The witness, over six feet in height and weighing 250 lbs., then began to breathe heavily and started growling like an animal. He then threw George and his own father, who had accompanied him, to the ground and ran crazily around the field swinging his arms and growling! Suddenly, he collapsed on his face into the manure-covered field. Dennis, too, began to feel light-headed and fell to his knees. Then Dave Barker began to complain that he was having trouble breathing. The air was now strong with the smell of sulphur. Yelled George Lutz, "Let's get out of here."

The entire event was tape recorded, but re-living the event on tape in no way can take the place of being there. . . .

I have discussed this case of seeming fantasy several times with Gordon. While the reports of the witness and police, and his personal experience, were no more fantastic than any of the cases I have investigated, I think it was the role of Bigfoot and the UFO *on one stage* that I found provocative.

Gordon is adamant about his case for Bigfoot and the UFO. "This one case helped convince me that Bigfoot, especially the kind we are finding in Pennsylvania, and the UFO are a part of the same psychic phenomena," he stated. "It's hard to explain the strange behavior of the one witness going ape, I know, but we have a tape of Bigfoot's screams recorded from an incident in Westmoreland and the sound is identical to his."

While on the pros and cons of Bigfoot's UFO connection, I told

Gordon about two cases I had checked on Bigfoot, without UFOs, in Ohio, in which gunplay also took place. But Gordon's endless catalogue of creature cases had more of this "wild West" feature than I had realized. Promptly I was referred to an incident occurring on February 6, 1974, near Uniontown, in Fayette County, Pennsylvania.

Mrs. A., who lives in an isolated wooded area, was sitting in her house alone watching TV. Hearing the sound of rattling tin cans on the porch, she thought of wild dogs on the prowl and got her 16-gauge shotgun. Her intention: scare the dogs away. The woman went to the door and turned on the porch light. Instead of a dog, she was confronted by a seven-foot-tall, hair-covered, ape-like creature standing just six feet away. Instantly, the creature raised both hands up into the air over its head. Shocked, the woman fired into the midsection of the creature, thinking it was about to leap on her. To her amazement, the creature "just disappeared in a flash of light." She said the flash was "just like someone taking a picture." There was no sound or smell.

She immediately ran into the house. While she was trying to recover from shock, her phone rang. It was her son-in-law, who lived with his wife and children in a trailer one hundred feet away from her house. He had heard the shot. Within minutes, armed with a six-shot revolver, he proceeded to his mother-in-law's residence. As he approached he observed near the edge of the woods "shadows of four or five hairy people." Suddenly they moved toward him, and he got a good, hair-raising look. They were seven feet tall, ape-like with long arms, and had "fire-red eyes that glowed."

He fired two shots, then ran into his mother-in-law's house. Looking out the window, they both saw a bright red flashing light hovering over the woods about five hundred feet away. They agreed that it looked like a Christmas-tree ornament and revolved like a beacon on a police car. Panic-stricken, they called the police.

The ground was frozen and no footprints could be found. The most convincing evidence to the investigating officers was the animal reaction. Four dogs were still shaking. Even when coaxed from their hideaway, they would not budge. The cats in the trailer were hiding under the couch. The horse refused to eat. And Mrs.

A.'s daughter in the trailer reported that her baby was so disturbed it cried all night, which had never happened before.

The only oddity about Ohio's Bigfoot is that their rare appearance predates their concentration in Pennsylvania.

Word about the "creatures" in Point Isabel, in rural Clermont County, Ohio, reached me through a social worker. There were two cases occurring on farm property in the 1960s, when Bigfoot was still an anthropological freak and well outside the fringe of UFO research. The case of Mr. and Mrs. Lew Lister is a good illustration.

I reached Mrs. Lister by phone on one of her visits to her mother's home. With her husband out of work due to an injury, she was unable to afford a phone on her farm. At first Mrs. Lister was reluctant to discuss her experience. She said repeatedly, "It was all too unbelievable." I assured her of anonymity, and when I mentioned Stan Gordon's research into Bigfootean phenomena, she took a deep breath and talked. Notes pertinent to Mrs. Lister's story were entered into my UFOLOG, February 25, 1975, as follows:

> Mrs. Lister's incident happened in 1964, when she was 18 years old. She prefaced her story with, "You'll never believe it," and "I hesitate even to tell you, because you'll think I'm crazy."
>
> The incident occurred on a road about a mile from the farm, then owned by her mother. She was dating Lew Lister at the time, sitting in the car talking about 11:00 p.m., with the lights out. Suddenly they both caught sight of a figure moving across the open field.
>
> "It didn't seem to see us until we turned on the headlights," she said. "Then it came toward us. It didn't walk, it just seemed to take large hops or leaps to our car."
>
> Mrs. Lister spoke excitedly, rephrasing her words trying to make an incredible experience sound true. "You won't believe this, but the thing moved through three strands of barbed wire. As it got closer, I screamed. Then it reared back and lunged forward as though it were coming through the windshield. It was so close, it tried to grab Lew, and I'm not sure if it touched him or not."

Mrs. Lister remembers that she and Lew desperately tried to roll up their windows and, vaguely, that Lew tried to start the motor. "I don't recall the motor turning over," she said. "All I can remember, even after it happened, was the feeling like I was being hypnotized by the creature's glowing eyes. I couldn't hear anything and I think I tried to scream, but I'm not sure if I did or not. I felt like I had a time lapse or like I was living in another time. . . . I just remember its eyes focused on mine."

At this point Mrs. Lister stopped. "I can't go on," she said. "It's too embarrassing; you won't believe me anyway."

She meant it; her voice wavered, her words melted. I offered to call her back, easing the tension momentarily, then in a maneuver to restore her lost credibility I countered with the details—the repugnant details—of another local case. She responded. Getting a new breath she said firmly, "The creature then changed into another form right before our very eyes."

"I have heard of this often in creature cases," I assured her.

"But this thing just crouched down; its hands became paws and it went on all fours," she said. "And it all happened like a slow-motion movie. Then it was gone. It vanished into thin air!"

For a brief full-conscious moment, Mrs. Lister got a good glimpse of the creature. It was at least six feet tall, had wide shoulders, which narrowed down to the waist. The body, upright, was covered with a yellowish fuzz in the glare of the headlights. "The head was horrible," she said. "It was pointed at the top and narrow at the chin and the brow was wrinkled—I'm sure of this—and its ears were large like pigs' and the nose was also like a pig's. I'm sure the eyes glowed orange, and the teeth were like fangs."

The second case I got on a tip from the social worker also occurred in the Point Isabel area, in the fall of 1968. I managed to reach Larry Abbott for the story, who was fifteen years old during the time of the weird encounter with Bigfoot.

About 10:00 P.M., there was a sound outside the farmhouse "like something hitting metal." Larry, his father, and a relative, Arnold Hubbard, went outdoors to look. Then, from the opposite side of the house, they heard a rustling of weeds.

"We got a flashlight," said Larry, "and then we saw it. It was a monster rising from the tall brush about fifty feet away. It was walking toward us, and my guess was that it was ten feet tall and about four feet across the shoulders. Its arms were long, like an ape's."

In the flashlight beam the monster's hairy body was a tannish color; its eyes glowed over a nose that was beyond Larry's ability to describe. The teeth were prominent and protruding, the ears pointed. But the feature that Larry remembered most was the thickness of the shoulders.

"The thing put me into a sort of trance," said Larry. "I couldn't talk. Maybe it was just fright, but I couldn't open my mouth. And nobody else talked either. Maybe we were all in a trance."

Larry said when he played the light beam on the monster it dropped down to the ground and was lost from sight. Then, a few minutes later, they could hear it again, near the garage. Alarmed, Larry's father returned to the house and brought back a .22 rifle and gave it to Hubbard, who wanted to stalk the beast. As the men moved across the open field, the creature suddenly stood up in clear view about fifty feet away. When Larry got it in the beam of the light, Hubbard fired. His first shot was a direct hit. The creature screamed hideously, a scream that Larry will never forget. Two more shots were fired.

Unbelievably, before the eyes of all three men, the creature was suddenly enveloped in a white mist. In less than a minute the mist vanished, then darkness.

"The three of us searched the spot where the creature was shot that night," said Larry. "We found no trace of it, no blood, nothing. The next day, we checked the whole farm. Still nothing."

Reports of Bigfoot activity continue through 1976 in many states; heavily in Pennsylvania, California, the Northwest, and Canada. Two policemen witnessed large, hairy, simian creatures separately within two weeks' time in the Woodlawn area, north of Cincinnati, in February 1976. On April 16, 1976, Caroline Morris called the police shortly after midnight to report that she was frightened by "screaming, screeching, and growling in a ravine below her hillside home near the rugged slopes of Mt. Tamalpais, on the north side of San Francisco Bay. Patrolmen Dan Murphy and Edward Johnson were dispatched to the scene.

"When we got there," Murphy said, "we heard the sounds, too. They were strange, high-pitched sounds. . . ."

With guns drawn, they hiked down the pitch-black, wooded slopes training their flashlights through the underbrush. "I heard heavy breathing ahead of us," said Murphy. "Then there were crackling noises, as if something was approaching."

In the beam of Murphy's light they saw a large, "dark-colored thing." Said Murphy, "It was walking on its hind legs. I saw it climb an eight-foot retaining wall and disappear into the brush."

At sunup the officers returned and found a thick trail of blood. Following it through the brush they came upon a slain deer, its neck broken, the body disemboweled and badly mangled.

But Bigfoot's UFO connection is rare, and so the beast remains on the fringe—unless we are to believe that there is more than one kind of anthropoidal configuration. Like the Loch Ness Monster, Bigfoot (or Sasquatch) is a freak. Unlike Nessie, landlocked in deep waters, Bigfoot is a promiscuous land rover of wild country, and, whatever his physical or metaphysical properties, he is not restrained by geography.

Loch Ness, in the highlands of northern Scotland, besides its natural charm, is a perfect place for the curious and tired mind of a UFO researcher. My wife and I visited the *loch* in April 1967, and despite the warning from our hostess, Mrs. James Penny of Inverness, I went to the water's edge and peered into its inky depths. Kneeling down to touch the water, I pondered its straight-down depth and the mystery somewhere beneath me still unresolved. The water was real, Urquhart Castle nearby was real, and the more than four thousand *reported* sightings of Nessie were real. Of that vast number, from mostly credible people, were many honest sightings of the *real* Nessie. I remember looking skyward and wondering about the mysteries of space and time, of the UFO and all the other fringe elements beyond my grasp to understand. From the waters I took a small, rounded stone covered with moss—this was my souvenir, my artifact from the waters of mystery. I did not see Nessie, and my stone proved nothing, but philosophically the stone was real and just as real as was Nessie to those privileged to see her.

Fortunately, Nessie is a zoological problem and is not a part of the UFO fringe. Although there are good reports of UFOs over the *loch*, Nessie, unlike Bigfoot, does not dematerialize into a mist or change into another form.

The act of transformation is not confined to creatures. On the fringes of UFO research is the reported or suspected change of one form into another of structural and mechanical hardware—the helicopter for example. Reports of phantom objects shaped like helicopters have been frequently witnessed by ranchers where animal mutilations have occurred—helicopters without lights, helicopters that suddenly vanish, and things shaped like the copter that are in places they don't belong.

One of the strangest UFO-linked helicopter events in my personal investigations occurred on a farm near Lynchburg, Ohio. Dan Richley, a teen-ager interested in astronomy and the UFO, had been seeing unusual nocturnal lights high over Lynchburg.

At 10:00 P.M., September 26, 1974, Dan saw a stationary object, which he described: "Looked like a star, but it was a bigger than a first-magnitude, and its rainbow of colors pulsated."

Promptly he got his father, Walter Richley, a UFO skeptic, who agreed "as an experiment" to use their portable searchlight of 132,000 candle power, mounted on their white pickup truck, to shine on the celestial light.

As the beam ranged on the object, the two Richleys stood in shock as a red beam was shot down engulfing them and the truck. "My white truck was as red as a fire engine," said Walter Richley. "And when I glanced up, the object in the sky also turned red and it was closer. It only lasted a few seconds, but I was scared out of my wits and turned off the searchlight. When I did this, the red light went out."

As the two ran to safety toward their house, Dan said he observed the UFO change back to its rainbow of colors and disappear into the horizon. Animal reaction during the light-beam interplay? Yes. Said the father, "We have two dogs and they both went crazy. One dog was tethered and nearly broke its neck trying to get loose. The other ran off to the barn and wouldn't come out."

It was not over for the Richleys. When I interviewed them at the home of James Carnes, near Lynchburg, on November 24, the father was obviously uncomfortable. Had it not been for Carnes, their close friend, I would not have gotten the whole story.

The following night, at 11:00 P.M., Dan was sitting up reading alone. His father had retired. Suddenly he was jolted by a terribly loud sound outdoors, near the barn. Running to the window, he saw a large helicopter about to land. On its side was a large silver star and many windows.

"It was like a flying boxcar," said Dan. "On its top were props spinning and blowing debris around the yard, which damaged our peach tree. But the copter had only one light, a white light. I watched for a minute or two and nobody got out. I then got Dad out of bed."

Together they watched the large craft climb vertically *amid many electric wires and trees,* and disappear.

Mr. Richley quickly assessed the meaning of the two-night episodes. "I think I put my light beam on something that was a military secret. That copter came here to warn me."

Walter Richley, out of fear of official reprisals, imposed self-censorship. I asked if he had ever received an official apology or remuneration for damage to his property. "No, and I'm not about to press it," he said nervously, "I'd rather forget it."

Among researchers baffled by the role of the helicopter fringing on UFO events is Ann Druffel, of MUFON, who wrote "The Mystery Helicopters," appearing in the February 1976 *Skylook:*

> Over a period of two or three years, there have been hints of helicopters of unknown source connected with UFOs and possible UFO-related incidents. Are these cases merely coincidence or misidentifications, or is there, indeed, mysterious helicopter surveillance of UFOs?
>
> A startling example occurred September 3, 1975, in Tujunga, California. Nestled in the foothills of the Angeles Crest Mountains are numerous homes built on steep, winding roads. The home of Mr. and Mrs. Cromwell boasts an east-to-west view of the mountains. About 8:00 p.m., Mrs. Cromwell heard a helicopter over a

nearby canyon. Since the helicopter is the first sign of jeopardy from brush fires, Mrs. Cromwell stayed outside to watch, accompanied by Mrs. Brandt, her sister.

Mrs. Cromwell was impressed by the extreme height at which this helicopter was flying. Her estimation, 1,200 feet. As she watched, she noticed a round, brightly lighted object above the helicopter, about 1,200 feet higher up. Intrigued, Mrs. Cromwell got binoculars. A vari-colored light pattern was clearly visible. The top was a vibrant blue-green, the middle portion white and the bottom a glowing red. The light pattern encompassed the entire disc.

The object remained stationary in the sky while the helicopter circled below in a tight surveillance pattern. Then the object changed shape from round to diamond, to chevron, and into a classic saucer. As it zigzagged over the canyon area of sky, Mr. Cromwell joined in watching the object. After a few minutes, the helicopter sped off. Then *two* helicopters returned, flying in tandem. The gyrations of the objects and the movements of the choppers were such that the witnesses were forced to watch from different areas of the yard to keep them in sight. . . . At about 11:00 p.m., the object disappeared from view in the west, still followed by the chopper.

All three witnesses reported that their eyes hurt after the incident. Mrs. Cromwell suffered blurred vision. All three witnesses' eyes were streaked with red that night and felt as though sunburned.

The next morning, Mrs. Cromwell made several phone calls to public-service agencies to report the incident. Griffith Observatory referred her to our organization, Skynet.

I called every known facility involving official and private helicopters within a 300-mile radius of Tujunga. No source would admit to sighting the UFO, or to having helicopters in that area at that time. Most of these agencies indicated that only rarely do their choppers fly in tandem, since doing so creates dangerous air currents. The only helicopter admittedly in the area was from the

Los Angeles Police Department. The pilot stated that he took off from the LAPD Heliport at 8:00 p.m. and was in constant communication with Burbank Airport. He did not see any unusual object in the sky or any other helicopters.

Equally strange is a recent NICAP case which concerned an oval-shaped object hovering low over a field in Enfield, Connecticut at 9:30 a.m., on March 4, 1975. The lights emitted were blue, green and red, reminiscent of the Tujunga case. It was seen moving slowly in view of two witnesses over a period of 45 minutes. During this time, the witnesses saw a helicopter flying close to the object. The NICAP investigator and the Enfield Police Department tried to find out the identity of the copter. All military and private installations were checked; all inquiries proved negative.

Real helicopters? . . . whose? . . . or illusions? Or, as Ann Druffel asks, "Which can we believe—the rational witness or the denials of official sources? Is it possible that the aerial displays were from a source inaccessible to civilian researchers? Were they from the military complex . . . ?"

Where is truth or fiction, and where is, or what is, the borderline? That amorphous borderline is also the fringe in ufology. Who is the authority to fit which event into what realm? We are at a crossroad: Maybe by taking one road or both we may find the eventual truth about Bigfoot, the bedroom visitants, the mystery helicopters, and all the other seeming freaks and behavioral grotesqueries that are tied to ufology.

We might ask which road, or is it both, that holds the answer to the mysterious force that made *time stand still* in Nazi Germany just before Hitler unleashed his armies into Poland in 1939. From a reliable source, son of a late member of the United States Department of the Interior who was on a secret intelligence assignment in Germany in the summer of 1939, an event of the highest strangeness befell the city of Essen. During the traffic rush hour everything mechanical and electrical stopped—cars, buses, street cars, motorcycles, clocks. His father, who was there, recalled that during the peak of the frustration, which lasted ten minutes, not one car was able to blow its horn!

The answer seemed obvious at the time—a test maneuver of Hitler's secret weapon! The German newspapers did not report the incident, but the information describing the effects of the suspect weapon was conveyed to the proper sources in Washington. Of course, time has proved that the Germans did not possess a weapon of this great magnitude, for the war would have ended less favorably for the Allies.

Whatever force immobilized Essen may well have come from the same source that controlled the foo fighters during the war, later the ghost rockets that shook Scandinavia in 1946 and 1947, the green fireballs over the southwestern United States in 1948, the electromagnetic mysteries in the Bermuda Triangle, and all the other incredible oddballs and entities *on the fringe* that mock and taunt man, erase his memory, perform Christ-like miracles, or, for no apparent reason, destroy.

An event similar to Essen, but with a UFO connection, occurred during Astronaut Gordon Cooper's Mercury overflight of Australia in 1963. According to a reliable and well-informed Australian businessman who visited my home in October 1975, a luminous green UFO with a red tail, witnessed by hundreds of Australians, flew in the opposite direction to Cooper's spacecraft. During the UFO's overflight, he learned from a military source that it caused an electrical outage at the Dry Creek Tracking Station and at the rocket range in Woomera, including a blotting out of radar. The low-level, football-shaped UFO was also witnessed by Australian scientists, and cameramen took sixteen thousand feet of color movie film of the object. My informant told me that he learned from a military soucre that the film was sent to Washington, D.C., for evaluation. No jet interceptors were scrambled, because the military feared they might be affected by the powerful force field created by the UFO.

I consulted Astronaut Cooper about the UFO incident. He denied reports that he had seen the UFO during his overflight of Australia. Also consulted was Astronaut Scott Carpenter, stationed at the time at the U. S. Muchea Tracking Station. He said he knew nothing about the power outages at Australian military-operated bases. Such information, he averred, was privy only to the Australian authorities.

Another "out of character" case, occurring on August 7, 1970, with a destructive UFO, was revealed by Dr. Hynek. A letter he had received from a medical doctor who worked for the United Nations in Ethiopia tells of a red glowing ball that swept through the village of Saladane, which destroyed houses, uprooted trees, burned grass, melted asphalt on the road, and broke the stone wall of the bridge to pieces. The object, making an "ear-splitting" sound, then became stationary and returned on the same path to cause more destruction. In all, fifty buildings were damaged and eight people were injured; one little girl died.

Commented Hynek, "This is one of the few documented cases where harm has been caused by something we must regard as a UFO. It was certainly flying, it obviously was an object, and it certainly was unidentified." To back up the incident, Hynek received many photographs showing the extensive damage.

Most emerging nations in Africa are stymied by poor communications; few UFO incidents, therefore, reach the news wire services, and fewer still reach the ufologist. Joseph Brill, with good contacts in some of the English-speaking countries, such as South Africa, manages to keep abreast of some of the developments. He received the following report from the Johannesburg *Star,* in South Africa, a case similar to the Ethiopian disaster. Occurring on September 13, 1973, in Roodepoort, it, too, defies rationale and deepens the mystery of the UFOs' intent.

Mrs. Chrissie Mans said she and the family had gone to bed at 9:30 P.M. at their home on Main Beef Road in barren country. The night was still and there was not a breath of wind. Suddenly their nine-year-old son, Johan, ran into their bedroom and said he could not sleep. He felt as though something was going to happen. Then Baskie, the pet dog, started barking frantically. "All of a sudden there was a thunderous explosion," said Mrs. Mans. "Something crashed on the roof. I shot out of bed, and my husband, Piet, followed me to the back door. Our plot was lit up as if the sun had risen. It was eerie. I shivered, then I saw a flaming, saucer-like object with a small golden ball beneath it emitting sparks and smoke. It disappeared over the trees about ninety meters from the house. I thought it was an optical illusion and wiped my eyes, but then my husband said he also saw the ball of fire."

Looking outdoors, the Manses saw the effects. The corrugated-iron roof of the double garage and storeroom next to the house had lifted and landed on the back of the roof of their home. Witnesses reported they had seen the object, which they took to be a burning aircraft, topple and fall, then take off again and travel in the westerly direction from which it had come. . . .

The Ethiopian and South African cases both show evidence of wanton disregard of man and his property. Are these destructive forces perpetrated by the same power that guides the uncanny behavior of Bigfoot and the little creatures, and causes aircraft and ships to fail and disappear? Are all the strange fringe phenomena tactics of diversion, staged for man to ponder, fear, and question?

Are the UFOs from different worlds or other realms? If from other worlds, are they united in their intent, or on conflicting missions with Earth their objective, while man, primitive and incidental, is being duped by hypnotically contrived creatures, mothmen, giant primordial birds, and the men in black?[1] Or is man the real prize, and what he has witnessed as fringe phenomena are but histrionics contrived to study his psyche?

There is no simple answer. Contrived or not, fringe or not, Bigfoot's mischief and all the other anomalies are no more baffling than the creatures that abduct human specimens into their craft for physical examinations and perhaps brainwashing.

Many abductions, new and old, are surfacing. While discussing the controversial Travis Walton case, which allegedly occurred in the Apache-Sitgreaves National Forest, November 5, 1975, Coral Lorenzen, of APRO, told me on January 22, 1976, "The answer to the UFO puzzle may ultimately be in the abduction cases. They provide the most information, if reliable, but we must carefully weigh all the evidence to make sure they are not planted or false. In this phase of research we are making progress, or let's say turning a corner. . . ."

Mrs. Lorenzen also told me about an abduction case, involving a military noncommissioned officer, which occurred August 13, 1975, but she was unable to disclose the details at that time. On May 11, 1976, the *National Enquirer* headlined the story about

---

[1] Mothman is a mysterious entity described by John Keel, in *Mothman Prophecies,* as a winged creature he believes is associated with the UFO.

The men in black, usually witnessed in groups rather than singly, are human-like entities clad in completely black attire. They are known to visit a witness after a UFO sighting and allegedly threaten UFO researchers.

Staff Sergeant Charles Moody being "Kidnapped by Humanoids in a Spacecraft" near Alamogordo, New Mexico.

Sergeant Moody, stationed at Holloman AFB, with security clearance, had driven to a lonely spot near the base waiting to see the Perseid meteor shower. He watched for forty minutes, saw no meteors, and decided to return to his car. Suddenly, out of the crystal-clear sky, a metallic, disc-shaped object flashed down, wobbled, and glided toward him. Moody tried to escape in his car, but the motor was dead. Then, he recalls, "An odd glow enveloped my car and I felt numb all over."

Later, when Moody reached home, he discovered he had lost an hour and twenty minutes, and later still he recalled his whole experience aboard the disc-like craft. "I remembered that while I was engulfed in the glow, two beings came toward me from the craft. They didn't walk," said Moody. "They glided."

The creatures were about five feet tall, with large heads and whitish-gray skin, with round, dark eyes—the size of a quarter—beneath an overhanging brow. "They wore a skin-tight white suit which covered everything but the head and hands. They spoke perfect English, but there was no lip movement."

Like the Betty and Barney Hill and the Hickson-Parker cases, Moody was allegedly taken inside the craft and physically examined on a slab-like table.

Said the *National Enquirer,* Moody's statements were analyzed by the Psychological Stress Evaluator, a lie detector so accurate that courts in eight states now accept its conclusions as evidence. After analyzing Moody's story, the PSE coinventor Charles McQuiston declared, "There are no signs of stress or deception. This man is obviously telling the truth—there's no doubt about it."

V

The Humanoid Factor

Little green men . . . the ageless whipping boys for the newspaper copy desk or a *green* reporter assigned to write a story about a UFO report—even though a little creature, green, purple, or silver was not a part of the incident. "Little green men," an easy, cop-out phrase as funny as the "flying saucer," the alleged craft that brought them to Earth from Mars or the moon made of *green* cheese.

Actually, little green men do not exist in UFO research, unless a writer wishes to allude to the leprechaun. So far, in the more than fifteen hundred cases of UFO entities catalogued, only a handful have been reported as green. One was a hoax, the others were reflecting a green light on the craft from which they landed.

It was in the early 1950s that the little men, and sometimes a monster, began to make the news. Quickly, the press painted them green. Even UFO research tittered and shied away.

By 1954, UFO-related creature stories gained some respectability among a few researchers as cases began to trickle in, mostly by mail, from Europe, mainly France and Italy. It was not until years later that U.S. research learned the full story of the "invasion" of France by UFOs and occupants of dwarfish configuration. Credit must be given to ufologist Aimé Michel, later to write *Flying Saucers and* the *Straight-line Mystery* (1958), for his record-keeping of the French incidents. Later Dr. Vallée in his *Passport to Magonia* (1969), borrowing from the Michel records and another pioneer, Raymond Veillith, editor of a French research bulletin, *Lumieres dans la Nuit,* cites forty-six "creature" reports in France alone within a six-week period, September 10 to October 27, 1954. From this number, many of which were dwarf encounters, we see again the scenario of the light beam and the paralysis victim. To show the intensity of this flap, random cases are cited from Vallée's compendium:

September 10, Quarouble. A metal worker, Marius DeWilde, came out of his house as a dog was barking and saw a dark object on the railroad tracks, then saw two dwarfs walking toward it. When he tried to stop them, he was paralyzed by a strong orange light beam. The creatures were under one meter tall, bulky, and wore dark "diving" suits.

September 17, Cenon. Yves David met a being in a "diving" suit who made friendly gestures . . . and had a voice "inhuman and incomprehensible." The witness could not move during the encounter. He saw the creature enter an object on the road. It took off "like lightning, throwing a greenish light."

September 28, Bouzais. At "Le Grand Tertre" Monsieur Mercier observed that someone had stolen grapes from his vineyard. He decided to stay late and catch the thief. He was amazed when he saw a luminous mass fall from the sky about fifty meters away and found himself paralyzed as three figures emerged from the light. He lost consciousness.

October 9, Lavoux. Monsieur Barrault was riding his bicycle when he suddenly saw a figure in a "diving" suit aiming a double beam of light at him. The figure, with very bright eyes, walked on the road and went into the forest. The witness was paralyzed throughout the incident. The entity had two lights, one above the other, in front of him.

October 11, Sassier, near La Carie. Messieurs Gallois and Vigneron, who were driving from Clamercy to Corbigny, felt an electric shock as the car headlights died. They then saw a craft in a pasture fifty meters away. It was cylindrical and fairly thick, and three dwarfs were standing close by. No light was seen, except a reddish point. Both witnesses were paralyzed until the craft left. A third witness had seen a lighted object fly over the woods at La Carie.

October 11, Taupignac. Three men got out of their car to observe an intensely red sphere in the sky. It was round, with a dome, six meters in diameter, giving off a orange light. Suddenly it moved for a short distance and landed behind a woods. Two witnesses went closer and saw four dwarfs, one meter tall, who seemed busy with the machine. When the witnesses arrived within fifteen meters, the creatures rushed inside the machine. The witnesses were blinded by a sudden burst of light, blue, then orange, then red, and the object took off vertically at great speed.

October 13, Bourrasole. Messieurs Olivier and Pérano and a third man (not identified) saw a reddish disc about four meters in diameter with a small being close by about 1.2 meters tall wearing a "diving" suit. One witness said, "His head was large with respect to the rest of his body and he had two enormous eyes. The suit was bright and shiny like glass." The craft was surrounded by a misty glow. One of the witnesses came within twenty meters of it and found himself paralyzed. The craft took off, throwing him to the ground.

October 16, Baillolet. Dr. Robert, while driving, saw four objects at low altitude flying slowly in echelon formation. Suddenly one dropped to the ground with a falling-leaf motion, one hundred meters away. The doctor felt an electric shock as his car's engine and headlights died. Incapable of moving, Dr. Robert saw a figure about 1.2 meters tall moving in the light of the object; then all went dark. Later, the headlights resumed operation by themselves, when the object left the area.

Hard on the heels of the southern European reports, the little creatures reared their ugly heads in South America. Venezuela and, to a lesser degree, Brazil were the geographic targets. Here the creatures were small, hairy, and more animalistically belligerent. Through excellent contacts made by APRO, the headlined stories in Venezuela reached the United States. Two books by the Lorenzens, *Flying Saucer Occupants* (1967) and *Encounters with UFO Occupants* (1976) provide full details of the long list of the early South American and updated worldwide incidents. One of our mutual contacts, the late Horacio Gonzales G., of Caracas, summed up the Venezuelan creature encounters in November and December of 1954 in a letter published in *Orbit* for March 1956:

There is a growing belief in Venezuela that the UFO, or *Platillo Volador* is of extraterrestrial origin. . . . Re-

garding hostility, of the six landings reported, three have
been of a hostile nature and one in which the hostility
was provoked. In the Petare incident, Gustavo Gonzales,
terrified out of his wits, grabbed the dwarf with the intention of taking it into the truck. The dwarf, drawing
strength from some unknown source, easily knocked him
fifteen feet away and he arose, jackknife in hand, to
combat whatever it was. His astonishment must have
been great when, on stabbing at the dwarf, the sharp
knife slid off some hard surface and an intense light
directed from the hovering sphere blinded him.

From the reports of the Carora case, this was definitely an attempt to kidnap one of the boys, and if it was
not for the desperate action of one of them, who knows
what would have happened. Gómez, one of the boys,
says, "I fainted when one of the dwarfs, with exceptional
strength, tried to drag me to the spherical apparatus and
push me inside." The other, Lorenzo Flores, seeing his
friend in the clutches of the strange being, acted in desperation; he did not think of shooting, but, seizing the
gun by the barrel, let the dwarf have it on the shoulder,
and the gun broke in two. What may have saved the
boys is that the lights of a truck came into sight. The
sphere then rose and disappeared and the boys beat all
track records in getting to the police station, where they
related their story.

The Zulia encounter is different. Jesús Paz might have
surprised the dwarf in some act or other, or perhaps the
dwarf, seeing the car stop and one person emerge, decided to wait in hiding and observe. But, then, why did it
attack Paz, clawing the whole length of his back?

Then we have the Valencia case. In this the jockey,
José Parra, really surprised the dwarfs when they were
pulling the boulders from the side of the highway and
loading them aboard their strange craft. Parra had not
the least idea of what was happening. He was out doing
roadwork to lose weight for the races and was stopped
short by the strange scene. He turned to run, the dwarfs
spotted him, and one of them shone some ray, which hit
Parra in the back, knocking him flat. Scrambling to his

feet and looking over his shoulder, he saw the sphere rising vertically into the air. He also lost no time in reaching the police station and relating what he saw.

My opinion is that these beings may not be hostile or have hostile intentions, *but will prove to be dangerous if provoked*. The geodesic survey of the Earth seems to be continuing and they may be planning to make contact with us. There is something on Earth which has obliged them to visit in such numbers. This *something* is what they are in need of or would like to have, and sooner or later they are going to make an attempt to get it. . . .

But all the yesteryear dwarfs in South America were not hirsute or hostile. Some were humanoid—in fact, *human,* except for dwarfish stature—if we are to believe the startling testimony of one witness with more than usual credentials to make his story credible.

The witness was Dr. Enrique Caretenuto Botta, who first related his story in April 1955, in confidence, to Horacio Gonzales G., in Caracas. Since I had gained the trust of Gonzales in the exchange of confidential matters, Dr. Botta gave permission in June to relate the full story to me, which, in part, follows:

Dr. Botta is a soft-spoken, cultured man about 40, of Italian nationality, ex-war pilot, aeronautical engineer, and now architectural engineer with a well-known real estate company in Caracas. In 1950, he was in Argentina engaged in a construction project on the Pampas, in a region called Bahía Blanca, where the incident took place. He was driving along the highway about 75 miles from his hotel in an isolated region when he saw the metallic, discoid object resting on the grass off the highway. He stopped the car to investigate. He watched it for a few minutes to see what it would do, but nothing happened. Approaching nearer, he saw an opening or door in its side. Peering inside, it seemed empty. There was some sort of red light pulsating in the dome at intervals of one second. Curious, he went inside and was surprised to see a curved divan with four seats, three of which were occupied by small beings covered in a kind of tight-fitting gray overalls. He estimated the height of the beings to be about four feet. Their faces were dark or charred. In front of them was a screen with rays playing on it, and on top of the screen was a globe of transparent material which was rotating. Irresistibly he touched one of the little occupants. Its flesh was rigid.

In the next instant, Dr. Botta rushed to his car and sped off at top speed until he reached his hotel. He related his story to two intimate friends and, armed with revolvers and a camera, they decided to return. But as night was near and because of the isolation of the region, they decided to wait until the next morning.

On reaching the spot, all they found was a heap of ashes. The doctor took a picture of the ashes and one of the group scooped some up with his hand. His hand turned purple, the color remaining indelible for several days after. They remained wandering around the site looking for tracks or clues; then one of the men looked up and spotted three objects. One was cigar-shaped, high up. Two others were discoid and smaller. One of the discs, about ten meters in diameter, was hovering above the group at an estimated height of 600 meters. Dr. Botta began taking pictures hurriedly. In all, he took five pictures, only two of which show the objects with any degree of clarity.

Dr. Botta said he and his companions must have been observed, for the two discs shot up and *merged* with the cigar-shaped object. It traveled for a short distance and turned blood red, made an 80-degree turn, and disappeared in a few seconds.

Dr. Botta also told me when the craft was on the ground it had a metallic appearance and that it felt resilient, like rubber. Also there were holes or vents in the floor. For weeks he suffered from a fever which no doctor in the area could diagnose, and his skin was covered with blisters. He had entered the disc with dark green eyeglasses (used by pilots) and the outline of the glasses was marked around both eyes. A doctor tested him for radiation but could not find any traces. No mention was ever made to the newspapers, and, except for his closest friends, he guarded his secret all the time.

Because of the character of the man and his professional standing, it is difficult to believe the story is a hoax.

In prompt follow-up, I asked Gonzales to impose on his friend to favor me with a personal account of his extraordinary experience. In a certified letter, dated October 25, 1955, Dr. Botta responded, apologizing for his "wretched English," to relate the following:

> . . . I have had a long scientific discussion with your CRIFO member, Horacio Gonzales G., with respect to the UFOs and, due to my technical training and the facts of the Argentina incident, I have dedicated myself to serious study. I do not think anyone believes in their existence more than I.
>
> . . . I am not in agreement with George Adamski. But nobody can say that Adamski is insane because the flying saucers may be coming from different planets of different sizes and different gravities which may allow for people with blond long hair! [Dr. Botta is referring to Adamski's contacts with human-like entities from Venus.] But for the present I am not in agreement with Adamski. In due time we will know the truth!
>
> . . . On our planet people have seen little men and large men, and [men] with and without oxygen masks, and with large eyes or without eyes! It is all so unreal. It is for that reason that I do not speak with everyone about my experience. Three persons know of it— Horacio Gonzales G., one other American researcher and you. Here are the facts concerning my case. . . .
>
> May 10, 1950. The Pampas, 64° Longitude West Greenwich; 37°45′ South Latitude. 800 feet above sea level.
>
> The object was resting on the ground in an inclined position. The disc was 32 feet in diameter, the surface was slippery and brilliant. The height was about 13 feet, the tower with windows was six feet high, while the interior of the craft was seven feet high.
>
> Three little men were seated in soft armchairs. They were dead. One of the three, the pilot (I believe) was

seated in the center of the tower. In front of him was a large panel with bright instruments. His hands were resting on two levers. They were about four feet in height. In appearance they were human, equal to ourselves with eyes, nose and mouth. The color of their hair was gray-chestnut, cut short. Their skin was bronze, their faces were dark. They were dressed in overalls of a gray-lead color. There was one chair vacant of the four. I touched the bodies which were rigid. In the tower there was a smell of ozone and garlic. In the roof of the cabin there was an intermittent small light of orange-whitish color. Very strange.

There were no cables, no pipes, only the panel of the controls. Above the panel *there was a small sphere with a circle*. To the right of the pilot there was an apparatus similar to a TV screen. I remained five minutes in the tower but the absence of the fourth person impressed me so much that I went out of the machine very stunned. The next day I returned with two engineers, but we found only a pile of ashes, very warm. . . .

Taken at face value, Dr. Botta's report does not make the work of research any simpler. The observation of the little men—dead or alive—does not prove his case, for he has not to my knowledge provided an artifact or even a sample of the ashes as proof of his discovery. On this premise his case becomes *one more* for the computer and *one more* for the catalogue of unexplained entity reports.

Conjecturally, however, the study of the humanoid factor in UFO research may yet uncover evidence to suggest that the precursory little men, like Dr. Botta's, are the real "spacemen." The little men at least provide provocative evidence—and perhaps specimens—to show that they are part of a nut-and-bolt universe. If we are to believe Dr. Botta and other reported cases of crashed UFOs and dead occupants, we may therefore deduce logically that the machines of this *"Homo ectosapiens"* race are fallible and that they are subject to *accidental* human-like death. Interestingly, the only reports of little human-like beings in the early days of the flying saucer all describe similar fates: *death in a crashed or disabled craft*. Some of these stories are now legend. One persists:

Following the crash of a "spacecraft" thirty-one feet in diameter near Aztec, New Mexico, in 1948, twelve human-like bodies, three to four feet in height, were found inside. They were moved surreptitiously to Wright-Patterson Field, where they had been stored in refrigeration in a secret building.

Frank Scully, in his book *Behind the Flying Saucers* (1950), revealed the intrigues of another crashed-UFO and little-men incident, but Scully's story was to be exposed as a fraud. However, some researchers have never given up and believe that Scully was the victim of official counteraction and that his smeared book was actually true.

Oddly, out of the hundreds of UFO reports received at my CRIFO desk before 1955, there were only two stories about close encounters with little men in North America—and one about a monster, with large, glowing eyes, that terrified a number of witnesses in September 1952 in Flatwoods, West Virginia.

One of the cases, occurring in 1953, involved two gold miners working a claim near Brush Creek, California. After their second encounter, one month later, on the same claim site, they went soberly to the police to relate that they had seen a little man dressed in a suit like a parka descend from a landed silver craft with tripods. The astonished miners said the "midget" scooped up a pail of water, saw that he was being watched, scurried back to the craft, and zoomed away.

The second case took place on a farm in Coldwater, Kansas, in September 1954. The lone witness, John Swain, a boy of twelve, was returning to his house from the wheat field on his father's tractor. Suddenly he was attracted to a "pint-sized" man about twenty feet away. The man had a long nose, long ears, was "dark-complexioned" and carried on his back two cylinders about a foot in length. To the boy's amazement, the little creature flew over a small hill to a saucer-shaped craft which was about fifty feet in diameter and hovering about five feet off the ground. The object opened, the creature floated in, and the craft flew away.

The next day, pear-shaped footprints, which were not animal or human, were found by the sheriff. According to a note I received from Rev. Albert Baller, a CRIFO member in Massachusetts who had written to the boy, a report was sent to "authorities" in Washington, D.C.

After the Swain case, the little men vanished—either literally or they were whiffed away by the whirlwind of a new elite, the chosen few who professed to have happy meetings with handsome space people from Venus, hidden planets, and faraway galaxies. These were the contactees, and the noblest was the late George Adamski, who had coauthored, with Desmond Leslie of England, *Flying Saucers Have Landed* (1953). Adamski was in great demand for lectures and traveled worldwide. He even had gained the audience of Queen Wilhelmina of the Netherlands to talk about his trip to Venus and back.

As the contactees gained a measurable foothold on the defenseless beaches of research, APRO's Coral Lorenzen and I, on behalf of CRIFO, resisted. But on one weekend occasion, in 1954, they probed and found a weakness in my defenses. Suddenly and unexplainably the hospitality of my home became the meeting place for a traveling lecture group from the West Coast. Among the dignitaries were Truman Bethurum and George Williamson, both contactees, and their flock. Scheduled to tell their stories before a "sold-out" audience at the Hotel Gibson in downtown Cincinnati, they came to get CRIFO's endorsement for their cause. I flatly refused.

After their departure I began to wonder about their *causes.* At one point during the evening's many *tête-à-têtes,* I chanced to overhear two "members" discussing the FBI. Pretending aloofness, I tried to overhear more. It seemed that one person was puzzling over the presence of an "agent" in the group. When I was caught standing too close, the FBI talk stopped. Whether or not I had reason to be suspicious, it was not difficult for me to believe that some of the contactees behind all this costly showmanship were official "plants."

During this period, of June 1954, UFOs were hot news. Despite a claim by the Air Force that UFOs were "ho hum," with only "87 sightings" reported since January, I learned by phone from Lieutenant Colonel John O'Mara, deputy commander of Intelligence at Wright-Patterson Field, that the Air Force was receiving an average of seven hundred sighting reports a week. When newscaster Frank Edwards got this news, he put it over the nation's airwaves. The O'Mara story had reverberations. . . .

Maybe, I reasoned, that was the ulterior purpose for the contactee visit, hoping that I would be mesmerized by Bethurum into believing that I, too, could rendezvous with a gorgeous saucer-ship captain like Aura Rhanes, as he had claimed. Once trapped into accepting contactee lore, my fate would be doomed. I would eventually be laughed out of research.

On August 21 and 22, 1955, a new kind of story broke into the headlines. Eventually, it was to put the Adamskis, Bethurums, Frys, and Williamsons out of the book business.

Datelined Hopkinsville, Kentucky, the story described little creatures storming a farmhouse, causing terror to eleven people, seven of them adults. The story is now a creature classic, a prototype of many reports since that year. Fortunately for history, the encounter was well investigated immediately, by Bud Ledwith, an engineer at radio station WHOP, Hopkinsville. Later the case was written into a one-hundred-page report for history by ufologist Isabel Davis of New York, after her on-the-spot investigation and comparing notes with Ledwith.

The obstreperous episode begins when Bill Taylor, a visiting relative, went outside to the well for a drink and spotted a strange lighted object land in a gully near the farmhouse occupied by the Sutton family. An hour later, the household was alerted by the barking of their dog in the yard. When two of the men went to find the cause, they were greeted by a small, glowing creature with huge, wide-set eyes, oversized ears and a slit-like mouth that extended from ear to ear. Described as about three feet in height, the creature had no neck, and its long arms, ending in claws, were extended over its head.

The two men, not trusting what they saw, retreated to the house for firearms. One with a .22 rifle and the other armed with a shotgun, they fired into the creature from about twenty feet away. To their amazement, the visitor did a quick back flip and scurried into the darkness.

This was followed by another creature's appearing at the window. He also drew rifle fire. The screen door bears proof of this attack on the intruder. Checking to see if they had killed the intruder, one of the men, stopping under the roof's overhang, saw a claw-like hand reach down to touch his hair. More gunplay. A shot was fired at the creature on the roof and another volley at one observed in a nearby tree branch. This one was hit directly, but it *floated* to the ground and dashed into the darkness.

Panic-stricken because of the ineffectiveness of their guns, the men bolted the doors. But the persistent creatures from time to time peered through the windows. After several hours of siege, the family of eleven piled into two cars and went to the police.

When they returned with the police, the only traces of the action were bullet holes. When the police departed, the creatures reappeared and the doors were again bolted. It was a night of terror!

While the nation's press tittered over the Hopkinsville incident, the little creatures dropped into Cincinnati. Like a plague, they began infesting the communities of Winton Woods, Cumminsville, Camp Washington, Mt. Airy, and Greenhills. Then, at the height of the furor, the police nabbed a fifteen-year-old boy who, clad in green-dyed long johns, admitted having fun in Cumminsville scaring his neighbors. The youth, however, denied leaving his neighborhood during his masquerade.

Another case coming to light during the fanfare was that befalling Mrs. Wesley Symmonds of Cincinnati. She claimed that, while driving through Stockton, Georgia, on their way to Florida, on July 3, 1955, while her husband slept in the back seat, she saw four "bug-eyed" creatures standing on the right side of the road. She turned her car sharply to avoid hitting them, and her husband was awakened but not in time to realize what had happened. "She was too frightened to stop," said her husband. "When we were at a good, safe distance from the area, I took over the wheel."

I made impressionistic drawings of the creatures. They were about three to four feet in height, wearing capes extending one-piece into thin arms and claw-like appendages. Two of the creatures, with rounded heads, were facing away from Mrs. Symmonds and standing in the background. A third creature, in the foreground, was bending over, with claw-like hands holding a rod that touched the pavement, and the fourth was standing upright in clear front view. This one had oval eyes, no visible mouth, long pointed nose and a chin that came to a point. On its head was a droopy-brimmed, flat-domed hat. Significant in this encounter is the creature facing her with upraised arms, a feature analogous to the first creature observed in the Hopkinsville case.

Just as weird as Mrs. Symmonds' encounter during the 1955 creature flap were cases that I had quietly collected in the Greater Cincinnati area preceding the well-publicized Hopkinsville incident. The most tantalizing of them all, which I got on a tip from Herbert Clark of the Ground Observer Corps, involved a Civil

Defense volunteer who saw four men three feet in height under a bridge in his community. The disturbing incident, I was told, brought the local police and the Civil Defense officials into action. Said Clark, *an armed guard was stationed at the bridge!*

Despite my special affiliations with the GOC and the Air Defense Command, I was unable to get any details of official action from the Loveland Civil Defense Authority, from Frank White-cotton, Coordinator for the Hamilton County GOC, or from the Loveland Chief of Police, John Fritz. However, I was able to learn from a member of the Loveland School Board that the incident had been investigated by the FBI.

In 1956, Ted Bloecher, intrigued by this one case, flew from New York to Cincinnati. As we had done the previous summer, when he visited my home to probe deeper into UFO reports in the Cincinnati "hot corner," we drafted a plan of action. First, I arranged a meeting with Frank Whitecotton at my home.

Bloecher stubbornly pursued this case for eighteen years, searching for corroborative data. He summarizes his investigation:

> During our meeting with Frank Whitecotton at the Stringfields' on August 26, 1956, we asked if he could give us more information about the bridge case. His response was neither enthusiastic nor informative. . . . He claimed that while he was "familiar" with the case, he was privy to "no details." He indicated that Police Chief John Fritz should know more about the report; that it was he who had ordered a cordon thrown up around the bridge when he received the report. But Whitecotton warned us that Fritz might not be willing to discuss the case.
>
> A meeting with Police Chief Fritz found him cordial, cooperative and businesslike. But, like Whitecotton, when the subject of the bridge case was brought up, Fritz seemed unwilling to discuss it.
>
> When I asked Chief Fritz about possible FBI involvement in the case, he began fiddling with coins and keys on the desk and shuffling papers. He denied any knowledge of such involvement, and changed the subject. . . .
>
> Chief Fritz was curious about my own, personal interest in the case. I told about my association with Civilian

Saucer Intelligence of New York and of my inquiries with Stringfield into the "little men" reports in the Cincinnati area. I referred to Isabel Davis' report on her Hopkinsville case and showed him the drawings that had been made by Bud Ledwith. Fritz examined some of this material and became somewhat less resistant.

According to Fritz, the bridge incident had taken place one evening early in July 1955, or possibly late in June. He made no attempt to locate the police report. The witness was driving a Civil Defense truck at the time, and as he was crossing a bridge in the Loveland area he noticed four small figures on the riverbank beneath the bridge. A terrible smell hung over the area. The witness drove immediately to police headquarters in Loveland and reported the incident. The Chief, however, was not in his office at the time and the witness' story was greeted with considerable derision. Fritz disclaimed any knowledge of a police cordon being set up around the bridge.

Toward the end of our interview, Chief Fritz caught me by surprise when he offered to drive me out to the witness' home. I quickly accepted. . . .

The Civil Defense volunteer lived in a farmhouse with his wife and her family. We arrived at an inopportune time—the family was ready to sit down for dinner. We spent no more than ten minutes with them, since it was apparent that our visit was being greeted with no great enthusiasm.

The witness stated at the outset in no uncertain terms that he would not discuss the incident with anyone at any time. He said that he had been ridiculed as a result of the report, and it was obvious that he was bitter about it. He said that, because he had made that report, he had been forced to quit his job with the Civil Defense. . . .

In an effort to elicit some degree of cooperation, I showed the man the drawings of the Hopkinsville little men. He looked at them with some interest and then volunteered the useful information that the figures he had seen bore no resemblance to the ones in the drawings. When asked if he had noticed details such as large eyes or claws, he merely remarked that he had seen "four more or less human-looking little men about three feet high," that they had been "moving about oddly" under the bridge, and that there had been a "terrible smell" about the place. He had seen them, he said, for a matter of only ten seconds or so. He would say no more.

It is impossible to speculate about the reluctance of everyone involved in the bridge case to talk about it. While both Fritz and Whitecotton openly spoke of other reports at least as strange as the bridge case, they drew the line at this witness' report. And the man's own silence, understandable perhaps because of the reaction of his associates, simply didn't seem justified under the circumstances of my own brief interview with him more than a year later. Trying to account for the uniform freeze-out by *all* participants merely increased the mystery and strongly suggests that it was a decision *not* of their own making. . . .

Bloecher's freeze-out strengthened his belief in FBI involvement in the bridge affair. Citing in his report my reference to a school board member's claim that the incident had been investigated by the FBI, Bloecher wrote, "A request by that agency for silence by people involved in 'sensitive' situations (in the interest of national security) would not be inconsistent with what we already know of its procedural policies. And it would not be the first time, nor the last, that the FBI has been said to figure in UFO and humanoid reports. . . . An FBI agent was present at the first official interview of Patrolman Lonnie Zamora following his sighting of a UFO and humanoids at Socorro, New Mexico, on April 24, 1964; and although the agency was not specifically identified, government agents quickly stepped in and silenced William Blackburn following his encounter with humanoids at Brand's Flats, Virginia, January 19, 1965."

Exhaustive search through newspaper libraries and files in three counties failed to produce the alleged news story describing the Loveland incident. Finally, in November of 1973, I phoned the witness again and found him at home ill with flu and irritably reluctant to discuss his "affair" at the bridge. He refused to relate any details, saying, "In no way do I wish my name used concerning the incident. It's all vague anyway. . . . I don't care to discuss it with you or anyone else."

In UFO research, a good case, or one with loose ends such as the Loveland Bridge Affair, is never closed. In January 1975 Bloecher wrote to the FBI office in Cincinnati asking for any information they might furnish about the case. Their reply: ". . . Although I would like to be of assistance in connection with your research, this office does not have the information you desire."

Bloecher's adventures into "Loveland" were not entirely wasted. The richest plum came quite unexpectedly when Police Chief Fritz, in what appeared to be a maneuver to circumvent discussion of his office's part in the "bridge" case, introduced another humanoid case he had investigated. Fritz offered every assistance in reaching the witness, Robert Hunnicutt, for an interview.

It was a hot, humid Saturday evening, September 1, 1956, when my wife, Ted Bloecher, and I met Mr. Hunnicutt at the 31 Club, in downtown Cincinnati. We met him early in the evening, before he was scheduled to go on duty as maître d'hôtel of another well-known restaurant in the city. We spent more than an hour with him, Ted and I taking extensive notes while I made an impressionistic drawing under his careful supervision of the little men he saw. Hunnicutt was well dressed, well mannered; his voice soft, undramatic; his eyes steady, never shifting. We were impressed by the cautious manner in which he constructed the details of his strange encounter.

About 4:00 A.M. on a warm night in May 1955, while driving through Branch Hill on his way to Loveland, Hunnicutt saw, in the beams of his headlights, what appeared to be three small figures kneeling at the right side of the road. His first impression was "somebody was hurt or some crazy guys having fun." Curious, he stopped his car and got out for a better look. To his shock, the figures were about three feet in height. "They were grayish in color," said Hunnicutt, "wearing tight-fitting garments" stretched over a "lopsided chest," which bulged at the shoulder to the armpit. The creature to his left stood motionless, his arms slender, one longer than its opposite member, which seemed to hang from its bulbous shoulder. Save for only a fleeting impression of "something baggy," the legs and feet were obscured by weeds and brush.

"Their heads were ugly," said Hunnicutt, reminding him of a "frog's face," mostly because of the mouth, which spanned in a thin line across a smooth gray face. While Hunnicutt thought that the eyes seemed far apart and the nose was indistinct, the pate of the head had a "painted-on, plastic-doll effect." He added, "It was corrugated or like rolls of fat running horizontally over a bald head."

The middle creature, said Hunnicutt, the one closest to him, was first seen with its arms upraised. "They were raised a foot or so above the head and holding a stick or chain which flashed blue and white sparks. The sparks jumped from one hand to the other."

As Hunnicutt got nearer to the trio, the creature with the chain suddenly lowered its arms "as if to tie the chain around its ankles." Moving still closer, he noticed that the creature with the chain made an "unnatural" move toward him, "as though warning me not to come closer." For about three minutes, Hunnicutt recalls, he stood still, just watching—too amazed to be afraid. As he got back into his car he was suddenly aware of a strong, penetrating odor. He compared it to a combination of "fresh-cut alfalfa with a slight trace of almonds." He drove directly to the home of Police Chief Fritz.

Fritz, with Hunnicutt at his side, and with gun and camera, drove to the site, made four or five passes, but saw nothing. Of interest, Fritz told Bloecher that on the night of Hunnicutt's encounter, the Loveland GOC post reported seeing UFOs in the area. The story, he recalled, got into one of the local newspapers. Several years later, when Bloecher revisited Cincinnati, he found the news item in the Loveland *Herald*. It described a flight of four UFOs in formation passing over Loveland. An observer in the GOC tower reported the UFOs to the Air Defense Command filter center in Columbus, Ohio. Jets were scrambled, which meant that blips had been picked up by radar. The date was May 24—on the eve of Hunnicutt's encounter!

We have been witness to a brief history of the early humanoid. We have seen the advent of the precursor, the controversial little man, through the eyes of Dr. Botta; we have watched the antics of the prototypes, of dwarfs wearing diving suits, of hairy little bipeds in Venezuela, of little nondescripts in Hopkinsville, Stock-

ton, Coldwater and Branch Hill; and we have been entertained by
the shenanigans of the contactees, who, notwithstanding, have in-
troduced the "acceptable" human-like entity—only later to appear
in silver crinkly suits—and we have gone behind scenes of official
intrigue at the Loveland bridge.

Now we leap unnaturally through the unimportance of time,
where man has affixed a numeral year to an event, to the present.

Today the reports of humanoids or nondescripts are replicas of
yesteryear, but they are more frequent and are not limited to
man's geographical boundaries or to any one of Earth's conti-
nents. Today's events don't make scary headlines because most re-
ports of alien entities surface to research, where they are quietly
computed and studied by scientific specialists.

It is beyond the scope of this book to examine the vast number
of unique humanoid cases that have come under the scrutiny of
UFO research since 1955. Scores of outstanding cases have been
recorded in two books by the Lorenzens of APRO, and John G.
Fuller in his *The Interrupted Journey* (1966) relates the poign-
ance of the classical Betty and Barney Hill abduction case, in
which professional regressive hypnosis revealed the couple's experiences of being physically examined by humanoids aboard a
large, saucer-like craft in Vermont in 1961. And one of the great
contributions to research, is David Webb's catalogue, *1973—the*
Year of the Humanoid, which includes Bloecher data.

The investigation of strange cases, especially with the humanoid
factor, is usually fraught with emotion. For the percipient, it is a
traumatic experience. For the investigator, great energies and time
must be exerted to gain the witness' confidence, extract accurate
data, recheck the data, and endlessly track down corroborative
details and vital statistics from extraneous sources. The more
complex the case, in some instances, the greater the chance of the
witness' transferring his trauma to the investigator, ending with
paranoia consuming both. John A. Keel, author of *The Mothman*
Prophecies (1975), who has been investigating UFOs since 1945,
said, "The UFO business is emotional quicksand. The more you
struggle with it, the deeper you sink."

Over the years, I have known a number of good, well-meaning
investigators who had become highly involved in paranormal
UFO cases, then became swept in by the lures of the contactee

cults to a point where they themselves put abstract meaning into commonplace events. Since 1973 I have been personally involved in the investigation of sixteen alien-entity cases, seven of which were in the Greater Cincinnati area. So far, I have been spared: no nondescripts have peered into my window, no mothman has soared over my house, and no threatening visits by the creepy men in black. . . .

Mrs. Heit's visitor came in the midst of the flap, October 21, 1973. It was witnessed inside a self-luminous capsule that rested on the pavement of a parking lot next to her trailer home in a western suburb of Cincinnati.

Mrs. Heit had awakened shortly after 2:30 A.M. to get a drink of water and was attracted to the window by a row of strange blue and silver lights outside. Drawing aside the curtain, she said, they were about two yards away, looking like Christmas-tree lights. Suddenly they blinked out and she found her eyes focused on a brighter light fifty feet away, resting on the asphalt pavement in the middle of the parking lot. It was a glowing object shaped like a "bell jar," which she estimated to be about seven feet in diameter when compared to a parked car nearby. Inside the luminous capsule, looking "like a light in an operating room," was an "ape-like creature with a heavy waist and no neck."

The hulking, gray creature, facing a large warehouse building about 150 feet to her left, showed only a side view. "It had no features," she said, "no eyes, no mouth, no ears—it was just smooth gray, except for a long, tapering nose."

Said Mrs. Heit, the arms were massive, protruding from a thick body, which moved alternately up and down with the "stiffness of a robot." Not believing her eyes, she tried to awaken her teen-age son from a deep sleep. In a half daze he arose to see the odd light but was not certain about the occupant. While her son was left to blink out the window, she called the police. "They wouldn't believe me," she said, "and when I returned to the window, it was gone."

The next morning, Mrs. Heit learned that a fire alarm had been mysteriously tripped in a nearby warehouse. I checked with the chief of the Fire Department in her district and learned that the alarm was tripped at about the same time she had seen the creature. Reporting to the scene were four fire trucks. I asked if the trucks had used the Brater Street entrance, which was on the opposite side of the large complex of buildings and out of view of Mrs. Heit. The chief's reply assured me he had used the opposite entrance, which eliminated the remote chance she had mistakenly seen a fire truck. Then he read me his report of the incident: "Compressor switch turned off. Sprinkler system lost air. Cause unknown. No fire." The chief added, "Something caused the electrical surge to trip the alarm. We could not find the cause."

The southwestern Ohio flap was ebbing on January 8, 1974, as John E. Justice, age fifty, night attendant for the Masonic Home in Springfield, Ohio, was departing in his car, after a night's work, at 3:00 A.M. He told me his car started normally as he drove out on the grounds' long driveway. Suddenly his headlights dimmed and his engine went dead. Within seconds, Justice saw a display of aerial lights descending a short distance in front of his car. The lights were like a "rainbow."

Then the rainbow blinked out, and in view was an oval-shaped light about six feet in diameter. It was so brilliant that he could not see any exterior body or appendages.

"The trees, the road, everything was lit up," said Justice. "And inside my car it was light enough to clip my fingernails."

As the object came in closer, within six feet above the front of the car, Justice got the shock of his life. He could now see inside the oval object. It was a gold-colored room with five occupants seated in high seats on the left-hand side. The occupants were sitting motionlessly in a "straight row"; their garments, like capes, were the same color as their seats.

"Were they people like us?" I asked.

"Not so sure," Justice replied. "They were small, maybe three or four feet tall." He tried hard to reconstruct a face, but he was unable. "I wish I could," he said. "I'm not sure, because their hair was so long and it covered part of their faces. They were all alike."

William Connors, staff writer for the Springfield *Daily News,* who investigated the incident on January 9, and I agreed that the strongest testimony in support of the Justice case came from Ray Fields, maintenance man of the Masonic Home.

Fields worked in the powerhouse, a half mile away from the Masonic Home. He carried a Motorola pager radio on his trips across the grounds to and from the home and the powerhouse. He related that, on the evening of January 7, his pager went dead while at the home. When he returned to the powerhouse, the pager came on strong as normal.

When he returned to the home, the pager went dead again. He replaced the batteries, still without response. Fields left the Masonic Home at 10:30 P.M., his radio pager dead. A check with the operator at the home's switchboard revealed that she had tried to reach Fields at least three times by radio but failed.

As Justice watched the UFO's departure, at 3:15 A.M., "shooting up at an angle very fast," his car started instantly.

Connors and I concluded: Probably the UFO was in the vicinity of the Masonic Home prior to 3:15 A.M. and was the cause of Fields's pager problem.

Another case involved an elderly lady, age eighty-two. Geri Wilhelm, who originally received the report, said Mrs. Page is a widow, "looks about sixty," is energetic, of sound mind, is always well dressed, and even contemplates marriage.

When I called our octogenarian, I found her surprisingly forthright—no ifs, ands or buts—about the UFO and its occupants she saw from her window in Fairfield, Ohio, on December 22, 1974.

At 10:30 P.M. Mrs. Page had retired but was still fully awake when she was attracted by a bright light shining under the partially open blind of her bedroom window. "It was very bright, shining on the walls of my room," she said. Looking through her window, in clear view she saw an oval object "shaped somewhat like a boat" hovering directly over her neighbor's house, about 125 yards away. She said the object was large, with green and white lights on its "base or rim." On one side were three small square windows through which shone a white light. The object, in view for about fifteen minutes, bounced slowly up and down.

Mrs. Page said the sky was clear as she watched the object move in a straight line slowly to the church on the corner, less than a city block away. Then, she said, it moved over the center of the church and started bouncing up and down again.

"The object stayed over the church for maybe thirty minutes," she said. It was during this period that she saw two dark figures, above the craft's windows, in what appeared to be a transparent dome. She opened the kitchen door for a better view, but it was too cold. While the door was open, she could hear no sound. The UFO then moved away, going north from the church in a straight line, and suddenly "shot off real fast."

"The figures in the craft were little people," she said. "I could see their two heads and down to their waistlines. Their arms were constantly waving. They seemed to be gesturing like people who talk with their hands. And while they waved they moved back and forth from one end of the object to the other and would seem to meet in the middle."

It is difficult to disbelieve Mrs. Page's report. We must either accept it in its entirety or dismiss it as a hoax or poor eyesight due to aging infirmities. She said she clearly saw the two little figures in the lighted object for about a half hour. It seems, on this premise, that to normally see people from her window moving on the opposite side of her street and recognize them as people, she should also be capable of seeing "people" at the same distance inside an aerial object.

While reading Webb's *1973—the Year of the Humanoid,* which had arrived in my mail on February 8, 1975, my daughter, Camille, was reminded that her friend Kim Davis and her two sisters and mother had seen a strange creature in the village of Mariemont just the past July. *My own back yard!* Without further delay, I phoned Mrs. Davis. Yes, she remembered the incident well. "It was probably the devil," she said with a trace of laughter. "We all have good imaginations, but we agreed on the details later among ourselves."

The story begins with an odor. Said Mrs. Davis, "We all smelled something like gas in the house." Outside, the neighbors were milling around, all complaining of the foul odor. The Cincinnati Gas & Electric Company was called, fearing a gas leak.

Discomforted by the smell and curious about the extent of its coverage, Mrs. Davis and daughters, Kim, age fourteen; Cindy, eighteen; and Dana, twenty, with baby, got into their car and drove around the neighborhood.

It was past midnight, under a clear sky, while driving on residential Homewood Street, that they encountered a strange being approaching their car. "It was about fifty feet away from us, moving unusually fast on the right-hand side of the street," said Mrs.

Davis. "It was about five feet tall and whether it wore clothes was debated among us. For sure, *it had no feet,* just a hoof, and it made a loud clicking sound on the pavement. It had a side to side motion, seemed to lunge forward and sort of hopped. I couldn't see its face. All I could think of was *no feet!"*

Stunned, the Davises drove a block away, then turned around for another look. The hoof-foot creature was gone!

Signed statements from Mrs. Davis' three daughters confirmed her report:

KIM: "The creature was about five feet in height, the feet were hooves and made a clicking sound. From the waist down to the hoofed feet there was a tight-fitting dark garment; the upper torso was nude. The bare parts and face seemed hairy."

CINDY: (Driver of the car) "The feet were like the hoof of an animal, which clicked as it moved. It was the way it walked that was so weird. Something dark covered its legs."

DANA: "The feet were without heels, like pigs' feet. It was walking fast and in long strides and making a clicking noise. It was bare above the tight-fitting pants and it seemed hairy, even its face."

On February 11, 1975, I went to the Cincinnati Gas & Electric Company to check on the reported gas leak for July 26, 1974. The official who reviewed the records recalled the mysterious incident. He said they had received about twenty calls complaining of the gas odor in Mariemont. Men were sent to investigate; their instrument readings were *zero.* The investigators were at a loss for an explanation.

Research records show again and again, when humanoids are near, so is an odor. Stranger than their odor is their diversity of size and features and behavior. Ted Bloecher and I have frequently discussed these factors. "They seem to be taunting us," I said. "How else can you explain their mischief?"

". . . Or perhaps their demonstrations are staged," offered Bloecher, "concocted for the benefit of the witness. Maybe they monitor our adrenalin. . . ."

PART II

Countdown to Crisis

VI

The Siege of 1973

When the great October 1973 siege was on, Americans who were only cursory readers of newspapers or failed to hang onto the tail end of a radio or TV newscast didn't know it. The more cognizant, even without past UFO interest, knew that the UFOs were back from wherever they had gone. But in the "hot" areas—and there were many throughout the United States—people by the thousands were feeling the brunt of the *UFO strike force!*

The many reports of UFOs witnessed by law-enforcement personnel are now one of the main sources of reliable input for serious research. Only a handful, because of the strangeness of the encounter, usually with entities or combined with a time-loss factor, have reached the plateau of controversy. The Center for UFO Studies, by use of its "hotline," depends largely on the cooperative input from police and sheriffs' offices in the United States and Canada. In 1975 the center received 505 UFO reports, 70 per cent of which came from police sources, 22 per cent involving police witnesses.

Although the eye of the law, so to speak, may be no more perceptively trained to detect and/or rationalize the true UFO than that of any other citizen, a police officer normally is less apt to waste his on-duty time chasing a doubtful UFO, much less take the risk of having it entered on the police blotter for exposure to the press. His official and personal reputations are on the line; a funny story in the local press could ruin his effectiveness as a law officer. Most lawmen will consider twice before reporting a light in the night sky that could turn out to be Jupiter dancing to the tune of atmospheric distortion or a searchlight beam playing on a rolling cloud.

Significantly, during the siege of '73, according to an estimate made by Dr. Allen Hynek, police personnel accounted for one third of the total of UFO sightings reported to the media or research groups. Many were close encounters.

One encounter, by two police officers who got within ninety feet of a UFO, stands out above the others. The incident occurred on October 17, 1973, during a one-night "spectacular" in, over, and around Chattanooga, Tennessee.

The report reached me from my brother, Jack, in Chattanooga on company business. When I got the story, which made front-page news there, I had already that day made a dozen phone calls checking into a rash of UFO reports in Louisiana. I had talked with sheriffs, deputy sheriffs, dispatchers, clerks—anybody who could relate information or new leads—in Slidell, Pine, St. Tammany, and New Orleans, following news stories scantily describing low-level UFOs charging down on cars on lonely roads. Weather-research balloons were being blamed for some of the sightings across Dixie, but in Chattanooga the UFO witnessed by two police officers at close range was not a balloon!

First I called Police and Fire Commissioner Gene Roberts for his appraisal of the alleged police encounter. Roberts was cooperative, commenting that he took a "serious view" of the incident, adding, "It was no joke."

Roberts had the highest praise for the integrity of the officers, Sergeant Lester Shell and Patrolman Harry Jarrett, who were sent to the scene to investigate a reported UFO that landed near a schoolyard. "Sergeant Shell is a reliable officer," he said; "I believe he saw what he thinks he saw." Shell was off duty when I called, and the commissioner encouraged me to call him at his home for a statement.

The incident began at 7:00 P.M. with a phone call from a woman who was described as "hysterical" when she reported that a large, bright, cigar-shaped object had landed in a wooded area near the Charles A. Bell Elementary School, in Alton Park. Officers Shell and Jarrett drove to the scene, hoping to "handle the case so it would not get on the air." Shell admitted that he wanted to reassure the woman that the light she saw had some simple explanation. Said Shell, "I never believed in UFOs. I always thought it was people's imagination, but now I know differently."

Shell told me that when he and Jarrett approached the wooded, swampy area, he was stunned to see that the bright light was still there, a "kind of light and shape that I had never seen before." Getting out of the patrol car, he and Jarrett got closer, for a better look. "It was definitely oblong or cigar-shaped and all bluish white," said Shell, "in fact, so intensely bright that I wasn't able to see any solid body behind it." Shell estimated that the luminous object was hovering about fifteen feet above the swamp and "well within one hundred feet" of where he and Jarrett stood watching, not believing their eyes. "The thing, whatever it was," he said, "was about two patrol cars in length in actual size." While the object hovered, making no motion, Shell said he heard a continuous, unfamiliar hissing sound.

I asked many questions, seeking out a significant forgotten clue. Shell's answers were straight, his voice unhesitating: He saw no red or green lights, there were no rotating lights or noticeable movements within the bluish-white, oval shape, no protruding parts or appendages outside of the luminescence, no strange odor in the vicinity, nor was his car's engine, or he and Jarrett, affected by the nearness of the object.

Finally, overwhelmed by curiosity, Shell said he got closer to the motionless craft, leaving his companion behind, who, out of fear of the unknown, would venture no farther. Said Shell, "The thing suddenly shot straight up, as though it were watching me." He said it climbed to approximately ninety feet elevation, then made a sharp angular turn and zoomed away at terrific speed to the east. Shell said as he watched the UFO traverse the sky, he observed an aircraft heading east toward the Chattanooga Airport. The UFO, however, seemed to stay behind and below the aircraft, "as though following it." Shell then called the control tower at the airport, hoping that the tower operators could contact the pilot and alert him to the presence of the UFO, but the tower report came back negative. Also, the tower operator looked skyward but could not see it. Both Shell and Jarrett returned to their car and, while driving in an easterly direction, watched the UFO disappear over Missionary Ridge.

Following the Shell and Jarrett encounter, Commissioner Roberts joined them in a search of the wooded area for possible trace evidence. Results were inconclusive; they found only scraps of paper and other debris dangling from the tops of trees. Roberts believed the debris had no connection with the UFO. Although he could not explain how the trash got into the tree tops, he said the sector in which it was found was a dumping area.

The Chattanooga UFO did not rest after Shell watched it disappear. Playfully, it touched down in several areas during the early evening and on into the next morning.

In St. Elmo, Captain Oscar Eaves and his crew of five firemen reported seeing a luminous oblong object hovering over a church after it came over a ridge from Alton Park. Eaves said they watched it take off from St. Elmo, then proceed northeast. Police said that the UFO's path would have placed it earlier in the vicinity of the Charles A. Bell School, where it was first reported by the woman who saw it land. After the Alton Park and St. Elmo sightings, numerous calls reaching police came in from North Georgia, East Ridge, East Chattanooga, and other outlying areas. County police said they got calls from an area extending eastward from Signal Mountain.

Early the next morning, sightings continued to reach police units in Cleveland and South Pittsburgh, Tennessee. Mrs. Carolyn Terrell reported a "big bright light" following her car from South Pittsburgh to her job in Chattanooga. She said the object was about the size of a star when she first saw it; then it came in close enough to "look as big as my car." When she stopped for a traffic light, she said the cigar-shaped object turned around and "went back the way it had come."

Near Charleston, several teen-agers on their way to high school told police they saw two "weird objects" hovering over houses and settling near the ground before heading north. One teen-ager, Annette Tinker, said the objects were cigar-shaped, with hazy lights. "I got scared and ran toward a house," she related. Charleston Police Sergeant Charles Parker reported spotting the two objects about fifteen minutes later, while he was directing school traffic.

The Delphos Ring, investigated by MUFON, was caused by a UFO touchdown on a farmyard on November 2, 1971. The ring's soil is still undergoing analysis by major laboratories in the United States and remains a mystery. Photos courtesy of Frank E. Shrimplin of MUFON.

A) The Delphos landing area on the day after the sighting.

B) A closeup of the Delphos site, showing that the snow will not melt on the ring area, two months later.

Photo of smoldering tree trunk discovered by police following a UFO incident in New Lebanon, Ohio, during the flap of 1973. Photos were taken during investigation by MUFON team of Larry Moyers of Akron, Ohio, and Richard Hoffman of Dayton, Ohio. Photos by Richard Hoffman.

(A) Physical trace marks in the soil help confirm Daniel VanGraans' encounter with a spheroid object that landed on the rocklike soil near Loxton, South Africa, on July 31, 1975. Near the UFO were four humanoids with high foreheads. As VanGraans approached the entities, thinking they were human, he was stopped by a beam of light that caused his nose to bleed. Following the investigation, the authorities are still mystified by the traces. Photos courtesy of Joe Brill.

(B) Marks left by craft in the soil at Loxton, South Africa

On the evening of March 29, 1976, ten teen-agers in Scaieni, Romania, witnessed a UFO while on their way home from school. The UFO was a large, luminous sphere and descended near the ground. The area was investigated by the school-teacher, who found strange, burnt marks in the grass about five feet in diameter which gave off a repulsive odor. After taking soil samples, he said that his hand became red and swollen and he suffered headaches. The sighting occurred near a high-tension wire system. Photo and story courtesy of Joe Brill.

(A) Japanese youngster indicates area near vineyard where a UFO touched down on February 23, 1975. The landing took place near Kofu City, Yamanshi Prefecture, Japan. An occupant allegedly emerged and touched one child on the shoulder, temporarily paralyzing him. The occupant then walked around the craft and reboarded. The boys, in hysterics, ran home to their parents, who observed a large, orange-red light hovering over the vineyard.

(B) Japanese youngster indicates landing traces and ring pattern near broken concrete piles where UFO landed. A schoolteacher found radioactivity within the circular patch. Both boys were questioned in depth by UFO investigator Masaru Mori, and one child claimed that there was strange writing on the side of the craft. Both photos courtesy of Dennis Hauck, director, International UFO Registry (IUFOR).

Said Parker, "I noticed the objects when I saw several students look up into the sky. What I saw was definitely not an airplane."

Sergeant Shell admittedly had come under some heavy ridicule from fellow officers for "chasing an outer-space thing." Talking with Shell at length about his experience indicated to me that he was a man of both firmness and wit, and could withstand any degree of kidding. Shell laughed when he said, "They've even written a funny song about me with words from the rhyme of *'Twas the Night Before Christmas* and it's getting wide circulation at City Hall."

The same date, October 17, another police officer, in Falkville, Alabama, about one hundred miles southwest of Chattanooga and twenty-two miles from the Redstone Arsenal, near Huntsville, suffered a different fate from Shell as a result of his encounter with the unknown. For Jeffrey Greenhaw, age twenty-three, chief of police in the town of twelve hundred, his deed of snapping four photos of a silver-suited and helmeted humanoid that he met on a lonely road about 10:30 P.M. cost him his job, allegedly wrecked his marriage, and was probably the cause of his trailer home being destroyed by fire.

Before Greenhaw snapped his ill-fated Polaroid photos, he had received a call from a woman who reported seeing a strange object land in a pasture near her rural home. Greenhaw said he drove to the area, saw no landed craft or anything unusual in the sky, and started to return to town, using the same gravel road. Suddenly his car's headlights flashed on something metallic, which emerged as a human form walking toward him in the middle of the road. Greenhaw got out of his car as the strange being, clad in "crinkled tinfoil," approached. He said, "Howdy stranger," and made a friendly gesture, but got no response.

Returning to his car, he got his Polaroid camera, snapped one photo when the being was about fifty feet from him and another photo about twenty feet away. Two more shots were taken when the non-communicative creature was within ten feet of him, and then it stopped. In the next instant, the "spaceman" turned around stiffly, almost mechanically, retraced his steps, and began running down the road. Greenhaw quickly switched on the patrol car's spotlight, aiming it at the retreating creature. "He was running as though he were on springs," he said. Greenhaw tried to pursue the speedy "robot," but after his car skidded in the gravel, almost upending into a ditch, he said, "I couldn't catch up with him. He was running faster than any human I ever saw." A search of the area later, using his spotlight played on the surrounding terrain, produced nothing.

Greenhaw's four photos made national headlines, but his life was to be changed by the diehard skeptics, who turned their ridicule into sadistic hate. The harassment he was to endure allegedly caused his wife to leave home, forcing him to consent to a divorce, and on November 15 of that year the Town Council of Falkville reportedly forced his resignation from the police department.

An incredible story, and photos to prove it! Plainly it was too incredible for the Falkville council and townspeople to swallow. We can easily call it a hoax—that Greenhaw and a conspiring friend did it all for laughs or for money—or that somebody was playing a joke on Greenhaw. Some serious UFO researchers have contested the photos, maintaining that the being was human and was wearing a silver fire-fighting suit taken from the Redstone Arsenal or an Air Force base. On the other hand, other researchers claim there is a distinct dissimilarity in the suits and that it was not Greenhaw's character to perpetrate a hoax. Also, there are other reliable cases, before and since the Falkville encounter, in which witnesses observed both a landed UFO and creatures wearing "crinkly tinfoil-like" suits and whose movements were also robot-like as described by Greenhaw.

In a cursory evaluation of the Chattanooga and Falkville cases it is easier to believe Sergeant Shell's encounter, mainly because a fantasy of light just may have a terrestrial explanation, and we can live with it subjectively as we have ever since the "foo fighters" of World War II. Greenhaw's humanoid, however, is a giant step into a new dimension of fantasy. In summary, we may add that if we accept Shell's case as valid—and it is certainly valid—then, why not the *next step,* experienced by Greenhaw, as equally valid?

If the UFO, and particularly its corollary, the humanoid, seems to belong in a realm of fantasy, to occasionally cause even the researcher to ponder its relevancy, there is also the strangeness of the "USO" (Unidentified Submarine Object), which left its mark in the siege of '73.

Far from the waters of the mythical Bermuda Triangle, where fact and fiction often mix to produce a spine-tingling air and sea tale, the waters near the city of Pascagoula, Mississippi, had their own "other world" mystery, which made national headlines twice within three weeks. On October 11, two *on-shore* fishermen (Hickson and Parker) were allegedly abducted by an interloper descending on them from the air, and on November 6, four *off-shore* fishermen, later joined by the Coast Guard, encountered a strange submerged object. Concerned, the Navy made a thorough investigation.

Not depending on the press story for all the facts, I called Raymond Ryan, one of the fishermen who chose to do battle with the submerged craft, and the Coast Guard in Pascagoula, who were called to investigate and also got into the action. Chief Bob Pace, on duty at the Coast Guard office, was cooperative and permitted me to talk with the two crewmen who, like Ryan, challenged the evasive USO with an oar.

Raymond Ryan, a fisherman in the Pascagoula waters all his life, said he made his living netting mullet and trout. Ryan related that he and his brother, Rayme, each accompanied by a son, had gone out to the brackish waters every night in the past week, and, encouraged by their big catch on the night of November 5, looked forward to a bigger haul on the sixth.

Instead of mullet and trout, the Ryans found a submerged metallic monster. In dark, shallow waters, said Raymond, he and his son, Earl, were in one boat, and his brother, Rayme, and his son, Rayme, Jr., were in another, all preparing to net. Suddenly he heard his brother, Rayme, shouting from his boat beckoning him to "come quick." Near Rayme's boat they all witnessed an underwater bright light in less than ten feet of water.

Raymond and his son gained quickly on the submerged light in their fast boat, using a high-powered outboard motor. As they approached, the light dimmed. Curious, Raymond first poked his long oar into the water. No response. Then he heftily swung his oar from overhead into the water. To his dismay, the light went out.

For a while the Ryans played a cat-and-mouse game, the light dimming when they were close, blacking out when poked at, only to reappear in superbrilliance elsewhere in the shallow waters. In the next close encounter, Ryan had a good look at the submerged craft. "It was large," he said, "maybe more than nine feet in diameter, and it was round and metallic."

Ryan said there was no question in his mind about the craft's metallic structure. "It looked like the rounded top of a parachute, with lines like ribs running from a dark hump in the center," he said, "and the lines went down as far as I could see to the outer rim."

Ryan added, "The whole object glowed a milkish white, and, when the light was on, it glowed above the water." When the Coast Guard boat came, he said the light headed for the channel, which goes into the gulf. "It's ninety feet deep there," said Ryan, "and whoever controlled it knew where the deep water was, to get away."

With so few close-encounter cases on record of man versus "USO," I was especially interested in questioning Ryan for his awareness of any electromagnetic or physiological effects occurring either during or after the incident. He assured me that he and others in the Ryan family suffered no ill effects, that the object made no audible sound, that his boat did not pitch or roll or vibrate, or have its engine stop or falter, and that he saw no wake or eddying on the water's surface during all the maneuvers.

Ryan, however, did have two disappointments: one, during the close encounter with the USO, he had the urge to strip off his clothes and jump into the water to get a good eyeball-to-eyeball look, but, upon seeing a young lady aboard a boat near shore, changed his mind, letting his modesty prevail; the other, when he resumed fishing after the object and the Coast Guard boat left the area, he found that the mullet and trout had also disappeared. "I caught no fish that night or the next," he said. *"The thing scared all the fish away!"*

When the Coast Guard's 16-foot Fiberglas runabout arrived on the scene with Boatswain's Mates Nations and Crews aboard, the "USO" was again pursued. During this stage of action, according to Ryan, the submerged object was in about ninety feet of channel water that led into the gulf. Luckily, I was able to reach BM3

Charles Crews, on duty at the Coast Guard headquarters following the incident, for a firsthand account of his experience.

Crews told me that on the night of November 6, he was asked by Boatswain's Mate 2/C Nations to check out a possible submerged UFO. He reported to the radio room, where he met Ryan and his son, who related their sighting of a strange underwater object.

At 9:45 P.M. Crews and Nations were aboard their sixteen-foot Fiberglas Coast Guard runabout on the way to the site where the submerged object was last seen.

About fifty yards away, Crews said, he could see another boat with a man gesturing, trying to attract his attention. As the runabout approached, he could see what appeared to be the man shining a large light into the water. However, as Crews and Nations got closer they were surprised to see that the light was *coming up from* the water. The light, he said, reflected off the front portion of the boat and the lower half of the man. The light was motionless at first, said Crews, but when two other fishing boats approached the area, it began to move in a straight course at about four to six knots.

Crews said that he tried to run up on the light from behind but could not because of the interference from the other boats. When he did manage to get closer, he got a good look. The light was about three feet by four feet and oval-shaped. As it passed under the fishing boats, he said he could see that the light was reflecting off a metallic object! Then all the boats followed the object, which Crews observed was still moving at the same speed and on the same course.

Said Crews: "We tried to make contact with it by using oars. One thing of interest here; when we put the oar into the beam of light, *it appeared that the light penetrated the oars. The oar didn't cast any shadow. I could not block out any of the light. I would compare it with an X ray.*"

Crews then observed that the light traveled several yards farther and blinked out. The boats, he said, sat still for about two minutes; then suddenly the light reappeared about thirty yards away, still on the same course and traveling at the same rate of speed. They again gave chase in the runabout, but the light dimmed and went out. Crews said he and Nations returned to their station at

11:00 P.M. Crews confirmed Ryan's testimony about no fish being caught that night after the object was sighted.

Boatswain's Mate Crews sent me two drawings of the submerged object. Figure I shows the object as it appeared passing beneath the Coast Guard boat. Figure II shows a brief, 2-second sighting of the USO.[1] Crews comments, "This observation occurred at the time we first came upon the light from behind. In the drawing of a fin-like protrusion, the light seemed to be coming from beneath the object. The edges of the object seemed to be blacked out by a shadow running completely around it. However, the rest of the object appeared to be reflecting the light. I reported this description to the Navy debriefing team who interviewed me."

Shortly after the encounter with the USO, fisherman Ryan disclosed that he was "told" instead of "asked" to appear before three Naval Intelligence officers who arrived at the Coast Guard headquarters from Panama City Naval Base. One was a high-ranking officer, he said; another was in plain clothes. Said Ryan, "I was being taped while the man in plain clothes took notes of everything I said."

The USO incident in Pascagoula waters remains unexplained. The two investigating Naval officers from Panama City offered no clues; nor the plain-clothes man, reportedly from "some" government agency. Certainly if these emissaries from Intelligence had some notion that the USO was a secret U.S. naval device they would not have made the trip to involve Ryan. Ryan's testimony would have been redundant. Also, it seems foolish to entertain the notion that a secret submarine device, manually or remotely controlled, would dare to enter shallow, heavily trafficked fishing waters, risking entrapment on sand bars or causing potential hazards to fishermen.

Not far from Ryan's underwater encounter and the nearby shoreline where Charles Hickman and Calvin Parker were abducted, the Navy was reportedly preparing to launch the U.S.S. *Spruance,* the first of a new fleet of multimission destroyers with highly sophisticated electronics. The *Spruance* was being built at the Ingalls Shipyard, and there are other shipbuilding facilities in the Pascagoula area, including a large nuclear facility operated by

[1] Boatswain's Mate Charles Crews's drawings of unidentified submarine object in waters of Pascaguola, Mississippi.

Litton Industries for the U. S. Navy. Perhaps USOs, like their aerial counterpart, the UFO, may have more than a casual interest in nuclear installations. As far back as 1952, a Project Bluebook report and map with indicator pins were released that showed that UFOs were seen preponderantly in the critical areas of nuclear development in the U.S.A.

Away from the Gulf Coast and its naval facilities and Alabama's Redstone Arsenal, both "touchy" targets with seeming cause for alien spy operations, the UFOs seemed equally interested in pastoral surveillance in their '73 master plan.

For a look at what a UFO did to one man's property, causing near panic to his household, we move to Columbia, Missouri. The incident occurred, outside the city limits, on June 28, 1973, and was thoroughly investigated by Ted Phillips of MUFON. Phillips made three on-the-spot investigations of the incident, one accompanied by Dr. Allen Hynek. Following is an abbreviated account of the in-depth report of the case that Phillips presented before the MUFON symposium in Akron, Ohio, on June 22, 1974.

The witnesses were James G. Richards, employed for ten years as an animal-care technician at the University of Missouri; his daughter, Vanea, age sixteen, and a baby son, Jamie, age three. They lived in a mobile home, surrounded by trees. Across the lane from the Richards' was a house occupied by an elderly lady who was asleep at the time of the incident.

The incident began thirty minutes after midnight, June 28, 1973, as Vanea Richards went into the kitchen to place a baby bottle in the refrigerator, by the north window of the trailer. The window was open at the time. Vanea heard a loud, thrashing sound in the direction of scattered trees just eighty feet north of the window. The sound seemed to be coming from a large tree nearer to the trailer, not far from a dark wooded area beyond. As the sound persisted, she became alarmed and called to her father, who was sitting with little Jamie in the living room. Richards stated that he was tired and was slow in getting to the window. Together, they looked toward the tree where Vanea heard the sound.

Near the tree, Richards noted two beams of light, silver-white in color, about four feet wide at the top, tapering to about two feet at the ground, and some five feet apart. He could not see any form above or behind the beams.

Suddenly the beams disappeared and a bright oval form was seen above the original position of the beams. Both Richards and his daughter estimated the glowing form to be twelve to fifteen feet in diameter. The object was described as extremely bright and silver-white in color, with fuzzy edges but no surface details. The only sound was a thrashing in the trees and grass, and both observed that the trees were moving back and forth as though blown by a strong wind. One tree, incredibly, showed an opposite motion. Vanea described it as a "tugging" motion. It seemed to her that something was pulling that one tree toward the ground. Shortly after the entire object was visible, the thrashing noise ceased; however, the tugging motion on the tree was still evident. Then they heard a loud cracking sound and the tugging motion stopped.

The area was then very quiet. Richards moved to the various windows around the trailer to get a better look. Suddenly he became aware that his dogs were unusually still, lying between the trailer and a shed nearby. He told investigator Phillips that his dogs would have normally barked at the movement of any other animals in the night.

Aroused by the strange sounds and then the silence, Richards went to the bedroom and brought a gun to the kitchen. He joined Vanea at the window once again and noted that the object was still there, in the same position. The light from the glowing form illuminated the trees as far away as one hundred feet. At this close position (about fifty feet) the object was silver-white or aluminum in color. Richards said, "It was real bright at the center, dull white at the edges, way beyond a normal light (such as an automobile headlight at the same distance) in brightness."

After several minutes of hovering in the same position, the object began moving away toward the north, passing below tree limbs through an open area some twenty feet wide. It moved parallel to the ground until it reached the edge of the field and then rose slightly and hovered some two hundred feet from the house. At this point it was not as bright, but it remained silver-white at the center with a blue band of light and an orange glow extending around the outer edge. It was still low enough to be below a line of trees. The object then moved to the west, stopped briefly, and then moved back to its original position over the field.

While the object was some distance from the trailer, Richards, alarmed, decided to call for help. He dialed 113 for Directory Assistance. The Directory Assistance operator took the call and later told Phillips that Richards seemed to be frightened as he described the event and asked her to contact the police, the F.B.I., or anyone who could help him. After about one minute she told him that she would contact the local operator and have her call him back. While he talked with the first operator, the house lights dimmed twice. Concerned, he hung up and returned to the window. While Richards and his daughter were watching the object, the Directory Assistance operator contacted the local operator and gave her the Richards' phone number. The local operator immediately dialed the number, but there was no ring—nothing. The Richards' line was dead!

During this time, Richards was concerned, as no one had called back. He tried to call again. At first he could hear no sound over his end of the line. Suddenly he could hear the operator, and, after a brief interval, he was put in touch with someone at the Flight Service Station (FAA) at the Columbia, Missouri, Regional Airport, who, in turn, called the police. By this time, Vanea, still watching the object, saw it move toward the trailer. The object moved to a point in the trees near its original position and remained there for an undetermined period of time. During this time, Mr. Richards admitted that he was terrified. "I got speechless," he said. "I had this cold feeling when it came back. I didn't know what to do; I just froze." After what seemed an eternity, the object moved away through the trees toward the field.

Both father and daughter noted that the trees did not move during the second close approach and there was no thrashing sound. As the object reached a point at the edge of the field, it rose slightly until it reached a point over the field some two hundred feet away. There it hovered motionlessly and the glow got dimmer, the size smaller. When the glow finally faded out, the object was not seen again.

Although it was comforting for Richards when a police officer arrived, nothing to indicate the presence of a UFO was immediately found. The broken tree limbs and the deep imprints in the soil were not discovered until later!

Following an on-site investigation on July 9, Phillips reported:

> I obtained brief details of the observation and spent most
> of the time obtaining measurements and taking photo-

graphs. The imprints and damage to trees are located in an area north of the trailer. A fence is 25 feet from the window and the first imprint was found some 50½ feet beyond the fence. This seemed to be a series of imprints rather than just one. There were four imprints measuring 6 inches by 5 inches with a depth of 2½ inches to 3½ inches. This first set of imprints was 9½ feet from a large broken tree limb. This limb is 5 inches in diameter and was still attached to the tree trunk. It appeared to have been twisted slightly and pulled toward the ground. The limb was broken at a point 16½ feet above the ground. Two smaller limbs, each 1 to 2 inches in diameter, located on the larger tree trunk at the point of the break, showed signs of being rubbed. All the breaks were fresh. Leaves in this area around the broken limbs were dying but showed no signs of scorching.

It was noted that three limbs on the tree 25 to 35 feet above the ground had leaves which were turning brown. To the north of the first imprint (along the alleged flight path) we found a complex series of imprints. It was hard to determine a pattern as the object moved through the area at least four times, coming in and going out. Bob Gassaway, a reporter with the Columbia *Tribune,* visited the site on the day of the sighting. He told me that he tried to make a heel mark by one of the imprints and although he weighs over 300 pounds, he could insert his heel to a depth of only ½ inch. As the imprints were generally 5 to 6 inches in diameter with a depth of 3½ inches, we must assume a weight on each imprint of well over 300 pounds. One other limb, near one imprint, had dead leaves. There were no marks of any kind in the field. The area was checked for radiation on June 28th, and none was detected.

On the site on July 14, Phillips, accompanied by Dr. Hynek, took additional photographs of the site. One change was noted: the three limbs of the tree were barren.

I first learned of the Columbia incident while conferring with Dr. Hynek in Columbus, Ohio, in October of 1973. He was being taped by a student reporter from Ohio Wesleyan University and was asked what he considered a "good" recent case. Hynek cited the Columbia incident. Ted Phillips, who frequently joins Hynek on investigations where physical traces may be found for study, told me in March of 1976 that he still regards the Columbia case as one of the best-documented. He had talked with the two witnesses several times since their experience. "They're believable people and the traces we investigated support all their claims," he said. "It was no hoax!"

Another close encounter occurred in Brownsville, Texas, on November 14. I reached Cameron County Deputies Eddie González and Frank López, who stated to me that they were still "shaking" after their experience the previous morning at 6:30 A.M. González related that they were driving three prisoners to the state penitentiary in Huntsville when a soundless round object, with a red light at the top and a yellow at the bottom, descended on their cruiser. Both officers agreed that the object remained about fifty feet above their cruiser, pacing them for about twenty miles.

"When we stopped, it stopped, and when we speeded up, the object stayed with us," said González. "On one stretch of road we opened the car up to 80 mph, but we couldn't get it off our back." The prisoners in the rear seat panicked. Distressed, González radioed police units in Harlingen and San Benito, who responded in time to see the UFO pacing the cruiser. Said Patrolman Arnold Riveas of the San Benito Police Department, "I could see it a half mile away from our car. It was round and orange and about forty feet above the deputy's car." Both officers agreed that the UFO changed to intense white as it sped off at an angle and then zoomed up and disappeared.

The sheriff's office checked with the Brownsville Airport. They had received calls from other witnesses, too, and they knew of no helicopter or other aircraft in the area at the time of the police encounter.

Calling Brownsville was like opening a can of worms. When I explained my UFO research to the sheriff, he said that the area had many UFO "complaints" in the past month. He referred me to several landing reports, two in Port Isabel, to the south. In one incident two people witnessed a square-shaped object land in an alley between houses. In another, a lady whom I called said that a large object was seen hovering a few feet over her six-foot-high fence. About the same time, she heard some strange sounds on her roof. She called the police. To her surprise, she found many papaya melons strewn over her yard. How they got there she could not explain, because she was certain that there were no papaya trees growing in her vicinity.

Human logic may question why a mission from another world is so monotonously repetitive in its tactical operations, yet remains so uncommunicative during its surveillance. Why does this "other world" intelligence persist in its monitoring of man, its study of flora and fauna, the atmosphere, the seas, and the geologic crust?

Perhaps in this "other world" there is a critical need for gathering so many soil samples and rocks from Maine, Montana, or Missouri. Perhaps, too, an aerial study of the sprawling night lights of a metropolis when compared with the lights of Falkville may reveal something about human civilization and its demographic patterns. Abstract, yes, but no less puzzling than any one of a hundred other repetitive acts of surveillance behavior. Perhaps, also, there was a certain attraction to the dazzling lights shining up from Disneyland, or something of great geologic importance about the San Andreas fault line, which drew UFOs into California in 1973. Whatever dictated that course of action, California came under heavy surveillance.

Headlined the *Register,* in Santa Ana, October 18, "Skies Thicken as Reports of UFOs Rise," and headlined the Los Angeles *Herald-Examiner,* on October 19, over a four-column story, "LA Joins UFO Mania." The stories were the same: mischievous reconnaissance over houses and cars, light beams affecting people and electricity, and silent little elfish creatures doing "crazy" things and, again, the "robot" wearing the crinkly metallic suit.

Mrs. Idabel Epperson, state director, southern California, for MUFON, sent me this note about the flap: "There are many sightings which may have been in the outstanding classification if we had the people to investigate them. I'm sure that there must be at least 50 reports just scribbled on my clipboard sheets . . . and there were many that I heard on the radio that did not give enough details to even write down."

One story not making the headlines came from Mrs. Epperson marked "names and addresses NOT TO BE PUBLISHED." The incident occurred on November 16 in Lemon Grove, near Los Angeles, at approximately 7:00 P.M., under overcast skies. The case report, as filed by the late Donald R. Carr, MUFON state section director, follows:

> The witnesses were two boys, both age 11. While playing outside, the boys went down into a vacant area next door to the group of four houses in which they live. This area is about 80×100 feet, is surrounded by a chain-link fence, contains a couple of small trees, and the ground is composed of hard clay covered by dead field grass. The area is surrounded by several neighboring houses, which are about 150 feet away.
>
> The boys passed through private property on the way to the field. After passing a clump of bamboo, they came out into the open, and saw an object sitting in the darkened field. They slowly approached it and, after about five minutes, one boy who had a flashlight in his hand walked up to it and rapped on it three or four times with the flashlight. The object, which the boys described as a dull gray, immediately came to life. The rapping had produced a metallic sound.
>
> A dome on top of the object, about as high as its diameter, became illuminated with intense red light which irradiated the entire area, including the boys. At the same time, the object, which had been about 18 inches off the ground, rose up to about three or four feet. A row of green lights around the peripheral rim of the object started to blink in sequence and the object started to rotate making a not very high-pitched sound which sounded like "woooo shooo woooo shoo." The rate of rotation became very high with the red light blinking on and off. Then the red light went off momentarily, came back on, and the object rose into the air, still making the same sound.
>
> The boys started to run, felt chills, tingly and weak. They agreed that they felt as if they were going to black out and that they were running in slow motion. They said the object took off toward the Southwest and, after

they got up to the street, they saw it disappear into the clouds.

When investigator Carr interviewed the boys a short time after the sighting, both their mothers were present. Both mothers stated that the boys were not in the habit of concocting tall stories. They stated that the boys were extremely excited when they came into the house.

The object was described as being about the size of their living room, kitchen, and bathroom combined, which would make the object about twenty feet in diameter. Later, in the field, they indicated a height against an adjacent tree of about ten or eleven feet. The investigation in the field revealed two holes in the ground six inches by six inches square by six inches deep, about six feet eight inches apart on centers. A third, partial depression forming an equilateral triangle with the two holes was apparent on a slight rise of the ground level. The holes were forty feet from the back fence, and the hole nearest the side fence was twenty-three feet three inches from it.

Dead field grass seemed to be lying in a counterclockwise circular pattern. The ground was clay, very dry and hard. The square holes appeared to have been sheared by something extremely heavy. Color slide photographs were taken of the reported landing area the next day, after a light rain had fallen.

Residual magnetism was checked in a piece of small-diameter pipe lying in the field, and in the chain-link fence surrounding the field. Reading on the pipe was —3.5 gauss at one end and +2.5 to +3.5 gauss at the other end. Residual magnetism of the fence was approximately +5.0 gauss. These are normal readings, so there was no magnetizing or demagnetizing field around the object.

A canvass of the Crane Street neighborhood revealed the following reports of TV interference at 7:20 P.M., Friday, November 16, 1973: Mrs. C.C. stated that intense TV interference occurred at approximately 7:20 P.M. on Channel 10; Miss T. noted TV interference at 7:20 P.M., just before the boys ran into the house; Mrs. C. reported intense TV interference, shortly after 7:00 P.M., so bad that she turned off the TV set; Mrs. R. reported her TV screen went white on Channel 6 at 7:20 P.M.; Mrs. S.

reported wavy lines on Channel 8 at 7:20 P.M.; twenty-five other neighbors who were checked either didn't remember or didn't have their TVs turned on.

We continue the siege of '73 on a case in which, once again, there is a fiery, "tracer-like" beam fired to the ground—with no apparent target—by a silent craft, spheroid in shape, leaving a glowing circle on the soil's surface. And, once again, we have the brief appearance of crinkly metallic humanoids. The incident occurred on December 14 about thirty-six miles north of El Paso de Robles, California. The case was ably investigated by David Branch and Robert Klinn, newspaper columnists, who taped one of the witnesses, Lance Mathias, who at that time was a student majoring in biology and who had served in Vietnam in the Marine Corps as a platoon sergeant. The other witness, Mike Andrews, was a computer programmer.

Mathias and Andrews were driving in open country in a Chevrolet van when, about 9:40 P.M., in a clear sky, they spotted an amber-colored spheroid less than a mile away at an estimated altitude of eight hundred feet. At the bottom of the sphere was a black, cone-shaped appendage that projected a red beam that looked at first like tracers from a Vulcan gun, used by helicopter gunships in Vietnam. The beam, which did not arc, as tracers do, caused great disturbance to a small area in the open field. Clearly visible, dirt from the beam's target was thrown as high as twenty feet into the air. Said Mathias, "The beam shot out, stopped, then shot again in intermittent spurts. When this was done, the cone was drawn into the sphere and a cloud of vapor became visible where the cone had been. I was ready to jump in the ditch along the side of the road," said Mathias. "I thought somebody in a helicopter gunship had flipped." But there was no sound from the craft at any time, nor by the "tracers" hitting the ground.

Mathias then described the object as stopping in its horizontal flight to hover, and then it shot away at incredible speed. It finally diminished to the size of a star and disappeared. Both men got their flashlights from the van, jumped over a fence, and ran to the area, where they saw the ground aglow. "It was a red, then a yellowish glow. In the center was nothing. It looked like a ring," said Mathias.

When the glow faded out, after about fifteen minutes, the two

men were swallowed up by darkness. It was at this time that
Mathias and Andrews turned their flashlight beams on two humanoid figures. They appeared to be metallic, like crinkly aluminum, about six feet tall. "The two were side by side," said
Mathias. "They startled me. I know I saw them."

Additional facts extracted by Branch and Klinn during their on-
site investigation indicated that the entities were cylindrical in
shape and were "waving" their arms from below their waist level.
Keeping the entities in view for about five seconds, both witnesses
saw a twinkling luminescence in the creatures' "eye" area. Branch,
learning earlier in the interview that neither witness had more
than a casual interest in UFOs, showed them a drawing of the alleged Pascagoula creatures. Said Mathias, "That's it! They looked
just like that."

Another striking similarity in this incident was the glowing ring,
reminiscent of the Delphos, Kansas, case, well known to research.
Here, on November 2, 1971, a UFO departed from a barnyard
area on a farm, leaving on the soil's surface an eight-foot ring of
"fire" that glowed far into the morning. The farm family, named
Johnson, was terrified by the UFO and the grotesque events that
followed. A flock of sheep stampeded; a tree was knocked down,
and a large limb of another tree was broken.

Soil samples from the Delphos "ring" have been analyzed by
several major laboratories. The ring remains unexplained. Like
the Delphos mystery, other "trace" cases occurring in 1973
remain analytically unexplained.

In the countdown to crisis, starting with the foo fighter of
World War II, the siege of '73 seemed to be approaching an ominous zero. It was the biggest concentration of UFOs ever to hit
the entire nation. But, as research gained provocative and useful
data, the people who provided the data share a common complaint: they will forever feel insecure!

VII

Situation Red:
a Regional Study

If we erase the boundary line between counties in southwestern Ohio—Hamilton, Butler, Warren, Clermont—and then to their north and east—Preble, Montgomery, Greene, Clinton, Highland, and Brown—we have a mix of dense industry and rich farmland not much different from any other region in the central states of the Midwest. In this mélange is Cincinnati, the City of the Seven Hills, its influence spilling across the Ohio River into hilly Kentucky and then sprawling almost house to house and industry to industry into Indiana; and again, to the north, into Dayton, with its technical nerve center, Wright-Patterson Air Force Base. In this complex are the giants of the soap and the machine-tool industries and the tiny Fernald atomic installation. Neither of the two principal cities is very different from any other American city. But this region does have a uniqueness, a fact long known by many ufologists: on its surface or under it, man-made or natural, there is something that triggers intensive UFO surveillance, something that is undetected by our human sensors.

In my twenty-seven years of research, I have witnessed and felt the anxieties of people in this region aroused by intensive UFO activity. In late July of 1955, Cincinnati and environs were in the direct path of the gathering storm. Just north of the city, in the town of Loveland, members of the Ground Observer Corps were reporting a heavy concentration of UFOs to the Air Defense Command in Columbus, Ohio. Strange, brilliant objects were frequently sighted hovering low over the residential section, and, on one occasion, a lone metallic disc was seen during daylight hours hovering not far from the GOC observation tower. However, it was not until August 5 that the public's eyes were opened and the press broke its silence.

At 8:40 P.M., a large, brilliant, teardrop-shaped object, flying south to north, crossed the city's skies. It moved swiftly and soundlessly in a straight horizontal path without visible arc. *Witnessed by thousands,* the object appeared as large as a dime held at arm's length. A notable feature was the sharply etched roundness of the device, which gleamed in a uniform, brilliant, white luminescence. Tapering behind this white mass was a short, fiery tail of bluish green—much like the tonguing flame of a rocket.

During the next few days, I interviewed over fifty witnesses. Almost all confirmed the description I had phoned to the Columbus Air Filter Center. Some described the object as "cone-shaped," like a "pear" or, as my daughter Colette, then seven years old, who saw it, told me, "a light bulb with a little blue tail." Reports poured in from every section of the city, mostly in the eastern half or from high ground in the west. One report, from Cold Springs, Kentucky, claimed that the object was exceedingly low and appeared to have windows.

In northern Cincinnati, at 1:00 A.M. on August 6, 1955, a witness was first awakened by his dog barking outside. Investigating, he was greeted by a blindingly white oval object about fifteen feet in diameter resting on the ground at the end of his driveway. About ninety feet away, the witness could determine the object's size by comparing it with the known width of his drive, which was twenty feet. He watched the object for about five seconds in this position, noting a distinct pulsation, which, according to the witness, severely irritated his eyes. Suddenly the object ascended soundlessly and streaked away with incredible speed toward the Fernald atomic plant, in the northwest. The man added that, during the excitement, he noticed that a car had stopped just ahead of the idling object on the road that crossed in front of his driveway.

The next day, he said, his eyes were extremely sore and he had to consult a doctor.

On August 14, 1955, a bright, kelly-green fireball streaking silently north to south lighted Cincinnati skies about 9:40 P.M., surprising hundreds of residents in several sections of the city. Walter Todd and assistant CAA officials on duty at Lunken Airport saw the fireball. Todd said, "It appeared about fifteen degrees above the horizon and was shaped like a drop of water flying through the air horizontally."

Following the appearance of the green fireball, Cincinnati's night skies virtually became a combat zone. Strange lighted objects swarmed in over a wide area. Jet interceptors gave chase and, in the confusion, one could hardly determine who had become the hunter and who the hunted. On August 17, strange orange-colored globes were witnessed over Reading and, later the same evening, over Mt. Washington. The Forestville GOC post later reported to the filter center an object moving in pendulum fashion before finally disappearing in horizontal flight. On the same night, I received an excited phone call from Anderson Ferry, the voice breathlessly describing a brilliant object "landing in the back yard." Another voice with urgency cut in, shouting: "Something's coming out of the bottom. Hurry." There was a promise to phone back, but none came. The writer's phone, unfortunately, remained busy the remainder of the evening with more UFO reports. To this day, I wonder what had happened that night at Anderson Ferry.

The sightings of UFOs continued around the clock, mostly at night, at a fantastic rate, from July through September. My "saucer post" telephone, designated Fox Trot Kilo 3-0 Blue by the Air Force, rang far into the night every night and, as requested by the Air Force, I screened and dutifully phoned in the reports referred to me by the news media, the police, the GOC, or an alarmed citizen who knew of my name from publicity.

On August 29, 1955, at 3:15 P.M., a metallic disc reflecting sunlight was seen hovering over the Ohio River. It shot away on the approach of an airliner heading toward Boone County Airport. In the days following, the city's peripheral communities were frequently visited, centering mainly in the western section at

Cleves, Bridgetown, and Hooven. Adrian Connelly, who knew this section well, repeatedly called the writer, reporting strange lights appearing as discs and spheres sometimes hovering, making square turns, swinging like pendulums or bouncing like balls. Landings were also reported in these areas—*not far from the Fernald atomic plant.*

Then, at 9:15 P.M. on September 3, while driving slowly over dark Boomer Road, west of the city, Frank Flaig and his wife were startled to see through the windshield a round, airborne object, appearing metallic gray, descending slowly before them. Awe-struck, Flaig stopped his car for a better look. Reflecting the moonlight, the spheroid had no protruding parts or lights. Its downward course, although slow, was constant and free of swerve, flutter, or suspension. Flaig desperately tried to follow the object, but it dropped out of sight behind an unlighted house, about 125 feet away. Leaving his car, Flaig then went to the side of the house to investigate and, to his surprise, *found the object suspended about a foot above the ground!* About this time, his wife, alone and frightened, called out. At that very instant, according to Flaig, the spheroid began to rise and, making no sound, continued its upward flight at a 45-degree angle. The object, Flaig estimated, was about four feet in diameter.

Looking back still further, 1952 was the first great UFO siege. It was the year the word "flap" was first used to describe a siege. Since that year, southwestern Ohio has endured countless flaps; flaps back to back, unending, while in other areas there were pauses or long lulls. My guess, looking back through the years to 1952: southwestern Ohio ranks among the highest for flap incidents in ratio to any region in the U.S.A.

Each flap, varying in degrees of intensity and range, has been treated by the news media like a child with a freak toy. Their readers and listeners have been the victims twofold: victims first when they encounter an unusual or frightening UFO, and secondly, while anxious to share their concern, think twice about calling the media, fearing "bad press" and ridicule.

The study of a flap must include the factor of communications. *The media can control it.* They can make it funny or they can scare the hell out of people. And they can stop a flap cold. In World War I, the British press, working with military censors, never told people on the home front that the losses of loved ones in the Battle of the Somme were appallingly high—such as fifty-seven thousand casualties in just one day. Instead, the press talked about the glorious battle and how they could see victory ahead. So the British fought on. Had the home front known the truth, they would have lost hope and maybe the war.

A notorious example of press control was Hitler's and Goebbels' propagandizing of the Germans into war. Still another example of effective control occurred during World War II, when the press worked in concert with the greatest kept secret of all time, the Manhattan Project. In Alamogordo the atomic bomb was produced and exploded without the public knowing it.

In my early years of research I often did battle with the city desks of all three Cincinnati newspapers to get a "straight" story before the public. Many times I stood my ground with a solid UFO report backed up by the strongest evidence, just short of bringing in the UFO's "steering wheel," but I lost. No story.

During the siege of '73, Cincinnati, like many cities, maintained an air of outward cool, a kind of business as usual during its day. But as the sun lowered into the horizon, anxiety about the UFO heightened. The press, the radio, and TV whipped up UFO news with such intensity that I wondered if Cincinnatians were being guinea-pigged as a test of psychological reaction. By late October I could sense the city's jitters as calls reporting sightings and close encounters poured into any authority who would take the time to listen. Cincinnati police phones were jammed.

Fortunately for long-range research, Charles and Geri Wilhelm, operating from their home in Fairfield, north of Cincinnati, tried to keep pace with the regional developments. Patiently, they listened to every anxious caller with a UFO report to make. Taking turns on the phone, Charles and Geri managed to take hasty notes, names, phone numbers; taped some of the more dramatic incidents, and tried to investigate them on site if time allowed.

On the other end for long-range research, and realizing Hynek's preoccupation and inability to reach by phone most of the better cases at their source, I volunteered to track down those with unusual police involvement, mostly in the Deep South. However, since October, I had been feeling at odds with myself for skirting so many good cases on the home front. Like the Wilhelms, I, too, had taken hasty notes from sighters with the promise to check back later for further investigation. Suddenly it seemed that every city in the U.S.A. had high-priority situations and not enough MUFON, APRO, and NICAP investigators to fill the gaps. As many researchers later confessed, countless potentially good cases have become only names with sketchy details on a pad, never to be followed up properly.

A typical sketchy case, dated November 12, came by phone from a Mrs. Long who said she was visiting relatives on a farm near Lynchburg, Ohio. She said that she was pulling into the driveway about 9:00 P.M. when a round, orange-colored object came in over her car and hovered. She said her lights dimmed, she screamed, and in the next instant the object was gone. Also gone was her pet cat, which had been in the car with her. She insisted that her car's windows were closed almost to the top!

But the missing-cat case was no stranger than the incident occurring on October 14, when the Greenfield, Ohio, police department responded to a hysterical call from a lady reporting that a UFO had landed on her farm and that her cow was missing. Unable to get a clear address from the lady, an officer, however, was dispatched to the area. He said he drove on an eight-mile stretch of road twice but could not find a stray cow—or the lady.

Panic calls were commonplace. A lady living near Florence, Kentucky, confided in me, the day following her experience, that she was in such a state of shock that she consulted a doctor and was given sedatives. She said she was awakened at 2:00 A.M. by a loud humming sound and went to the back door to look outside. There, hovering over her patio, which extended ten feet beyond the door, was a large spheroid object with blinking red and green lights in the middle of it. She said that the object was wobbling and moving from left to right. Terrified, she ran upstairs to join her teen-age children. "I screamed all the way up the stairs," she said. When the teen-agers checked the back patio, nothing was there.

Law-enforcement personnel were generally cooperative in southwestern Ohio during the panic, even though their patience was sometimes tried to the limit. The police chief in Greenfield, Ohio, cited a case, following the missing cow episode, involving a terrified lady who reported that she had seen a red-lighted object making strange sounds in a pasture. "When we checked," said the chief, "we found that she was right. The object on the ground was a self-propelled combine with a red light on the top."

The chief admitted he could not explain all the reports in his area but offered some restful views on some of the nocturnal lights people had been reporting. "I think some of the lights are a part of the Israeli airlift from Dayton," he said. "There's been a lot of air traffic over here since the Mid-East war broke out."

But the chief's "air-traffic-to-Israel" view could hardly apply in the New Lebanon, Ohio, case, which captured local headlines. The incident, a UFO aerial display occurring on October 10 about twenty miles northwest of Dayton, caused crowds to gather to watch and brought police to the scene to maintain order. Patrolman Robert E. Bales, who was dispatched to the area, had a good look at the UFO's performance, took photos, and later worked cooperatively with MUFON state director Larry Moyers of Akron and Richard Hoffman, state section director of Dayton, in putting the puzzling facts together.

The New Lebanon story began at 6:05 P.M., when a family of five watched for three minutes as an unusual glowing object headed south, then, to their surprise, made a sudden and complete reversal in its flight. Before it disappeared, the witnesses said the UFO made continued maneuvers that seemed impossible. The police were called but did not respond.

Another witness, Robin Thompson, age seventeen, was watching TV alone about 8:00 P.M. when she heard a strange, loud sound outdoors. Stepping to the door, she saw an oblong object with several bright-red horizontal lights that radiated an eerie glow. Robin estimated that the object was about one hundred feet away from her house. Quickly she got her Polaroid camera and took one photo. Hoffman told me later the photo was sent to the *National Enquirer* but never published. Robin did not call the police, but others in the area of Holderman Street about 8:00 P.M. had been calling. Paraphrased are Hoffman's notes, which record the unfolding events as recounted by Patrolman Bales.

> Bales was dispatched to Holderman Street about 8:10
> P.M. and found several teen-agers exclaiming excitedly
> that a strange object had just passed over the rooftops
> making a strange sound like a "twirling jump rope."

Bales was unable to see the UFO, but, within minutes, he was radioed to report to Lawson Street, just two and a half blocks away. Arriving, he found a group of adults standing outside their homes staring skyward. They also had been shocked by the strange, loud "twirling" sound. Then, according to Bales's testimony, a car suddenly pulled up alongside the crowd and a man yelled out that a low-level object was again in view from Holderman Street. Bales returned to the site and found a growing number of people watching a glowing red object in the southwestern sky. Reporting back to the dispatcher by radio, Bales learned that his office had received several UFO reports and that the dispatcher had been out to see it for himself. He also heard that Ed Stoner, sheriff's deputy in Montgomery County, had seen the same UFO while patrolling in his cruiser.

In a matter of minutes the amber-colored UFO, "with five lights in a straight line in the center," became closer and brighter. As the object maneuvered back and forth low and at increasing speed across the sky, Bales could sense the crowd tensing up. Hoping to avoid panic, he tried to explain it away to witnesses: that it was an airplane. He said he even tried the "ridiculous" ploy of calling the UFO a blimp.

While Bales was trying to disperse the nervous crowd of about twenty-five people, he suddenly remembered he had two cameras—an Instamatic and a Polaroid—in the back of his cruiser. Shooting two photos on each camera, he managed to get only one Polaroid shot, which showed the UFO near a star, just before it made a fast dive; then it leveled off and shot past him, out of sight. Minutes later, both the Madison Township and Randolph Township police on patrol saw the same amber-colored object.

A week later, unknown to the press and the public, a smoldering locust tree was discovered in the same area where the UFO had been seen at low level. It was spotted glowing in a far-off field by Police Lieutenant Orville Freeders, of the Perry Township Police Department, while on routine patrol. Investigating,

Freeders concluded that the smoldering tree had been split by a violent force and knocked to the ground.

Fire Chief Bernard Faldorf, who was called to investigate the glowing tree, stated that *it was not struck by lightning, nor was there any evidence to suggest human mischief to be the cause.* Chief Faldorf found that the trunk of the tree was smoldering inside solid live wood, about four feet above the base. When Moyers, Hoffman, and Bales examined and photographed the tree, they removed about two feet of white ashes and extracted a section of unscathed fiber. Hoffman said it was hot to the touch and suddenly emitted blue sparks. "It looked like a Fourth of July sparkler," said Hoffman.

In the Greater Dayton area, between October 10 and 14, twenty-seven policemen and well over a thousand citizens watched in puzzlement as glowing, pulsating UFOs darted, made angular turns, and hovered in the nighttime sky. Descriptions of the UFOs were remarkably similar: red-orange, fast-moving, and disc-shaped.

Sergeant Fred Shaner of the Union Police Department told the *National Enquirer* that he had tried to calm an excited crowd of forty to sixty persons who claimed they watched four UFOs being chased by six jet aircraft on October 14. Shaner made this statement: "I didn't believe them until about half an hour later; I saw two bright, oval, orange objects in the sky. I radioed in what I saw, and within minutes there were twenty officers on the spot and we all saw the same thing. The UFOs were the shape of a flattened-down football. . . ."

On the same night, October 14, the UFOs returned to New Lebanon. This time, Police Chief Richard Winkler, accompanied by five police officers, watched an oval object hover for forty-five minutes, then shoot "straight up" at tremendous speed, without noise, and vanish. Said Winkler, "I radioed through the Sheriff's Department to ask nearby Wright-Patterson Air Force Base to check the object on radar. Base officials will probably deny it, but personnel there said they had picked up something which they couldn't explain."

Sergeant Stanley Kavy of the Dayton Police Department summed up local activity: "For days we had so many people calling in to report UFOs, we couldn't cope. One night we had sixty to eighty calls."

South of Dayton, the tempest continued. Said the Cincinnati *Post* on October 16, "UFOs are flying rampant over the country-side and over Cincinnati. . . . Police stations have received calls galore." In one night's recap, for October 15, Middletown police had fifteen reports, Franklin had nine, Springboro one, and the State Highway Patrol had twenty, mostly from Trenton, Le-Sourdesville Lake and the Monroe area. Butler County deputies said they had too many to record. Cincinnati police on October 15 admitted they were overwhelmed with reports.

On the night of October 16 there was no letup in the UFO thrust in southwestern Ohio. At 6:00 P.M., in Northside, a lady phoned the Wilhelms exclaiming excitedly that her neighbor's boys had seen an orange ball, with orange flame pouring out of its tail, zoom over her rooftop. During this time, the lady said, she was talking over the phone when she was interrupted by a "terri-ble noise" over her house. To her dismay, she found that whatever caused the noise and her house to shake had also cracked her ceil-ing, bringing down chunks of plaster.

Then, at 9:45 P.M., Mrs. Raymond Belcher, living in Mt. Repose, just east of Cincinnati, managed to inject a frantic call into the Wilhelms' busy lines. Mrs. Belcher, speaking in a heavy German accent, said that she had just returned to her home from the shopping center and, while getting out of her car, she saw above her tree tops a large, multicolored object with a white dome on top. Also watching the UFO were a number of neighboring children, all yelling and pointing skyward.

When Mrs. Belcher got to her door, she was instantly mystified by strange sounds of music in her hallway. Then, suddenly, the lights in her house went out. Groping in darkness, she went to the phone to call the police. The phone was dead! Adding to her frus-tration, her pet poodles, tethered in her back yard, were howling furiously. "I brought them indoors," said Mrs. Belcher. "They were shaking all over. I've never seen them act like that before."

In a daze, Mrs. Belcher, whose husband was out of town on a business trip, was comforting her poodles when her house lights were restored. Immediately she called the police, who, busy with other UFO calls, did not respond. Nervously she called the Cincinnati Observatory. Speaking in her German accent, she related her UFO story to the man on duty. According to Mrs. Belcher, the man unsympathetically asked, "Does it look like a *Braunschweiger?*"

Baffled by the "authority's" lack of interest and chagrined by his insult by relating the *"Braunschweiger"* to her German accent, Mrs. Belcher hung up. "I was ready to call Washington to see what was going on," she said. Later that night, she was comforted by a friend, Mrs. Shoemaker, who came to stay overnight. "I would not stay in that house alone," declared Mrs. Belcher.

The next day, Mrs. Belcher said, another strange thing happened, but she wasn't sure whether or not it was related to the UFO. When she and Mrs. Shoemaker returned to the house from the market, where they had been shopping for groceries, she found that her front door had been bashed in. A section of paneling was crushed in, and on the door's framework were heavy scratches. And the lock was broken! *Curiously, nothing in the house was missing.*

Also on the night of October 16, Cincinnati police received a call about a mystery craft that landed on the railroad tracks near the downtown district. Police checked but couldn't locate it. "We're getting more calls than we can handle," said Sergeant Raymond Davis of Station X of the police department, adding, "people are just seeing *things* instead of UFOs."

The next day, October 17, to my surprise I made the front-page news of the Cincinnati *Enquirer*. Featured was a comparison of the creatures described in the recently released "hot" Pascagoula story with creatures in a case that Ted Bloecher, of New York, and I investigated in 1955 occurring in Branch Hill, near Cincinnati. Also, on the top of the front page was a drawing I had made of the three Branch Hill creatures during an interview in 1955 with the witness, Robert Hunnicutt. The Branch Hill case was taken from my book *Inside Saucer Post 3-0 Blue,* which I had lent to an *Enquirer* reporter, Graydon DeCamp. The *Enquirer* story went on to relate scores of other UFO calls reaching the paper from every corner of Cincinnati: Springdale, Mount Lookout, Finneytown, Batavia, Milford, Middletown, and as far away as Connersville, Indiana, where fifty people saw a UFO land near a factory.

The front-page story only served to inflame public concern, and the Cincinnati police switchboard became completely jammed. Even crime calls couldn't get through. On the morning of the seventeenth, Patrolman Jake Isaacs of the Police Research & Development Department called me at my office. My name in the news reminded police officials that I had worked with them on behalf of the Condon project in 1967 to 1969, at which time I was issued a special pass to investigate UFO reports received by the police. Isaacs got right to the point: The police need your help!

I explained my affiliation with MUFON and my recent association with Dr. Hynek and suggested a diversionary tactic. To take "the monkey off their back," I said I would agree to accept a certain amount of publicity, hoping to pull the reports from the police. Although I decried publicity, which meant having my home phone clanging all night, I knew it afforded me an opportunity to get some good reports worth follow-up.

By noon the plan was in effect. When I returned to my office from lunch, my secretary had placed a memo on my desk requesting that I call Mrs. Charles Murdock, President of WLW Radio. Before I knew it, I had agreed to go on the air, using my company phone linked up with the station's disc jockey, Joe Kelly, all afternoon, to answer the concerned public's questions about UFOs. Kelly would play a tune or two, then it was my turn to talk. In the main, I tried to placate the mood of crisis, make light of the landing reports, and rule out the possibility of an attack or invasion from outer space. Kelly told me the public-interest program brought endless calls long after I had gone home, where more calls continued to reach me far into the night.

The next day, although weary of UFOs, I found that my involvement of time to perform a public service had just begun. By eleven o'clock I was "co-starred" on Channel 12's Nick Clooney show with his sister, Rosemary Clooney. After my favorite songstress sang, I again explained Pascagoula, the landings, and official secrecy. After that, I hit all the TV and radio news programs and many more across the country. In fact, the requests for appearances became so great that I was featured on separate TV stations on different subjects in one evening. On WCPO, I was shown first in line getting a flu shot on Fountain Square, while on

WLW, I was being interviewed with Mrs. Wesley Symmonds, who had had a previous encounter with three humanoids on a road in Stockton, Georgia. For certain, my strategic publicity was helpful to the police . . . they were able to breathe easier, but my home phone never stopped ringing.

Records of the UFO incursion for the night of October 17–18 are as heavy as the previous night's. Many were taped by the Wilhelms; many remain as brief notes in my files. On the night of October 19, it was SITUATION RED from sunset to sunup. The Wilhelms' log lists twelve incidents reported by phone between the hours of 6:45 and 11:15 P.M.

The Wilhelms later apologized for their inability to follow up every call. Although many of the reports may have had conventional explanations, the Wilhelm records, and mine, serve to show not only the intensity of the flap but a human behavioral reaction in time of traumatic conditions.

In the midst of the flap, the Greater Cincinnati hotbed shared in the nation's crop of humanoid reports—none, however, getting the news coverage we have seen for the Pascagoula and Falkville incidents.

On October 19 came the "Sam" case, occurring in Goshen, Ohio, amid a night of heavy activity. When Charles Wilhelm went to "Sam's" house unannounced, he found him reluctant to answer any questions. Said Charles, "Upon talking, and finding that we both grew up in Kentucky, he opened up. But first he made me promise like a southern gentleman that I wouldn't use his name or let any news people or anyone else come to his house and ask him to tell his story."

Wilhelm first learned of the "Sam" incident from a Mrs. Norman Wright, Sam's neighbor in Goshen. She phoned in to report a bright ball of light descending about 8:30 P.M. near Sam's farm property. "It was moving in an easterly direction and went over a hill," she said. "It looked like it landed."

I asked Wilhelm how he sized up "Sam" as a witness. "Alert, agile, in his sixties, probably retired, but farms and has a few head of cattle and pigs. He looks honest," he said.

Sam's case begins outdoors with his two "coon"-hunting dogs on their usual evening walk. The dogs, on leashes, were tugging Sam up a slope not far from his house. Then, according to Sam, they began "acting funny" and had to be "dragged" to reach the top. There, to his shock, he saw a strange craft, about three hundred feet away, settled near the base of the wide ravine below him. The craft, saucer-shaped with a bell top, was about fifty feet in diameter and dimly lighted. There were two white and two blue lights, and it made no sound.

The craft was resting on three "stilts," said Sam, and underneath were three figures that looked human in the shadows. Sam could see one of the figures climbing up a ladder, while another was standing by the third, who seemed to be "bending over as though reaching for something." Sam's dogs by this time were almost uncontrollable, and their barking, he said, made the figure on the ladder stop and look in his direction. The figure then disappeared inside. In a matter of two minutes, he observed, the other two figures went up the ladder and drew it up after them into the ship. Sam said the craft then rose slowly, made a sound like a "train whistle," and shot up and away into the sky.

When Wilhelm checked the alleged landing site, he found it moss-laden and spongy. It was Sam's opinion that there might be water underground. Commented Wilhelm, "When I walked across the area my foot impressions would retract. It appeared as though I didn't walk there at all."

Five independent reports from northern Kentucky on October 21, all described an orange object emitting smoke, cavorting in the night skies, hovering, jumping up and down, then moving north descending toward the Ohio River. One observer said she saw it dive into the middle of the river and disappear.

UFO concentrations in the southwestern region of Ohio have sparked scientific interest. Dr. Saunders has speculated that the high volume of UFO activity compiled since the early 1950s may be due, in part, to CRIFO's early research publicity and subsequent team work with other groups operating with an effective "collection net."

One researcher guessed that southwestern Ohio lies under a "time-dilative window," or corridor, through which the UFO travels from deep space.

Whatever the answer, the UFOs, humanoids and grotesque creatures, and all the other tandem anomalies use and "mis-use" the Ohio region with alarming frequency.

VIII

The Intent—a Priority Question

A dense fog was lifting over the coastal waters off Binn, Korea, on a fall day in 1974. On shore, for the men of the Air Defense Artillery, the day was starting like any other day. In such "attack" units it is always a matter of wait-and-see and being in fit preparedness in the event the North Koreans should strike south. Hawk missiles, three to a pad, were always on a "ready alert."

About 10:00 A.M., the base radar unit picked up a blip. It was a "bogey" moving in fast from out at sea toward Binn's shore-line defense system. At seven hundred yards there was a visual contact. The men on duty could see its massive form in the haze. The form was oval-shaped; a glowing metallic disc, estimated to be one hundred yards in diameter, ten yards high, with red and green pulsating lights moving around the rim counterclockwise. Suddenly the huge craft stopped, at less than seven hundred yards range, its lights blinking rapidly. It was not a missile or a conventional aircraft, nor was it marked by any insignia. For certain, the craft's lack of identity and its menacing position in the Binn area meant SITUATION RED. The command's decision: the craft is hostile!

The captain of D Battery gave orders to fire the first Hawk missile. Ignited, it started off the pad. In clear view of the men waiting anxiously from a remote-control zone, the missile, according to my informant at the scene, "never made it." It was hit by a beam of intense white light and destroyed! So was the launcher! Both were melted down like lead toys. In a matter of minutes, the unidentified craft, making a sound like a swarm of bees, departed from Binn at extraordinary speed and disappeared from the radarscope!

Without statistics in this sensitive area of missile defense, where security is tightest, we cannot speculate about rumored UFO incidents or what the UFO's vital interest may be in the U.S. missile system. In the Binn case the known facts about the action suggest that the UFO, by standards of human warfare, was the aggressor, But it may be argued that the UFO had stopped in its flight just short of its presumed target—and it withheld its fire until fired upon! Summarily, we are left to guess whether the UFO had intended only to *spy* on the missile base and fired in self-defense, or that it intended provocative or outright offensive action.

Whatever the purpose, the UFO was an *armed vehicle* prepared to operate either defensively or offensively. Certainly the superbrain behind the mission to Binn must have known of the dangerous circumstances, and also that it had the upper hand, with the ultimate weapon.

My informant relates that the captain of D Battery was dumbfounded by the action. And, in everyone's view, was a melted mass representing millions of dollars of highly sophisticated equipment. Fortunately, because of the missile base's remote-control mechanism, there were no casualties. The next day, all members of the battalion on duty were summoned to a secret meeting and told by the commanding officer that the disaster was *absolutely hush-hush*. But, regardless of UFO secrecy, the men on the base never felt secure again.

Security, understandably, conceals other rumored UFO-missile incidents. They persist whisperously among researchers, minus solid data, with no hope of getting substantiation. In 1966 I heard of an incident from a reliable source that a Nike missile was in position to be launched from a base near Felicity, Ohio. Its target: a radar-confirmed UFO. I was told that the Nike was not fired, because of the UFO's great evasive speed. There were similar reports of Nike action in the 1950s. One even claimed that a Nike was launched at a UFO and was "swallowed up."

A surprising number of UFO-related commercial and military aircraft mishaps and disasters reach the hands of researchers. The most publicized military disaster was Captain Thomas Mantell's 1948 flight, when his P-51 disintegrated as he chased a UFO flying high over Louisville, Kentucky. The event to this day is haunted by many elusive facts and others that contradict the official answer: Mantell died of anoxia while chasing Venus! Later it was changed to chasing a Skyhook balloon. Researchers are still trying to assess the real facts in this classical disaster.

I have heard a number of exotic stories about the Mantell incident, but one stands out that comes from a reliable source. My informant, preferring anonymity, related that he had talked with Mantell's wing man, who witnessed the incident. The pilot stated that Mantell pursued the UFO because he was the only pilot equipped with an adequate oxygen mask. The pilot also related that he saw a burst of "what appeared to be tracers" fired from the UFO, which hit the P-51 and caused it to disintegrate in the air! Since the Mantell case, all other military encounters ending in disaster have been hidden from the public.

From the beginning of my UFO research—actually, since my own experience over Iwo Jima—I have pressed for raw data, hard facts, even the sickening details about ill-fated aircraft encounters with the UFO. Back in the early 1950s, when I knew of the jet scrambles that sometimes led to disaster, I agreed with Major Keyhoe's writings that in these we may know the *intent* of the UFO. I also agreed that "losing our aircraft to the UFO" may have been the reason for official secrecy, fearing that the public would panic if they knew the whole truth.

Robert C. Gardner, a knowledgeable UFO investigator, writer, and lecturer residing in California, visited my home for a weekend in 1955. During our chats Gardner reiterated his concern about "our losing aircraft to the UFO." He described several cases in detail. Impressed by the papers he carried with him, with names, places and dates, and other supporting data, I decided to pin him down and asked for a written statement. In the November 1955 issue of *Orbit,* I published Gardner's eye opener:

> In the latter part of February, 1953, I carried a letter
> of introduction and recommendation from a New York
> official in charge of our Eastern Air Defense to General

Benjamin Chidlaw, then in charge of all our continental air defenses at Ent Air Force Base in Colorado. The letter concerned a plan I had which the Eastern Air Defense considered important to our national defense. Out of courtesy to General Chidlaw, who has since retired, I have withheld until now the vitally important information herewith revealed. In the course of the half hour private interview the General mentioned, among many interesting items, the following, "We have stacks of reports about flying saucers. We take them seriously when you consider we have lost many men and planes trying to intercept them."

Two months before receiving the statement from Gardner, a major in the Air Force Reserve who lived in Cincinnati had related to a GOC supervisor that the "Air Force was losing about a plane a day to the UFOs." The major had frequently dropped hints of off-the-record information about UFOs, but this one I took with the proverbial grain of salt. Also, about this time, during the '55 flap, still another Air Force officer, an active major and in a better position to get his facts *on the record,* told me in private, "What bothers me is what's happening to our aircraft."

The major, who had recently returned from an overseas assignment, had visited my home to hear about the big flap. He said that his brother knew of my research and suggested that he see me for details. After hearing my recap of "good" cases and my work with the Air Defense Command, I observed, he shifted uneasily in his chair, stared at the floor, and became silent. I could feel the strain of quiet as we sat in the basement at my work desk full of CRIFO mail. Then, abruptly, he rose and walked in short, measured steps toward the opposite wall.

"I have a case I want to tell you about," he said, stopping about a foot short of the wall. With his back to me, he added, "I can't give you all the details, you understand, but one case scares the hell out of me. And, for God's sake, don't use my name."

The major, maintaining a rigid about-face posture, continued, "This case happened in Iceland while I was stationed there with the Air Force. It began when radar picked up two UFOs approaching our base at fast speed. In the area we had a jet fighter on a routine mission, so Operations vectored it in for intercept. We heard the pilot confirm the UFO on radio, then suddenly we lost contact. The next thing we saw was the jet plunge into the water. The waters were shallow and we recovered the jet and the bodies of the two airmen."

The major then turned slightly, became less rigid, but still did not face me at my desk, across the room. "We couldn't explain the crash," he said, "and there were a number of other things we couldn't explain. Anyway, the case was closed when the adjutant notified the next of kin that the officers were killed while flying on a *routine training mission.*" Then the major returned to his chair, smiled furtively, and said, "Of course I have been talking to that wall, not you!" He assured me he felt no guilt in breaching security regulations.

I said kiddingly, "Even the walls have ears."

In the 1950s there were many parallels to the Iceland incident. Although they reached me less dramatically, I sometimes wondered whether they were leaked to me to enlighten my *Orbit* readers—or to make me appear paranoid.

One military case that might be the product of a paranoid's dream predates Mantell and even the gremlin foo fighters of World War II. It might well have been a classic today, like the *Marie Celeste* of sea lore, except that it had no fantasied UFO to blame and because *dead men tell no tales.* The case comes from the Gardner files, dating back to the summer of 1939, before the outbreak of World War II.

At 3:30 P.M. on a late-summer afternoon, a military transport plane with thirteen men aboard left the Marine Air Station in San Diego for a routine flight to Honolulu. When three hours at sea, the aircraft was in distress. Mayday calls were radioed back to the base, then nothing more was heard until the craft came limping back and executed an emergency landing. The first men to reach the craft were shocked by what they saw: all thirteen members of the crew were dead save for the co-pilot, who had managed, miraculously, to steer the transport in safely. Three minutes later, he was dead!

Examination of the bodies showed remarkably large, gaping wounds that indicated whatever hit the aircraft from the outside had unusual destructive power. Another discovery was that the side arms, Colt .45 automatics carried by the pilot and co-pilot, had been emptied; their spent shells were found lying on the floor of the cockpit. Lastly, and possibly akin to UFO phenomena, was the characteristic rotten-egg odor, which pervaded the plane's atmosphere. It was later learned that personnel who handled parts of the aircraft showed a mysterious skin infection. Security measures, Gardner was told, immediately blanketed the affair and cameras were restricted. Corpsmen were barred from removing the bodies, and the job of identification and diagnosis was limited to three medical officers only.

In the strictest sense, the case does not belong to ufology. It is devoid of UFO testimony and its strangeness lies only in mute evidence. But in that evidence may be clues to determine *what did not* happen to the transport. The most farfetched is that the warlike Japanese had tried to provoke an incident, as they had done in 1937 when their aircraft attacked the U.S. gunboat *Panay* in Chinese waters. But using aircraft for an attack in "American" waters would have required an aircraft carrier with escort vessels. Another remote possibility was that the transport was inadvertently hit by gunfire during U.S. naval maneuvers. But such maneuvers were never confirmed, and certainly the flight would have been advised beforehand of this action and rerouted. Also, it is difficult to believe that the pilots would have used Colt .45's in revenge against a U. S. Navy ship. Even if they had been unable to identify the hostile vessel, it would have been futile, if not ridiculous, to fire small arms. The only other mundane answer would have been mutiny, and negating this notion is the fact that holes were blasted into the *outer surface* of the craft. Perhaps the truth lies in the spent shells of the Colt .45's, which suggests that in final desperation the pilots had directed their fire at *something airborne* at close range.

Reports of air mishaps and disasters caused by UFOs and other mysterious forces showed an ominous upswing in the early 1950s. Their impact shook research, and as its news filtered into the literature of the day, its chilling effect was soon to take the fun out of "flying saucers."

Unlike the ill-fated transport carrying thirteen servicemen into San Diego in 1939, a mysterious air disaster occurring near Calcutta, India, slipped through the news wires.

On May 2, 1953, five minutes after leaving Dum-Dum Airport, at Calcutta, a Comet jetliner crashed and burned, killing forty-three passengers. While the press blamed it on structural failure, the real facts were hidden. On May 20, the Civil Aviation Ministry reported to U.P.: "A BOAC jetliner was struck in the air by a 'fairly heavy body' before it crashed and burned early this month. A preliminary investigation did not indicate the failure was due to poor construction or workmanship." Also ruled out was the liner's possible collision with another aircraft or lightning. Later, on January 20, 1954, Dr. P. B. Walker, chief of the Structure Department at The Royal Aircraft Establishment for Research at Farnborough, said that examination of the starboard and port main planes of the airliner, and the tailplane, gave an impression as "if they had all been torn off by a giant!"

In March 1975, Henry Perry (name changed by request), from a community near Cincinnati, came to my home bringing six slides, showing progressive shots of an orange, tear-shaped object in the evening sky. The photos, which Perry had safeguarded until he heard my name connected with UFO research on the radio, were taken on May 19, 1972, using a Nikon camera with Soligar zoom. The slides were of exceptional quality, but the photographer was unable to identify the object. Nor could I, although suspect was a high-flying bomber reflecting the setting sun. I admitted I was puzzled by certain features in the object, and he agreed when I asked to have the slides analyzed. They were sent to the Center for UFO Studies, MUFON, and to Bill Spaulding of the Ground Saucer Watch. After careful analysis, all agreed that the tear-drop UFO was a high-flying bomber at seventy thousand feet. Perry readily accepted the verdict, just as I had accepted him as a person of highest integrity.

During our several personal chats about UFOs, I learned that the photographer had more than a passing interest in UFOs. He had been an assistant crew chief in the 64th Fighter Intercept Squadron, with top security clearance, while stationed at Selfridge AFB, in Michigan, in 1952. He recalled a number of UFO alerts at the base and the great interest in UFOs among pilots whose aircraft he serviced. One incident he remembers clearly. A jet returning from a UFO chase had photos to prove it. Said Perry, "Before the film was channeled to Intelligence I saw the processed photos, when they were an hour old. One was especially clear. It showed an oval white object just like the kind you see in books."

Perry had more to tell about UFOs during his tenure in the 64th Fighter Intercept Squadron. He spoke hedgingly at first; then, when I offered a promise not to use his real name in writing, he said, "It's not that so much as the story itself."

It happened in the summer of 1953, when Perry was stationed at Ernest Harmon AFB, near Stevensville, Newfoundland. He recalled that two F-94 jets were scrambled after base radar picked up an unknown blip on its scope.

"I was in the alert shack at the time," he said, "and one of the jets stalled in a 'hot start' and went off onto an apron. The second jet got off O.K. and in a minute it was up in the clouds. In the shack several of us were waiting and we heard the pilot radio that he had visual confirmation of the UFO and then he said he had it locked in on his short-range radar. He gave his speed and altitude and then said he was going into a steep climb to give chase."

Perry paused and lit a cigarette. "That was the last we heard. No mayday, nothing. The next thing I knew was the jet going straight down in a dive. It crashed into a mountain." Perry said that a special detachment of men went to investigate the crash site. They dug forty feet to get the remains, and the case was hushed up. "The base was put on Red Alert," said Perry.

Had Perry's eyewitness disaster been released through the news media, it would have had a shocking effect on public opinion. Despite the clamp on military disasters, the Gallup Poll of November 1973 reported that 51 per cent of adult Americans believed UFOs were real. Surprisingly, 11 per cent, or a projection of 15 million people, said they had seen a UFO—more than double the 5 per cent figure of 1966. Another statistic showed that 95 per cent of the adult population in the United States had read or heard about UFOs.

Despite these remarkably high figures, middle-of-the-road America is still standoffish about the UFO. Because of the demands of the workaday world, the nation's "backbone" has not yet been "psyched up" to read any of the UFO books or magazines that flood the market, and only a few give more than a cursory glance at an occasional sighting report in their hometown newspaper. Some even have been witness to a UFO, but, fearing ridicule, they clam up. The more abstract the experience the greater the reluctance to discuss it with friends, neighbors, or at work. Eventually, a few hard-data cases circuitously reach the researcher, who must then delve to get hard facts.

Nameless cases abound in the files of research. MUFON, CUFOS, APRO, NICAP, GSW, each have "locked file" cases that have never surfaced for the public eye to see or to be shared with their fellows in research.

Regrettably, because of fear of ridicule or reprisal, the real names of some witnesses who represent exemplary cases in this book must be listed anonymously. But it was the major who faced the wall to relate the Iceland story who risked the most. He knew that talking out of turn about UFOs could have cost him ten thousand dollars or a one- to ten-year prison term. Air Force informants who defy Joint Army-Navy-Air Force Publication (JANAP) 146 because of antipathy to the UFO cover-up, have found a champion of their cause in Keyhoe. Providing him with informative leaks, they feel they have anonymously joined in his fight to tell the world that the Air Force knows that the UFO is extraterrestrial.

Since 1953, Major Keyhoe and I have maintained close working ties in the exchange of UFO information. He has often entrusted me with bits of news, mostly from leaks from Air Force insiders. But Keyhoe sits tight on much of the data entrusted to him about certain aircraft incidents.

"They have given me many cases, knowing I will keep my word," he said, "but they are the kind that I could never use. To describe them would tip off the source."

Then, in 1975, in one of our many chats, I learned that Keyhoe hit the Pentagon jackpot! It was a top-secret case, and he could reveal only the rawest details. The case involved three jet interceptors that vanished from the radar screen while pursuing a UFO.

"This is a powerful case, similar to the Kinross incident," he said, "but the location is secret. I can't even tell you on which coast it happened, or when it happened. But it was over two years ago."

This incident begins with radar picking up a blip that appeared on the scope as the UFO circled over the airbase. Three jets were scrambled. As the jets climbed skyward, the UFO continued its circling maneuver; then it leveled off, heading toward them. Trying to avoid collision, the jets spread out. Then the UFO accelerated to a higher elevation, leaving the interceptors under it. Suddenly and inexplicably the jets vanished from the scope. Said Keyhoe, "It was as though the UFO swallowed up the jets. Then the UFO made a turn and streaked off the scope. The radar had over a 200-mile range, but there was no trace of the three jets or the UFO."

The Air Force made the usual extensive search for the missing jets. Nothing! Said Keyhoe, "My Pentagon sources, in complete trust, gave me this, but they were uneasy about it."

Then Keyhoe, suspicious of sudden ticking sounds on his phone, which I also heard, added cautiously, "There is another officer who believes that the truth should be bared, and is considering trying to line up two or three others who would sign a joint statement on this case so that he won't have to bear the brunt of the backwash. His wife is very much against it, and thinks he would be court-martialed."

In March of 1976 I again queried Keyhoe about the three missing jets. He still would not name the coast where it had occurred. But he did have news about a big battle going on in the Pentagon about the rights and wrongs of secrecy. When I told him I was preparing a regular column for MUFON's *Skylook* he sent me this note for publication:

". . . Pressures are increasing to force a reduction in the AF censorship, if not a complete end to the cover-up. I know certain informed persons in the Pentagon who have been trying to persuade HQ highups to act soon, before anger over the recent Archives deal causes high court actions forcing the AF to turn over the original UFO reports without planned deletions. . . ."

While Keyhoe was privileged to know the facts behind the case of the three interceptors missing over an unmentionable coast, I was still trying to put the pieces together in a "privileged" case occurring in my own back yard. Only a few details were known about it, but the *known* facts were sobering:

On May 15, 1975, my wife, Dell, and I met Dr. Hynek at the Greater Cincinnati Airport and drove him directly to the University of Cincinnati, where he was to lecture at Sigma Xi's annual dinner. On the way, I told Hynek that I had just learned of a shocking case occurring on May 6 over the restricted military air corridor north of Cincinnati and east of Wright-Patterson Air Force Base. I gave him the high points of the incident: a near disaster involving a jet testing a highly sophisticated new instrument. The jet, I said, had been harassed by three UFOs, which caused the pilot to panic. I filled him in on the details as they were given to me by Geri Wilhelm. She got the story straight from the engineer who helped develop the instrument—but, again, no name!

Laying his briefcase aside, Hynek focused his eyes on me sharply. "Three UFOs, May 6?" he asked. "Are you sure you're not talking about the Mexican case?"

I knew about the Mexican case, and for a moment I almost felt embarrassed, because the cases were strikingly similar in details and occurred within three days of each other. But I stood by my source even though I knew how easy it was for cases and facts to get garbled in research, especially when the information comes second or third hand. I assured Hynek that the Wright-Patterson incident was valid, because the engineer who gave the Wilhelms the information said the aircraft was testing an instrument that was manufactured by his company, in Cincinnati. Also substantive was the fact that the engineer was on the scene when the pilot came in for debriefing.

The test-pilot incident occurred in clear weather during daylight hours. Somewhere east of Wright-Patterson Air Force Base, the pilot, making his routine test run, suddenly caught sight of three unidentified silverish objects, flying in formation at an unknown distance ahead. They were closing in fast toward his aircraft.

The UFOs, described as huge silver discs with portholes that had a mirrored effect, suddenly moved in menacingly close. The pilot, fearing a collision, tried to evade the objects by descending to one thousand feet, a dangerously low level. But the three UFOs hung tenaciously close—one on each wing tip, the other above the fuselage.

The stunned pilot again tried evasive action: leveled off and then shot up in a vertical climb to three thousand feet. But the UFOs stuck to his aircraft and continued their harassment for more than one hour. During this frantic period, all the instruments on the pilot's control panel went "haywire," and he admitted later that he lost all sense of time. According to the engineer, the pilot, during debriefing, said he was terrified by the action and confessed that he broke down and cried. The UFOs were confirmed by base radar, probably by a portable unit of the Air Systems Division.

As we neared the Seasongood Faculty Center, where Hynek was to talk, I dropped the test-pilot case. During his talk, he referred to the incident, but the overflow crowd was too absorbed in his other revelations to give it a second thought. When he finished talking, a file of people came up to the podium to ask questions. Standing nearby was a tall man casually dressed in a blue sweater, silently waiting his turn. Finally, when the crowd broke up, he came forward, talked to Hynek briefly, and, in the next instant, had whisked him out the door. I learned later that evening from Richard Hoffman, MUFON investigator in Dayton, who attended the lecture, that the man wearing the blue sweater worked for the Air Matériel Command at Wright-Patterson. Curious, the next day at lunch I asked Hynek if he was able to get confirmation of the Wright-Patterson case from his companion.

"He never heard about it," he replied.

The Mexican case confused with the test pilot's encounter near Wright-Patterson happened over Lake Tequesquetengo, not far from Mexico City, May 3, 1975. In this case there were early, contradictory reports depending on the news source; however, the stories agreed on the essential details. Impressed, Dr. Hynek flew to Mexico City to get firsthand information. The August 1975 issue of *Skylook,* quoted in part, summed up the case:

> Carlos Antonio de los Santos Montiel, age twenty-three, was flying at 120 mph in a Piper Comanche from Zihuatanejo to Mexico City. He was at an altitude of fifteen thousand feet, and while passing over Lake Tequesquetengo, at 1:34 P.M., he felt his plane vibrating in a strange manner without apparent cause. Then, along the right side of his plane, a 10–12-foot disc appeared. Another disc appeared to the left of his plane. He described them as being about 4½ feet high and dark gray in color. At the center was a protuberance. Just above this was a small window, and on the upper part a kind of antenna. A third disc was reportedly spotted coming at

the plane head on. This disc hit the bottom of the plane, according to the pilot, "giving it a light blow." A report from the Center for UFO Studies by Dr. J. Allen Hynek, in *Physical Traces Associated with UFO Landings,* states:

"Soon a third object like the others appeared above and in front of his plane, and dropped down and collided with the under part of the fuselage, jolting the plane and the pilot, and disappeared from his view."

On seeing that one of the objects was going to pass underneath his plane, the pilot instinctively pulled the lever for lowering the landing gear so as to touch it, but the mechanism failed to operate. The pilot reportedly felt the plane was being magnetized, as though it were being lifted up, and he believes this may have caused the malfunction of the landing gear.

The pilot reportedly attempted to wobble the wings of the plane, but the controls would not operate. The pilot also tried to slow the plane, but it continued at 120 mph. The pilot, quite shaken by the experience, began weeping and was unable to speak at times, but he maintained reasonably constant radio contact with the Mexico City Airport. The airport cleared traffic for the pilot, and after awhile he was able to manually lower his landing gear and land. The plane was checked, and a dent and possible scratches were found on the fuselage.

The *National Enquirer* checked into the case and reported that two of the objects made an impossibly sharp turn, which baffled air traffic controllers who were tracking them on radar. The paper quotes air traffic controller Emilio Estanol López as saying, "The objects made a 270-degree turn at 518 mph in an arc of only three miles. Normally a plane moving at that speed needs eight to ten miles to make a turn like that. In my 17 years as an air traffic controller I've never seen anything like that."

Dr. Hynek states, "It was reported that the objects on the wings rose up and merged into one and moved off in an easterly direction, whereupon the radar operator

could see the object for the first time. It disappeared in
the direction of the mountain Popocatépetl."

By phone, on April 7, 1976, Dr. Hynek gave me this roundup
commentary: "This appears to be a valid visual-radar case. There
was only one witness, but on the basis of my conversation with
personnel in the control tower, who confirmed the UFOs, the case
seems solid. Still open to question are the physical dents caused by
the close encounter, but the case itself joins the ranks of other
visual-radar cases."

In both the Wright-Patterson and Mexican cases, the UFOs' te-
nacious, gnat-like behavior are reminders of World War II's foo
fighter. The UFOs, whether in groups of three or singly, seem to
playfully challenge aircraft of all kinds, military, commercial, and
private, with seeming disregard for human life. Like so many
other aspects of the persistent UFO, it is difficult for research to
rationalize the marauder's ceaseless surveillance of a commonplace flying machine. What new data can be gained, especially if
we are to believe that aircraft "specimens" have already been abducted for examination? Pointless it seems, but so is human rationalization!

Down to Earth, the UFO seems just as senseless in its harassment. Shattered is any immediate hope to put all the anomalies of
cases together into a single hypothesis. Ufologists are stumped by
the diverse data on hand and retreat from labeling any belligerent
segment of it as a sign of the UFO's long- or short-range intent.

During a warm September day in 1974, near Hobbs, New Mexico, a huge disc-shaped object suddenly descended over a tract of
farmland and stopped to hover about five hundred feet over a
barn. A farmer was in his pickup truck driving toward his house
nearby when he glimpsed the object and stuck his head out the
window for a better look. Also watching the strange object in
amazement were his wife, his daughter, and a neighbor. Suddenly,
before their eyes, the pickup truck with the farmer in it was lifted
vertically from the ground and vanished into the underbelly of the
disc. Hysterically, the farmer's wife called the police.

The facts of the case, still incomplete, are in the confidential
files of the International UFO Registry. The investigator in this
case, a radio newsman, prefers anonymity. Through a good source

he got the basic information about the incident from an officer only on the basis that the names and most of the data be kept confidential until the victim was found, dead or alive. A little more than a year later, an unidentified body of a man was found in unusual circumstances in the small town of Ruidoso, about 150 miles from Hobbs. Investigation showed that the body was that of a man from Hobbs, but it was not the farmer. The investigator is still working quietly with the authorities, hoping someday the abducted man will show up, possibly alive.

The mystery of missing persons linked to the UFO is a sensitive subject, much like animal mutilations. Most publicized cases involving missing persons and UFOs turn out to be cultish shenanigans. Occasionally, one like the Hobbs case takes on serious overtones.

In October 1976 another incident with a possible UFO connection surfaced in Albuquerque, New Mexico. A family of three—wife, husband, and a teen-age son—was last seen May 26, 1976, vanishing without leaving a trace. Quiet investigation is continuing by the author, working with Dennis Hauck, director of IUFOR, and with other members of the concerned family, who prefer anonymity. One major clue is that the missing wife told her mother, prior to disappearing, that she had established contact with an alien being aboard a UFO near the Sandia Crest. According to the mother, her frightened daughter predicted, "You'll never see us again."

In November 1957, during a period of one of Ohio's many flaps, which included a number of landing reports in a farm region, Mr. and Mrs. James Allen (name changed by request) were watching TV. Suddenly there was interference, the picture going into waves then blacking out. Seconds later, a strong, eerie light came through their window. The Allens rushed to the window and saw to their shock a large, "squat" object about twenty feet in diameter hovering over their back yard. As Mrs. Allen watched through her window, her husband went outdoors to investigate. The object moved directly over him as he stood frozen in disbelief. Regaining his senses, he fled indoors, feeling almost instantly ill and feverish. Within forty-eight hours James Allen was dead, his insides fried as though by the heat of a microwave oven. Medical examination showed intense radiation. Depressed, Mrs. Allen sold her farm and retired to Arizona. She related the story of her husband's death to a physician, who in turn gave the details to one of the nation's foremost researchers.

Like the archaeologist who looks for artifacts of man's past by digging into ruins, the ufologist digs into the past for UFO cases "Before Arnold." Ted Bloecher's painstaking work *Report on the UFO Wave of 1947,* published in 1967, records many uncelebrated UFO cases occurring in 1947, many before Ken Arnold announced to the world that he sighted "nine saucer-like things" near Mt. Rainier. Bloecher missed it by one year in unearthing one of the most horrifying cases ever to reach my desk. My information comes in anecdotal form from Ray Stanford, director of Project Starlight International, Austin, Texas, a case he occasionally uses in his lectures. The case was originally published in the British *Flying Saucer Review,* as reported by Professor Felipe Machado Carrion.

The alleged incident happened in February 1946 in a small village of Brazil called Aracariguama, in the state of São Paulo. Curiously, the region's people had been witnessing strange nocturnal lights in the sky, causing them concern. During this time, a man named João Prestes had gone fishing in good weather with a friend and, on leaving the house, advised his wife, who was planning to attend a carnival in a nearby village, to leave the house window unlocked so he could get inside on his return. At dusk, after fishing, Prestes departed from his friend and went home. As he entered his house through the window, he was suddenly hit by a shaft of light from a light source in the sky. Dazed, he ran frightened to his sister's home in the village.

Three members of the family came out to help Prestes as he stood in what appeared to be a trance. Then, to their horror, they watched the skin on his face and arms begin to change. His skin began to blister and pop open, widening into gaping lesions. Then his muscles sagged from his arms and face. But Prestes showed no sign of pain, made no grimaces, uttering just guttural sounds. As his neighbors stood horrified, too shocked to do anything but offer him food and water, the flesh on Prestes' face began to roll off like hot butter. His nose slipped down his face, his lips fell, exposing his teeth, and, as he literally melted away, his eyeballs slid down from their sockets onto the ground.

Prestes still showed no pain nor uttered a sound as his neighbors put his broken body into a car to rush him to a hospital. He was dead on arrival. João Prestes' body, it was learned, was exhumed by Brazilian authorities in 1974 for further research, but there have been no disclosures of their findings.

The range, intensity, and aggressiveness often displayed by the UFO is indicative of a military strike force, but strangely it leaves no widespread destruction normally associated with a totally hostile attack. Here and there, in a strange pattern of randomness, someone suffers injury or discomfort and even inanimate objects are damaged with seeming wantonness. This "warlike" behavior—bizarre and inconsistent as it is—stops short of *open* hostility. Because of the seemingly massive forces available to the interlopers, it would seem that they could destroy our civilization at will if that were their intention. Maybe that is what they are trying to tell us. Or maybe there is some more profound —or sinister—answer.

In my files are many disturbing UFO incidents befalling mankind. Conceivably, in some, the belligerence hypothesis may find strong support. However, not to be overlooked are the eighty thousand cases in Dr. Saunders' computer bank, UFOCAT, which show that most UFOs are of a more curious and evasive behavior. In these cases, it can be conjectured that if man has been frightened "out of his wits" or physically harmed by a UFO, the cause may not have been an act of belligerence but an *inadvertent* situation in which the victim was in the wrong place at the wrong time.

It is the hope of many scientific researchers that Dr. Saunders' UFOCAT can establish a pattern to put the UFO in its place—or in a better perspective to determine its source, nature, and intent.

IX

". . . Above Top Secret"

Said Senator Barry Goldwater in his letter of December 3, 1974, responding to mine, which asked for his comment on the charge that he knew about the alleged "twelve little men" preserved in a secret building at Wright-Patterson Air Force Base, ". . . I made an effort to get in the room at Wright-Patterson where the information was stored, and I was denied this request, understandably."

Senator Goldwater answered another researcher's letter, March 28, 1975, reiterating his being denied access to the stored UFO information and added, ". . . It [the UFO information] is still classified above Top Secret."[1]

Indeed, these unminced words coming from a powerful political figure have the clout to beat down every denial of secrecy ever made by the Air Force since 1948, when they were first charged with concealing the real UFO evidence from the public. With the Air Force ostensibly removed from the responsibility of UFO investigation since 1969, the question that remains unanswered is which government agency, if any, since that year, still holds the key to the locked-up evidence such as the Air Force's gun-camera photos showing UFOs spotted during intercept missions.

A small number of key people have worked and breathed within the existent policy of secrecy. Some work in abject silence;

[1] A copy of Department of Air Force letter addressed to Senator Barry Goldwater, dated June 10, 1976. (See letter in Appendix IV.)

Sketch of the author's sighting of three unidentified luminous "blobs" seen from imperiled C46 during flight from Ie Shima to Iwo Jima, en route to Japan, on August 28, 1945. The author, on an intelligence assignment, landed safely in Atsugi, Japan, three days prior to the official surrender of Japan. This incident with the "foo fighters" triggered the writer's interest in the UFO mystery. Sketch copyright 1957 by the author.

A video-modulated laser beam pierces the night sky as Ray Stanford, director of Project Starlight International, watches the aiming monitor while he controls the movements. The laser beam is not normally visible to the naked eye when viewed from the side, but a fine water mist was sprayed into the beam to scatter the coherent light and allow it to be recorded in this photo, a time exposure with flash. This unit is one of numerous monitoring and recording instruments being used by PSI specialists to gather sophisticated UFO data. Photo courtesy of Project Starlight International (PSI).

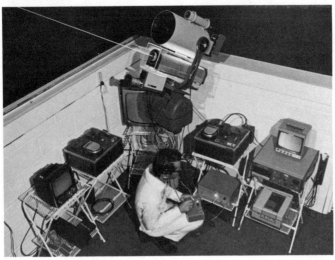

Physical damage caused by a low-level UFO near a residence in Columbia, Missouri, on June 28, 1973. Limbs of the tree were twisted and broken, and later the leaves withered and fell. Photo courtesy of Ted Phillips.

Drawings by the author showing a variety of humanoid entities reportedly associated with UFOs during close encounters. Mona Stafford, of Stanford, Kentucky, with the author during posthypnosis in February 1976, pointed to the encircled head, which she claimed looked similar to the entity she witnessed during her alleged abduction. Significantly, Elaine Thomas pointed to the same head while under hypnosis, in June 1976. Drawings copyright 1977 by the author.

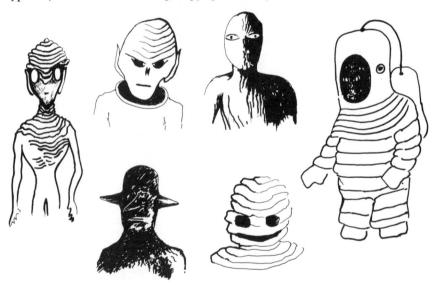

a few, ever so cautiously, will drop a hint of their work—but never before a third person.

"It is an incontrovertible fact that credible, sane people whose testimony in a court of law would be accepted on any other subject continue to report UFOs," said Dr. J. Allen Hynek, director of the Center for UFO Studies.

At my home on May 22, 1976, the day after he had addressed a large group of Northwestern alumni in Cincinnati, Dr. Hynek and I honed down our discussion to the sphinx-like official attitude.

"Len," he said, "it's quite possible there has been closed government concern about UFOs. In fact, I hardly think our government could be so stupid as *not* to pay attention. In the face of the Gallup Poll indicating that fifteen million Americans have seen something in the sky they couldn't explain and that the majority of Americans believe that UFOs are real—well—these are big numbers, important both sociologically and even politically. A government that would ignore these figures would be stupid indeed!"

Dr. David Saunders, of UFOCAT, stated by phone on January 22, 1976, "I certainly operate on the assumption that there has been, and may still be, official secrecy."

At the Chicago conference sponsored by the Center for UFO Studies, April 30–May 2, 1976, I often brought up the sticky question of secrecy before a knowledgeable confrere and I usually got a quick response. Shared were many UFO incidents, military and civilian, involving official cover-up, cases of photo confiscation, knowledge of a secret NASA movie showing UFOs, and stories of official sources admitting high-level secrecy. But always lacking were names—to protect the informant. . . .

As I retired to my room after the second night of late-hour, off-the-record informative chats—so different from getting "news" by phone or letter—I again wondered, as I am wont to do, about our world's freak, the UFO . . . and I wondered even more in long, sleepless quiet about the reasons for the colossal secrecy. In my mind churned all the uncensored revelations added to all the technical data from papers presented during the long day from learned ufologists. I also wondered if we as a group knew as much as *or more than* the people enforcing the colossal secrecy.

Mainly my thoughts were on Bill Spaulding, director of Ground

Saucer Watch. In his pursuit of a computerized photo analysis project, he had reopened an old controversy over the Ralph Mayher movie film allegedly confiscated by the military authorities in 1952.

In my book *Inside Saucer Post . . . 3-0 Blue* I wrote, in 1957:

> Another act of hocus pocus involves the Mayher film, a 16 mm. movie which shows a bright object streaking over Miami, Florida, July 29, 1952. Accompanied by friends, Ralph C. Mayher, a Marine Corps photographer, shot 40 feet of film, but today he owns only a few frames, thanks to somebody's sleight of hand. After shooting the film, Mayher phoned the Marine Air Station. Sent to the scene was a Lt. Aldridge who, on departing, took the film roll with him.
>
> Although denied the right to show his film while in uniform, copies were sent to the Air Force for analysis. However, a letter addressed to Mayher dated April 13, 1954, revealed, "This is to advise you that a search of the ATIC files has failed to show that the Air Force has ever received the film you mentioned. It is our belief that since this film was originally submitted to a Naval Base, it must still remain with Naval Intelligence."
>
> The letter was signed by 1st Lt. R. C. White. Mayher then wired the Marine Corps Air Station in Miami where he was stationed as a service photographer the night he caught the UFO on film. The reply, dated April 19, 1954, stated, "Saucer film turned over to Air Force, July 31, 1952." The telegram carried the name of Colonel T. G. Ennis, C.O. of the air station.

On June 7, 1975, Spaulding, in an attempt to procure important data on the Mayher film, wrote to the CIA, known to have had a finger in the film's fast handling. As it turned out, Spaulding and the CIA exchanged many letters, but, in the end, he did not receive the data requested. Some of the CIA memoranda he received indicated that portions of the data concerning the Mayher film were still classified.

Research groups are familiar with official legerdemain in handling UFO film, both stills and movies, and they know about the secreted gun-camera photos taken by military pilots during UFO intercept missions. And it is known in some instances that major film processors have played a *sub rosa* intermediary role in monitoring UFO film. Following a taped TV performance featuring the UFO, in January 1975, for Junior Achievement of Greater Cincinnati, a student, working part-time for a film developer, told me she saw on her boss's desk a directive from the studio's parent company which directed that photos received showing pornography *and UFOs* were to be destroyed! The student, with no interest in UFOs, seemed sincere, but I could get no confirmation from local developers that such a directive existed. Fact or hearsay?

The seasoned heads of the major research groups hear many strange stories, many of them twisted rumors and baseless hearsay, but they are also aware of the long, sedulous arm of secrecy. I asked each for a statement:

John L. Acuff, president, NICAP: "There is no doubt that the decision was reached by the Air Force to classify most of the case material relating to UFOs. This classification took place throughout the operation of Project Bluebook. The recent decision of the Air Force requiring the deletion of witness names, investigator comments, etc., before UFO records are made available to the public through the National Archives, will make these files almost worthless for research purposes. The real question is not whether secrecy did exist, or still exists; the question is why was it imposed. Many people have speculated that a 'conspiracy' exists on the part of the Air Force with the intention of keeping the general public from learning the 'truth' about UFOs. I seriously doubt that such a conspiracy does exist or that the federal government learned much more about the true nature of UFOs than NICAP. It is still a mystery deserving of well-conducted research."

William H. Spaulding, director, GSW: "Throughout my years of active UFO research and investigations I have constantly been exposed to sour comments, from both concerned witnesses and ex-governmental officials, that directly infer a UFO conspiracy by our various governmental departments. The elements of foul-up and cover-up openly exist in the UFO story. I have seen repetitive reports citing film confiscation and editing, a landing area being plowed under and the witnesses receiving cruel and unnecessary official ridicule.

"There is something big behind the total UFO report, something big enough to hide like the size of America's atomic arsenal. This is well displayed in the official documents and statements uncovered since 1947.

"I cannot understand why a sincere UFO witness, who generally is placed in a situation by chance rather than choice, must be treated like a juvenile by 'Big Brother' just because he has unfortunately observed an unidentified flying object, the same type that do *not* officially exist."

L. J. Lorenzen, international director, APRO: "A few years ago (at the APRO symposium in Littleton, Colorado, July 1974), I predicted that government sources would begin to ease up on UFO information, making it more accessible than in the past. I predicted that this would take place through a gradually accelerated program over a three-year period. I was wrong. Essentially the same information had been leaked to me through three separate channels, giving me confidence that I was onto something real. In retrospect I feel either that I was 'set up,' i.e., fooled into thinking I was onto something real, or that such a plan did exist but has since been reversed.

"Since the closing of Project Bluebook, an act which ostensibly took the Air Force 'out of the UFO business,' I have noted an unobtrusive addendum to many Air Force press releases to the effect that they continue to investigate UFO cases through normal intelligence channels. This of course has always been true—under the assignment of defense responsibilities. Since 1953, Bluebook had merely served as public-relations diversion. Its purpose was to solve P.R. problems for the Air Force (relative to UFOs), and it was closed when it began to create more problems than it solved.

"Recent information has come to my attention which indicates that the military establishment, having apparently learned a lesson from Watergate, now rewrites history in connection with UFO incidents to the extent of altering and purging records and framing individuals within their ranks to make sure (apparently) that no telltale material exists for further investigative committees to uncover. Hopefully the purged material is preserved at some higher echelon, as normally happens when classified material is upgraded and called forward; otherwise it is lost to science forever."

Ray Stanford, director, Project Starlight International: "P.S.I. takes the position that if there is censorship of the UFO hard evidence by the intelligence community, it is undoubtedly for what they deem to be very good reason—like the secret duplication of an advanced technology. We do not care to attack any such position but, instead, to continue to do instrumented UFO hard-data monitoring and recording. That kind of research will eventually speak for itself even without governmental authority having to verify it."

Dr. D. William Hauck, director, International UFO Registry: "Shortly after Kurt Waldheim lost his bid for Chancellor of Austria, I questioned him concerning the concealment of UFO reports by Austrian authorities. He replied that the Austrian Government would not hesitate to release significant material should it become available. This approach shadows the official position of West Germany based on findings of a government commission headed by Dr. Hermann Oberth.

"The Oberth Commission found that '. . . UFOs are conceived and directed by intelligent beings of a very high order, . . .' and the West German Government has proved very open in its handling of the phenomenon.

"To my knowledge, the British Air Ministry has taken a less serious approach and is only too happy to pass UFO reports along to U.S. authorities. All Canadian UFO sightings must be reported to U.S. military communications stations under a Joint Chiefs of Staff directive, although the Minister of Defense, Mr. James Richardson, has denied all knowledge of such an arrangement. The Australian Department of Air also works closely with U.S. authorities in what appears to be a continuing effort to debunk UFO sightings.

"Czechoslovakia has an extensive UFO research effort underway, which remains completely classified. Without doubt, the Soviet Union is involved in the study of UFOs, although in 1968 the Soviet Academy of Sciences pronouned the study of UFOs 'unscientific.' In view of Soviet research into 'unscientific' psychic phenomena, it would seem as if that announcement was as politically motivated as our own Condon Report's conclusions. In reality, the All-Union Cosmonautics Committee is a secret UFO study group connected with the Soviet Air Force. In addition, several civilian scientists, notably Dr. Modest Agrest and Dr. Felix Zigel, carry out private UFO research in Russia. China has a very large radio network through which UFO sightings are reported by simple codes. The U.S. has monitored several mini-flaps on the Chinese mainland, and the Chinese are acutely aware of everything that goes on in their skies.

"Now that Kurt Waldheim is secretary general of the United Nations, there is hope that a concerted international effort to solve the UFO problem can be initiated, provided, of course, the various national groups pool their findings to convince the UN member nations of the international nature of the problem. I would be happy to work with anyone interested in attacking official secrecy, under the guidance of the United Nations."

Walter H. Andrus, international director, MUFON: "Historical events during the U. S. Air Force study of UFOs, starting in 1947, have been 'earmarked' with letters, investigations, news releases, and official reports, giving credence to the so-called 'secrecy,' when the incident being reported in no way resembled the actual event, facts, or data.

"An example may be taken from a Department of the Air Force letter dated March 29, 1967, from George P. Freeman, Jr., Lieutenant Colonel, USAF; chief, Civil Branch, Community Relations Division, Office of Information. Quote: Regarding the 1948 'Estimate of the Situation,' the late Captain Ruppelt in his book, *The Report on Unidentified Flying Objects,* provides the answer. The top secret estimation was working its way up to the higher echelons of the Air Force. It got to the late General Hoyt S. Vandenberg, then chief of staff, before it was 'batted down.' The general wouldn't 'buy' interplanetary vehicles. The report lacked proof and the estimate died a quick death. Some months later, it was completely declassified and relegated to the incinerator. Colonel Freeman then concluded by saying, 'I am sorry, but we have no copies of this document.'

"The new Freedom of Information Act has made many formerly secret reports by the Central Intelligence Agency available to the general public. Classified 'SECRET Security Information,' the report of the CIA Scientific Advisory Panel on Unidentified Flying Objects meeting on January 14–17, 1953 (commonly known as the Robertson Report) was declassified in segments starting March 28, 1975. Mrs. Ann Druffel, MUFON field investigator and director of SKYNET in Pasadena, California, was able to secure the declassified report, including names of all the participants, some of which had been deleted in the original release.

"The United States Air Force Project Bluebook, and its predecessors, has received its share of condemnation for its unprofessional administration and investigation of UFO sighting reports. Having had 'a tiger by the tail' since 1947, the Air Technical Intelligence Center was relieved of this responsibility at the end of 1969.

"As the international director of MUFON, I would like to consider several hypothetical policies that may have influenced the so-called 'secrecy' associated with the UFO phenomenon by the U. S. Air Force, the United States Government, and the Central Intelligence Agency:

"1. Failure to take the phenomenon seriously enough to assign adequate and competent personnel to obtain the scientific facts and data.

"2. An underlying belief that the citizens of our nation would panic if they were exposed to the reality of extraterrestrial visitation by advanced intelligent beings.

"3. The inability to face the possibility that we may be dealing with some form of psychic manifestation not presently understood by modern science.

"4. C.I.A. or Department of Defense delaying strategy in which the United States may have tried to use counterintelligence to confuse the U.S.S.R., while diligently seeking the technical answers to the propulsion methods of UFOs, in an endeavor to 'win the space race.'

"5. And last, but not least. The agency responsible for the investigation of UFOs was so baffled that they came up with a big zero for a logical explanation. This reluctance to disclose the identity of the phenomenon could be construed 'secrecy' by some people. The latter may be the most significant hypothesis proposed.

"In all fairness to our government, the Joint Chiefs of Staff of our Armed Services are not idly 'sitting on their hands.' Even though the U. S. Air Force was publicly and officially released from its responsibility to investigate the UFO enigma, on December 31, 1969, the study is continuing under the auspices of other agencies. In the latest manual issue of the 'Joint Chiefs of Staff Publication 6, Volume 5, Joint Reporting Structure,' dated February 1975, 'U. S. Air Force Reporting Instructions' still specify the method for reporting 'unidentified objects' via the CIRVIS report (Communications Instructions Reporting Vital Intelligence Sightings). This manual explicitly explains how the CIRVIS report shall be made out, by whom, and to the appropriate responsible agency within the governments of both the United States and Canada.

"The CIRVIS report is similar to the UFO reporting instructions contained in the 'MUFON Field Investigators Manual,' edited by Raymond E. Fowler, in 1975, for the Mutual UFO Network. Pilots who observe unidentified flying objects and report them in detail as prescribed in the CIRVIS instructions will provide some unknown agency within our government with an unlimited source of raw reports for an ongoing study."

John B. Musgrave, of Edmonton, Alberta, Canada, affiliated with MUFON, CUFOS, and APRO, is preparing a documented history of the UFO in Canada, for which he received a Canada Council grant: "With few exceptions, official Canadian policy toward UFO reports and the UFO phenomena consistently reflects official U.S. policy. This is hardly a surprise. Canadian military is subservient to the U.S. military through so-called joint commands such as NORAD and NATO, and police bodies such as the RCMP are closely linked to their U.S. counterparts through networks such as FBI and CIA computer centres. As in the U.S., UFO sightings that have become public are downgraded, and sightings that have come to the private attention of military or police personnel are covered up.

"In theory, since 1968 any unclassified report compiled by military or civilian authorities eventually is forwarded to the Upper Atmospheric Research section of the National Research Council, near Ottawa. Although often believed or stated that this section is actively engaged in UFO study, this branch is only interested in these reports as potential sightings of meteorites. Hence, all reports sent to NRC are classified as either 'meteoritic' or 'non-meteoritic.' Needless to say, for their purposes, any potential UFO sighting is part of their garbage-can file.

"The Criminal Investigations Branch of the RCMP is involved with carrying on UFO-type investigations (UFO percipients are referred to as complainants, and are often asked about potential criminal acts, such as previous use of drugs, during the interrogation), and, again in theory, pass on any UFO reports of unclassified nature to NRC. It has been the experience of a number of field investigators that they know of many reports collected by teams of RCMP or military personnel that never show up in these files. Whether conscious or not, the net effect of the data-gathering network ending at the NRC is to stifle or cover up UFO reports. Reports either are not passed on to NRC or are passed on to secret investigatory bodies such as the CIA. In addition, it seems routine for these official investigators to strongly advise all witnesses to keep silent.

"While there has been cover-up, there have also been some notable Canadian contributions to UFO research which have enjoyed at least some support from governmental agencies. The most famous of these, Project Magnet, was authorized in December 1950 by Commander C. P. Edwards, then Deputy Minister of Transport for Air Services. The project was in fact headed by Wilbert B. Smith, who was largely the inspiration for the project. Although no monies were allocated, facilities and electronic equipment were provided at Shirley Bay, Ontario. Although the gravitometer was tripped off on August 8, 1954, no UFO was actually sighted, and this part of the project remained inconclusive. In his Project Magnet Report, Smith concluded after analysing twenty-four cases from 1952 that 'It appears, then, that we are faced with a substantial probability of the real existence of extra-terrestrial vehicles, regardless of whether or not they fit into our scheme of things.'

"Project Magnet was not continued, but its existence still generates some heat from opposition members of Parliament who wish to attack the government for wasting funds on flying saucers. Its death knell was sounded in part by Project Second Story, a pale cousin of the CIA-sponsored Robertson Panel. The Canadian equivalent was convened in 1952 at the instigation of the Defense Research Board. Like its cousin, it concluded that UFOs pose no threat to national security and every effort should be made to downgrade UFO reports and UFO speculation. There has been no major change in Canadian policy toward the UFO phenomena since then."

Clandestine studies of the UFO go beyond the joint operations of the United States and Canada. All technological nations *are* involved; some and perhaps all are interlinked at various depths in the exchange of information with the United States. While publishing *Orbit* in the 1950s, I was told by a reliable source that each edition was translated and distributed among key officials of the Venezuelan Government. On the other hand, Argentina openly exchanged UFO incidents with CRIFO.[2]

Knowing of the great number of UFO incidents occurring in Brazil over many years, I phoned the Brazilian Embassy in Washington, D.C., May 21, 1976, for their government's official position. I was referred to the air attaché, Colonel Adelio del Tedesco. The cooperative colonel indicated his interest in the UFO and said that just prior to acceptance of his present post as air attaché, fifteen months before, he had been asked by his Air Force to establish a UFO investigative unit. He said orders had been prepared to send to all federal agencies and police units to cooperate with the project, which would include the investigation of sighting reports from the public. He had no new data on the project, or on whether it was in effect, but from another reliable source who had been in Brazil in recent months I learned that Air Force authorities there had tightened up their security on the UFO.[3]

Joe Brill's exchange of letters with Dr. Felix Zigel, professor of mathematics and astronomy at the Moscow Aviation Institute, in the Soviet Union, has produced some outstanding reports of UFO incidents. In a letter dated June 24, 1975, Zigel disclosed that he was completing a book entitled *Interplanetary Vehicles and UFOs*. Enclosed with the letter was a prospectus which stated, "In the new 'Program of Investigation of Problems Concerning Extraterrestrial Life,' published by the Academy of Sciences of the USSR (1974), on page 19 there is a point concerning interplanetary vehicles, where the following is stated:

Special attention should be devoted to the discovery of vehicles of extraterrestrial civilizations that may be found

[2] Letter from Argentine Air Attaché. (See letter in Appendix V.)

[3] A letter from Air Force Lieutenant Colonel Durval Osvaldo Tomcyak, dated June 14, 1976, in response to my inquiry regarding the official status of UFO research in his country, states in part, "The Brazilian Air Force has adopted throughout the years a position of observer and analyst. In accordance with that position the Air Force takes care of those cases which present, *ab initio,* a certain mark of credibility."

in the solar system or in orbit around the Earth. For such a search for quickly moving objects, the system of continuous surveillance of all the heavens must be supplemented by creating a special radio directional-bearing system. In the initial stage, use could possibly be made of the already existing complexes intended for cosmic link-ups and radio location.

Coincidentally, on the same date as Dr. Zigel's letter, June 24, 1975, Dr. A. A. Kulakov, director-in-chief of the Academy of Sciences of the USSR, Foreign Relations Department, answered my letter of inquiry:

Thank you for your letter of April 15, 1975, giving me the opportunity to inform you about the attitude of Soviet scientists toward the problem of unidentified flying objects (UFOs).

In the USSR there is no agency or other special organization that studies the UFO problem. At the appropriate time our Academy of Sciences considered this problem and came to the conclusion that in those cases when communications on UFO appearances merit confidence those appearances can be interpreted either as atmospheric phenomena or as phenomena of technological origin. It is well known that also many American scientists hold a similar point of view, for example the well-known astronomer D. Menzel.

From time to time communications from Soviet citizens about observations of phenomena involving the descent of UFOs are acted upon. Such communications are customarily directed to astronomical observatories or geophysical institutes, where they will be examined and a reply made to the author. The common appraisal of such communications has been as stated above.

We have no data on the question as to whether UFO appearances were noted by Soviet troops in World War II.

Soviet scientists share the hypothesis of the possible existence of intelligent life beyond the limits of the earth, but it is doubtful that they would agree on considering UFOs as manifestations of such life.

The TASS report mentioned by you is, apparently, the consequence of a misunderstanding or wrong translation. It is not known to us whether a special search for signals from an extraterrestrial civilization was conducted in the city of Gorky and whether, furthermore, those signals were detected.

In the joint program the flights of the cosmic ships *Soyuz-Apollo* are contributions and will yield extensive information.

In conclusion, I wish to emphasize that our astronomers and geophysicists do not consider the real existence of UFOs and, furthermore, communications with intelligent life outside the earth as having been in any degree established.

In a letter, with enclosures, dated September 2, 1976, Dr. Zigel informed Joe Brill that his twenty-year study of the UFO phenomenon has convinced him that they are of extraterrestrial origin.

Said Zigel, "A number of specialists have gradually entered into UFO research in my country. It has been proposed to bring out a symposium on the problem and to publish its works. . . . In reality the UFO phenomenon is a tough nut to crack for any scientist of high rank. I am afraid that we are still very far from correctly understanding the nature of the UFO. However, I don't see any alternative hypothesis to the one which explains UFOs as being manifestations of extraterrestrial space ventures."

Communist China is also sensitively alert to the UFO, but officially has said nothing. Confirming Dr. Hauck's statement, my Australian informant, who had met the late Chou En-lai while serving with the first Australian trade commission to China, told me that his peers talked about UFOs—*but only in guarded privacy*.

The official British position is unclear, but, from many well-informed sources over many years, I have heard that the Ministry of Defence has been working in liaison with the United States in some areas of intelligence, much the same as Australia and New Zealand.

In my early years of collecting UFO information internationally, I had developed lengthy correspondence with Lord Dowding, air chief marshall of the R.A.F. during World War II. In one of his letters, February 18, 1956, he wrote, ". . . I am sorry that I cannot tell you anything about the British official attitude to UFOs. I don't think there is one. . . ."

For an updated view of the British position, I called their embassy in Washington, D.C., on September 10, 1975, and talked with Dr. Terrence Moynehan, scientific attaché. He said he knew that the R.A.F. maintained an office in the Ministry of Defence in London for this phase of research and suggested that I send a letter with my questions through his embassy office, which he would forward to the R.A.F. Their reply, signed by J. A. Peduzie, S4 (air), November 27, 1975, follows:

1. I am replying to your letter of 26 September 1975, addressed to Dr. Terrence Moynehan at the British Embassy, Washington, since responsibility for investigating reported UFO sightings within the United Kingdom rests with the Air Force Department of the Ministry of Defence.

2. The Ministry of Defence investigates UFO reports, which are received from various sources, such as members of the public, the police and service units, solely to see if there are any defence implications. The Department has no organization specifically concerned with the study of UFOs as such. Reports are examined by various specialist staffs within the Ministry of Defence and RAF commands as part of normal staff function. They have access not only to the full scientific and professional resources of the Ministry but also, if necessary, to the expert advice of other Government and non-Government bodies.

3. Since the Ministry's interest in unidentified flying objects is limited to the defence aspect, investigations into the scientific significance of the phenomena have not been carried out. Indeed, the pressures on our budget are now so severe that we could not justify expenditure on

scientific studies which would go beyond the defence interest.

4. Reports of UFO sightings are not normally regarded as classified material. However, in common with all forms of correspondence received from the general public, the reports are treated as confidential and are closed to public scrutiny until such time as they would become available in accordance with the Public Records Act—i.e., at the end of 30 years. I should add that we hold no reports earlier than 1962.

5. During the years 1962 to 1974 inclusive, 2,360 UFO reports were received in the Department; this figure includes 380 in 1971, which was the peak year. These figures include reports from all sources, and in order to state the number originating from military sources a special examination of all the papers would be necessary. I regret that we have not the resources to undertake such a task. However, you may be interested to know that by far the great majority of reports are made by the general public, although we cannot say what number of reports were received from military sources in 1973.

6. Once it is clear that there are no defence implications, we do not pursue our research further—for example to a point where positive correlation with a known object might be established. I regret, therefore, that we are unable to state the percentage of unexplained reports for past years, including 1973 and 1975.

7. With regard to your enquiry about "Foo Fighters," we are unable to comment on this phenomenon. As I have said, we hold no reports prior to 1962. However, had the Ministry been in possession before 1962 of any reports which had any implications for the air defence of the United Kingdom they would certainly have been retained.

8. I hope this letter will be of some help to you. We do not dismiss the possibility that intelligent life could exist in outer space. However, the UFO reports that have reached us to date contain no evidence to support this hypothesis. I am sorry I cannot answer your specific questions more fully.

In the United States, before the demise of Project Bluebook, in 1969, the battle of the UFO raged between research groups and Air Force officials. Dr. Hynek, working with Bluebook while I was publishing the CRIFO newsletter, has since told me that my name was considered "anathema" to the front-office Bluebook heads such as Captain George Gregory, Captain Charles Hardin and Major Hector Quintanella. My problem: it seems that I was too persistent in my demands to get the real facts on questions they preferred not to answer.

Said Major Andrew Wood, executive, Public Information Division, in his letter of December 14, 1956, "We have just completed a review of the considerable file of correspondence that has accumulated over the past few years between you and various units and offices of the Air Force. Our conclusion is that a continuation on the subject would be of little value to the United States Air Force investigation and technical analysis of UFO studies. . . ."

Said Lieutenant Colonel Lawrence J. Tacker, Public Information Division, in his letter of July 26, 1960, ". . . There is absolutely no truth in the charge that the Air Force or any other governmental agency is withholding information on the subject of UFOs from the general public. . . ."

Scores of other letters I received from various Air Force officials all denied withholding information. With each letter came a copy of their latest Fact Sheet, which explained away all the UFO sightings except the usual 2–3 per cent.

Irate citizens with an above-average UFO sighting were caught up into the emotional controversy. One, a Cincinnati businessman, the late Thomas Eickhoff, having witnessed a UFO, threw down the gauntlet. In a letter he prepared for publication in *Inside Saucer Post . . . 3-0 Blue,* he describes his attempt at legal action as follows:

> . . . At present, in the UFO controversy, there exist two diametrically opposed factions; one, the various government agencies who make statements explaining away the UFO as *hallucinations* and scientific improbabilities; the other, a group of persons who claim personal contacts with people from other planets. . . .
>
> In 1954, I took the initial steps toward ending this comedy of errors. There were two men slated for speak-

ing engagements in our city. Both had made contact claims in books and were here primarily to promote sales. I could not see why the officials would let these men, if their word was false, speak here; that is, if a citizen should actively object. I did object, and to the FBI, Air Force and other agencies of authority. The rebuff I received from the FBI was that the men were only stating personal opinions, which they were entitled to state. However, the books which these contact claimants offered for sale were headed by such sales clinchers as "documentary," "fact," "truth," etc.

It was during this time that my wife and I made a personal visit to Lieutenant Colonel John O'Mara, then chief deputy commander of Air Intelligence, Wright-Patterson AFB. While we talked, O'Mara once again branded these men as obvious hoaxers and also made disparaging remarks about Major Donald Keyhoe. He also stated that "there are no such things as the Tremonton or Montana motion-picture films showing flying saucers in flight. However, many Americans, today, have seen those very pictures which were shown on public movie screens. The Colonel did admit that grid cameras had been placed on many jet pursuit ships and indicated they were for further study of the UFO problem. . . .

In the next year, there were more sightings and more claims of personal contacts. Saucer books, magazines and direct-mail circulars were being published in increasing numbers. My thoughts were, how was it that the "charlatans" were going on their way busily fleecing the people unapprehended by, and by the audacious use of, the U.S. mail system at that? At any rate, I purchased one of these books via the mail system, called *Inside the Space Ship,* written by George Adamski. However, prior to purchasing this book, I had examined it and found a very vulnerable legal Achilles' heel. Adamski's "heel," in this case, reads as follows:

"I do have witnesses to one of my journeys in a space craft. Both are scientists who hold high positions. Once they are able to make a statement the picture will change overnight. However, the way things are nowadays, with everything classified as security, for the time being they must remain in the shadow. When they believe they can release the substantiation they have without jeopardizing either the national defense or themselves, they have said they will do so through the press."

On the strength of this statement, which in a sense is scientific corroboration of his experience, the book ceases to be a product of his personal opinion and becomes a statement of fact open to question by legal means!

Irate with the government's lassitude in challenging the "charlatans," I decided to force the issue myself. The book in question was George Adamski's. It was my opinion that he should be brought to Federal Court, where he could prove by use of testimony of his two scientists that he really had been on a space ship from another planet. Of course, this would also have given the government their opportunity to press the case, and therefore, when he was unable to produce the aforementioned scientists, they could prosecute him (Adamski) for the act of fraud committed by illegal use of the U.S. mail system.

I called an attorney friend and explained the situation. He answered that in his opinion I had a case. Out of respect for various agencies involved, my lawyer decided to call in a certain federal representative to act as a go-between. At first this representative thought that we were just kidding, but my lawyer convinced him that we were serious. We gave him our plan of action. "Do nothing until I check" was his advice. We waited and finally he suggested a letter of inquiry be sent to a certain agency in Washington. This we did and the answer that was forthcoming was so evasive that it even angered my very conservative lawyer friend. "They can't do this to us," he said. "We're going through with it." However, when he called the representative, he was advised to please hold off once more until he could get to Washington. Within the week, my attorney called me to his office. He had received the answer which also included instructions for all

parties concerned to deny any connections with the statement. The statement itself came from Allen Dulles, director of the CIA. Said Dulles: *Yes, I did have a case
for Federal Court. However, by use of the injunction if
necessary he would prevent anyone from testifying in
court concerning this book because maximum security
exists concerning the subject of UFOs.* My lawyer, after
carefully pointing out the fact that if the injunction was
used I would be left high and dry and would be open for
countersuit, suggested we drop the case.

Realizing that an iron door of security stood between me and
the hidden UFO evidence, I visited the Air Technical Intelligence
Command at Wright-Patterson Field, August 13, 1957, hoping to
get data on certain UFO cases in their files from Captain George
Gregory of Project Bluebook. He was absent from the base. The
registration desk then connected me with Dr. Miley, whom I was
told was "in charge" of Section 4E4, but he refused to be interviewed. Next, I was directed to Mr. Spencer Whedon, the head of
ATIC Information Services Offices.

While waiting for Whedon's arrival, his secretary, aside from
her many courtesies, kept a watchful eye, even following me to the
drinking fountain. Ushered into a small office with only a desk
and several straight-back wooden chairs, I waited. Suddenly,
Whedon, a robust man in khaki, and his assistant, in plain clothes,
stormed into the room, both looking as if they were rushing to
battle stations. Abruptly, they squeaked chairs across the floor,
flanking them against mine. Hemmed in the middle, and eyeball-
to-eyeball to my left and right, I watched my hosts both in unison
swing one leg over the other. Then silence. I got directly to the
point. "I understand from certain sources that the Air Force is
coming out soon with a new and different statement on UFOs."

"Don't know of any," boomed Whedon, pressing tobacco into
his enormous pipe. "Unless it's a slight modification of its present
text—but nothing big or different that I know of."

As time elapsed, in which we had covered several debatable
subjects, I could feel that Whedon was rambling into valuable
time. In the middle of one of his standard Air Force replies I decided to cut in, asking why the Air Force persisted in stating that
UFOs do not exist.

Appearing nettled, Whedon relit his pipe, and finding a new balance in his chair, he boomed, "All but 3 per cent can be explained—and we'd explain those if we had more data." Half smiling, he then recalled some personal experiences in which he himself had been fooled by the optics of light. "Just recently," he said, "while driving my car in Dayton I came to a familiar intersection and was surprised to see two red traffic lights." Pausing momentarily, drawing heavily on his pipe, he went on. "I thought this was odd, but as my car got nearer—guess what?" In the next instant, Whedon was laughing so gustily that he even failed to notice that his pipe had burned out. Knowing the answer was going to be funny, I edged closer. Even the wry face of his assistant creased into a traceable smile. Finally, Whedon, reeling back in his chair, said, "There was only one red light." He then explained that anyone can be fooled by lights and so can people who see saucers!

Whedon admitted that the Air Force had never ruled out the interplanetary theory, but that he knew of no evidence that would support it—"unless," he said, "they aren't telling me everything."

Thinking this perhaps was the case, I next hit on the subject of secrecy. "We're not hiding a thing," he countered. "Everybody seems to think we are, but there's nothing to hide." I then asked if I could see the military reports, especially those by pilots.

"We can't show these," he said, "because we don't have the personnel to handle all the requests to see the reports," adding, "besides, it isn't our policy to supply material for commercial purposes. . . ." Relighting his pipe, Whedon continued, "Air Force pilots are free to say whatever they please about UFOs. They are not muzzled and I can show you this in black and white. . . ."

Time having run out, I thanked Whedon and his assistant for the interview and departed. I thought about Whedon's denial of secrecy and wrote him the following: ". . . In one of our topical avenues which concerned the 'muzzling of pilots,' you stated that such charges are not so, and that you could prove this in writing. Although I did not request this proof at the time, I would now like to see whatever reference or directive you had in mind."

The terse, hazy reply to my letter was signed by Captain Wallace Elwood: "In answer to your letter of 14 August 1957, Mr. Whedon believes that you may refer to his statement that the

Air Force regulation which alone governs the actions of Air Force personnel with respect to UFOs clearly does not muzzle pilots."

I have since framed Elwood's letter as a masterpiece of ambiguity.

UFO incidents, internationally, which effect a single person or a large group of citizens can quickly and dramatically become a military matter.

One of the better-documented UFO cases on record is the Norwood searchlight incident. It has photographic evidence, plus thousands of witnesses including scientists, Catholic clergy, press, and military. Since I first published part of the incident in my book *Inside Saucer Post . . . 3-0 Blue,* new evidence has surfaced to reveal military cover-up.

The incident began on August 19, 1949, during a carnival on the grounds of the Saints Peter and Paul Church in Norwood, Ohio, a city of thirty thousand population, adjacent to Cincinnati. For such occasions, the late Reverend Gregory Miller, pastor of the church, had purchased from army surplus an 8-million-candle-power searchlight. Borrowed to operate it was Sergeant Donald R. Berger, of ROTC of the University of Cincinnati. It was during the height of festivities when Sergeant Berger's sweeping searchlight suddenly flashed across a stationary circular object in the sky. Father Miller was called to the scene; later others joined in. From that date until March 10, 1950, when the object was last seen, Sergeant Berger, who thought he had picked up a "space platform," maintained a detailed log of the events.

I first learned the full significance of the incident during a TV appearance in 1952 as a featured guest with Father Gregory Miller. After the program he called me aside and from his pocket he handed me several photographs clearly showing the spheroidal UFO caught in the beam of the searchlight. "If you have time," he said, "I'd like to show you and your wife the movies of the saucer."

Needless to say, the studio attendants didn't need much persuasion to run the reel. Dell and I watched the screen in amazement as the giant, stationary disc glowed intensely in the sweep of the searchlight.

Cameraman for the movie, on request of Father Miller, was Sergeant Leo Davidson of the Norwood Police Department. Filming most of it on October 23, he used three rolls, twenty-five feet each, and a Hugo-Meyer F-19-3″ camera with telephoto lens. Having observed smaller objects leave the giant UFO, Davidson commented, "They were visibly the size of pinheads, but they didn't have the intensity to register clearly on the film." He pointed out, however, that, to the naked eye, he and all others present *saw two groups of five small objects leaving the parent object,* each with halos brighter than the searchlight beam. Said Davidson, "We watched each group fade out of view."

Davidson also took ten "still" photographs using a Speed-Graphic camera with a 14-inch Wallensach telephoto lens. Two of these were exceptional shots, said Davidson, showing both the parent object and its brood. . . .

But the two prize shots had the usual mysterious fate. Last to see them was the late Harry Mayo, who, as a correspondent for *Time-Life* had prepared a feature story for *Time,* that included the two photos. But Mayo's story and Davidson's photos were not used in *Time* or *Life,* and in spite of requests by Father Miller or Mayo to the publishers, the photos were never returned.

The most eventful night, according to Berger's log and according to the testimony of others, was October 23, 1949. Again the point of observation was the church grounds, this time about fifty persons witnessing the phenomenon. Using a telescope, William Winkler, a businessman, said he observed one of the two groups of five smaller objects leave the parent object, describing them as "triangular." Father Miller and his brother, the late Father Cletus Miller, agreed they were shaped "like the apex of Indian arrow heads." When I interviewed the late Robert Linn, managing editor of the Cincinnati *Post,* he admitted that he saw the searchlight beam "bounce off some definite object" but said the smaller objects were "fluttering like bits of paper." Concerned, Linn joined Father Miller in reporting the incident to Intelligence at Wright-Patterson Field. The Cincinnati *Enquirer* was also called about the giant Norwood object, and while they did not publish the story of the night's activities, they did admit receiving numerous reports of unidentified lights in the sky over Greater Cincinnati. Air Force interceptors were scrambled but could not come close to the large, stationary object.

On the scene on December 20, 1949, were astronomer Dr. Paul

Herget and physicist Dr. D. A. Wells, both of the University of Cincinnati. Herget told the Cincinnati *Post,* "It's not a fake. I believe it may be caused by the illumination of gas in the atmosphere. We need an explanation to squash people's fears."

Dr. Wells, busy with protractors and in frequent hush-hush huddles with two special military investigators using oddly similar names, "Eichleberger" and "Eichlebarger," computed the object's size. Unbelievably, the object was approximated at ten miles elevation and ten thousand feet in diameter!

The mayor of Norwood, the late Ed Tepe, told me during an interview in 1954 that he was standing near Dr. Wells during the computing and heard him relate the object's incredible size. Tepe firmly believed that the object was a solid body. "It had ridges or ribbing," he said, "which were very discernible."

It was not until February 19, 1975, that I learned of a more dramatic event about the incident. On the night of October 23, 1949, a youngster, Paul Koch, and his mother, who lived a block away from the church, were on the grounds watching the searchlight stab at the moon-like object. Like the other witnesses, he saw the small, disc-like objects dart down the light beam, make 90-degree turns and shoot back up. Then, suddenly, his attention was turned to a military jeep arriving on the grounds. Two men in uniform jumped out, one a four-star general.

The general went directly to the searchlight and ordered Sergeant Berger to switch off the light. Father Miller intervened. Hot words were exchanged. Then the general again ordered Berger to switch off the searchlight and put his hand on an unbuckled holster at his side. Said the general, "If you don't turn off the light, I'll shoot it out." Berger, in uniform, obeyed his superior officer despite Father Miller's protest.

The witness, Paul Koch, twenty-six years later, recalls that Father Miller at the following Sunday's sermon condemned the military interference with his rights on church property.

During the 1950s I asked public information officers at the Pentagon—and Mr. Whedon at Wright-Patterson AFB—about the case. All denied having any record of it in their files.

Still another case clammed up by the officials involved a UFO and a toxic red spray that killed a peach tree and physically affected the witness.

About 6:00 P.M., July 22, 1955, Edward Mootz was loosening the soil around a fruit-budding peach tree near his home, a high-elevation point close to downtown Cincinnati. Mootz, a quiet, affable man, living alone, spent most of his spare time beautifying his fabulous gardens terraced into the hillside.

Suddenly, from out of the sky, Mootz was splashed by a liquid red spray looking like cream soda. His arms, bared, were covered with the substance; also the nape of his neck. A billed cap prevented its hitting his face. Looking up, he spotted a strange object passing over, heading toward Eden Park. Guessing its height to be more than five hundred feet, Mootz described the soundless object as a pear standing on end, bulbous side upward, with a metallic fin appended to the rear. The object's colors were vivid: red and green, divided at the midsection.

While watching the object, Mootz said that he became aware of a sharp tingling sensation on the exposed parts of his arm and neck. "It felt like phosphorus burning into my skin," said Mootz, "and the pain was intensifying." Wasting no time, he ran to his house, removed his clothing and washed thoroughly. Mootz told me later that what saved him, in his opinion, was his heavy perspiration, which helped dilute the spray.

The next morning, Mootz revisited the ill-fated spot. To his amazement, the peach tree was dead! The branches and twigs were shriveled grotesquely, the leaves curled and crisp brown, and the once-healthy buds of peaches looking like prunes. A little digging showed that the tree was killed to its very taproots—overnight!

During the on-the-spot interview, Mootz carefully recounted the details of the incident, gave me samples of the mummified peaches and twigs, showed me the many white pinprick scars on his arm "where the substance burnt in," and finally explained that *the authorities, three men, had visited him after the incident and had taken away the tree and its dead fruit.* Mootz would not identify the authorities, except to say they were dressed in plain clothes and courteous. Said Mootz: "They promised a report of their analysis within six weeks."

I lost no time in getting the "pruned" peaches, the twigs and other chunks of root I dug up into the hands of a friend of mine who offered to take them to the Physics Laboratory at Villa

Madonna College, in Covington, Kentucky. There tests were made, one which involved a comparison of seeds, the Mootz specimen and another, provided by the lab, that had been allowed to dry out sufficiently. Under controlled conditions, the comparative seed sprouted normally. The Mootz specimen was completely dehydrated!

Follow-ups with Mootz in the fifties and sixties produced no comment on the official laboratory analysis. In January 1975 he gave me the full story:

The three plain-clothes men, he said, were from Air Force Intelligence. They removed the entire peach tree for analysis, except for a couple of "mummified" peaches he retained in a jar as a souvenir. Although they promised a written report of the lab results, he was instead informed by phone. In brief, he was told that the chemical sprayed on the peach tree was "extraordinary." They admitted, he said, that the "lab was stumped" but analysis indicated that the substance was a *"severe poison."* While many other questions by Mootz were left unanswered, he was told to keep the analysis results confidential.

Another sinister event, said Mootz, happened two weeks after the authorities removed the tree.

During daylight hours, a black Chrysler Imperial with New York license plates was seen to drive up and park on the opposite side of the street from his house. He saw three well-dressed, heavy-set men alight from the car and remove a movie camera and other equipment from the trunk. Immediately, they trained the camera toward his home and hillside garden. "They were there for about an hour," he said, "so I became disturbed and went out to ask them what they were doing?"

One of the three, speaking in broken English, responded that they were taking pictures of Cincinnati industry at the base of the hill. On his challenge, said Mootz, they quickly departed.

Mootz called the FBI, who said they could not answer his complaint because it was beyond their jurisdiction. He then called the police, who drove up too late to locate the mysterious car.

When I talked with Mootz on May 26, 1976, he said he still has the white flyspeck scars on his arms where the toxic spray started to eat into his skin. "Good thing I was perspiring, and washed off the chemical right away," he said, "or I might have been killed like the peach tree!"

Secrecy may stop a church-carnival searchlight and cover up the removal of a mummified peach tree—*and it may hide some outer-space little creatures.*

Until the 1970s, the little creatures were more amusing to UFO research than a subject meriting serious study. Official agencies scoffed at the charge they were hiding twelve refrigerated little men from a crashed UFO inside Building 18-A, area B, at Wright-Patterson AFB.

Unlike the UFO, hard evidence for its occupants is lacking; there is no radar confirmation of their earthly mischief, there are no bona fide photographs of them peering through the UFO's portholes or exiting from a sliding door, and no such trained eyes as a pilot's have ever seen them. Yet, everyone in research knows that the occupant—humanoid or bestial, found dead or captured alive—would constitute the *final proof* of the UFO's extraterrestrial origin. If, indeed, there are bodies already hidden as evidence, this one fact, above all else, must be kept secret—*ABOVE TOP SECRET*.

When I visited the Center for UFO Studies in February 1975, I spent an evening with Sherm Larsen, president of the organization. Somehow we got on the subject of the little men allegedly hidden at Wright-Patterson AFB. Said Larsen, "I've got a story just as good."

Following one of Larsen's recent lectures on UFOs at the Adler Planetarium, Chicago, he was approached by a Presbyterian minister, about thirty-five years of age, from Wisconsin. In confidence, the minister related a singular experience occurring to him as a young boy escorted by his father, also a minister, when they visited the Museum of Science and Industry in Chicago. In their meanderings from the main lobby, they strayed off into a labyrinth of corridors and became lost. Hoping to find an exit, they entered a room in which they encountered a large, glass-covered case. Peering inside, they were shocked to see a number of preserved small, humanoid bodies. The minister recalled that instantly his father was grabbed by several men and forcibly taken into another room. Detained for some time, his father was forced to sign papers before they were allowed to leave the museum.

Years later, said Larsen's informant, his father, on his deathbed, revealed to him the whole story, the facts that for so long he had relegated to secrecy.

Part II of the mystery: A close friend of Larsen's, during Larsen's wartime years in the Counter Intelligence Corps, was an attorney who worked for the government. In their chummy days, his friend never revealed the confidential nature of his job, even though he was aware of Larsen's work in the CIC.

By happenchance, Larsen, during a recent social get-together with his old friend, recalling his World War II experiences in the CIC, learned to his surprise that his friend served in the Security Intelligence Corps during the war. He also learned that *his friend's SIC office in Chicago was in the Museum of Science and Industry!* Perhaps forever unanswered is the question: Was there a secret link between the SIC and the preserved little creatures?

The legend of twelve refrigerated little men from a crashed UFO, hidden in a building at Wright-Patterson AFB, has been categorically denied by the Air Force, and most researchers tend to believe the story is a fabrication. But the story persists.

Researcher Charles Wilhelm perhaps offers the best testimonial in favor of its actuality from two separate "deathbed" confessions.

One came firsthand. In 1959, a lady living alone in Price Hill, Cincinnati, had hired young Charles to cut her grass all summer. She knew of his interest in the UFO but said little about it until she became ill with cancer. Knowing that she had a short time to live, she called Charles to her bedside to reveal a startling story.

She said that she had had a Top Security Clearance in her past work at Wright-Patterson Field and had seen two saucer-shaped craft in a secret hangar. One craft was intact; the other, damaged. She also knew of two "small creatures" preserved inside another secret building, and had personally handled the paperwork on their autopsy report. She told Charles, "Uncle Sam can't do anything to me after I'm in the grave."

The second revelation came to Charles Wilhelm in 1966. He got the story from a friend in the Army Reserve whose father worked with Project Bluebook at Wright-Patterson Field and held high security clearance. On his deathbed, he related to his son that he had seen two disc-shaped craft, *one intact and one damaged,* and four preserved small alien bodies "packed in chemicals."

The saga of the UFO and its occupants closes with the story, from Ray Fowler, that was published in part in the April 1976 issue of *Official UFO.*

I, Fritz Werner, do solemnly swear that during a special assignment with the U. S. Air Force on May 21, 1953, I assisted in the investigation of a crashed unknown object in the vicinity of Kingman, Arizona.

The object was constructed of an unfamiliar metal which resembled aluminum. It had impacted 20 inches into the sand without any sign of structural damage. It was oval and about 30 feet in diameter. An entranceway hatch had been vertically lowered and opened. It was about 3½ feet high and 1½ feet wide. I was able to talk briefly with someone on the team who did look inside only briefly. He saw two swivel seats, an oval cabin, and a lot of instruments and displays.

A tent pitched near the object sheltered the dead remains of the only occupant of the craft. It was about 4 feet tall, dark brown complexion and had 2 eyes, 2 nostrils, 2 ears, and a small round mouth. It was clothed in a silvery, metallic suit and wore a skull cap of the same type of material. It wore no face covering or helmet.

I certify that the above statement is true by affixing my signature to this document this 7th day of June, 1973.

> Signature: *Fritz A. Werner*
> Date Signed: June 7, 1973
> Witness: *Raymond E. Fowler*
> Date Signed: June 7, 1973

Commented Fowler:

I watched Mr. Werner incredulously as he carefully read and signed the above affidavit. It was the final piece of documentation to a 65-page report that I had prepared for the National Investigations Committee on Aerial Phenomena (NICAP). My attempts to substantiate this account had put me in contact with the Atomic Energy Commission, Stanford Research Institute, Wright-Patterson Air Force Base, former Project Bluebook personnel, and a number of persons employed within the military-industrial complex. Although no additional witnesses could be found, the peripheral names, positions, tests, dates and places mentioned within Mr. Werner's personal account of the incident checked out very well.

Fritz Werner had kept his experience a closely guarded secret for almost twenty years before deciding to confide in me. His story, which follows, is incredible and, if true, indicates that the recovery of UFO hardware and our government's attempts to duplicate such have been kept secret from the public for more than twenty-two years.

Mr. Werner had held several engineering and management positions at Wright-Patterson Air Force Base, near Dayton, Ohio, between June 1949 and January 1960. During that period he worked in the Office of Special Studies of what was then the Air Matériel Command Installations Division. His specialties included the engineering design of Air Force engine test cells, and research and development techniques for determining blast effects on buildings and structures. Later, he also designed aircraft landing gear and became chief of alighting devices within the Aircraft Laboratory at the Wright Air Development Center. At the time of the alleged incident, he was on assignment to the Atomic Energy Commission at the atomic proving grounds in Nevada. Let's hear about what happened in Mr. Werner's own words.

"I was project engineer on an Air Force contract with the Atomic Energy Commission for "Operation Upshot-Knothole" at the atomic proving ground, Nevada. This operation was comprised of three atomic explosions; the first, an air drop; the second, a tower shot; and the third, an artillery shot. My job involved the measuring of blast effects on various types of buildings especially erected for the tests.

"On May 20, 1953, I worked most of the day at Frenchman Flat. In the evening, I received a phone call from the test director, Dr. Ed Doll, informing me that I was to go on a special job the next day. On the fol-

lowing day, I reported for special duty and was driven
to Indian Springs Air Force Base, near the proving
ground, where I joined about fifteen other specialists.
We were told to leave all valuables in the custody of
the military police. We were then put on a military
plane and flown to Phoenix, Arizona. We were not allowed to fraternize. There, we were put on a bus with
other personnel, who were already there. The bus windows were all blacked out so that we couldn't see
where we were going. We rode for an estimated four
hours. I think we were in the area of Kingman, Arizona, which is northwest of Phoenix and not too far
from the atomic proving ground in Nevada. During the
bus trip, we were told by an Air Force full colonel
that a super-secret Air Force vehicle had crashed and
that since we were all specialists in certain fields, we
were to investigate the crash in terms of our own
specialty and nothing more.

"Finally, the bus stopped and we disembarked one at
a time as our names were called and were escorted by
military police to the area that we were to inspect. Two
spotlights were centered on the crashed object, which
was ringed with guards. The lights were so bright that it
was impossible to see the surrounding area. The object
was oval and looked like *two deep saucers, one inverted
upon the other*. It was about thirty feet in diameter,
with convex surfaces, top and bottom. These surfaces
were about twenty feet in diameter. Part of the object
had sunk into the ground. It was constructed of a dull
silver metal, like brushed aluminum. The metal was
darker where the saucer "lips" formed a rim, around
which were what looked like "slots." A curved open
hatch door was located on the leading end and was vertically lowered. There was a light coming from inside
but it could have been installed by the Air Force.

"My particular job was to determine, from the angle
and depth of impact into the sand, how fast the vehicle's
forward and vertical velocities were at the time of impact. The impact had forced the vehicle approximately

twenty inches into the sand. There were no landing gear. There were also no marks or dents, that I can remember, on the surface—not even scratches. Questions having nothing to do with our own special areas were not answered.

"An armed military policeman guarded a tent pitched nearby. I managed to glance inside at one point and saw the dead body of a four-foot, human-like creature in a silver metallic-looking suit. The skin on its face was dark brown. This may have been caused by exposure to our atmosphere. The face was not covered but it had a metallic skull-cap device on its head.

"As soon as each person finished his task, he was interviewed over a tape recorder and escorted back to the bus. On the way back to the bus, I managed to talk briefly with someone else going back to it at the same time. He told me that he had glanced inside the object and saw two swivel-like seats, as well as instruments and displays. An airman who noticed we were talking separated us and warned us not to talk with each other.

"After we all returned to the bus, the Air Force colonel who was in charge had us raise our right hands and take an oath not to reveal what we had experienced. I was instructed to write my report in longhand and not to type or reproduce it. A telephone number was given me to call when the report was complete. I called the number and an airman picked up the report. I had never met or talked with any of the investigating party. They were not known to me, although I think I recognized two officers. One was from Griffith Air Force Base, at Rome, New York, and the other was involved with an Air Force special weapons group based at Albuquerque, New Mexico. I later saw and recognized the colonel in charge in a movie concerning Project Bluebook."

In summary, Fowler states:

Mr. Werner confided in me that a year after his experience he was assigned to serve the U. S. Air Force

UFO Project Bluebook as an official consultant. He said that he sympathized with the Air Force's secret handling of the UFO problem and added that the Air Force did not know where UFOs originated. He felt that they probably still do not know, although he said that the Air Force did believe that UFOs were interplanetary vehicles, but that they did not know how to handle the situation. They did not want to create a national panic.

Fritz Werner's credentials are impressive. I personally checked out his résumé by calling former employers during a careful character check. Neither of the two former "Bluebook" officers with whom I talked would confirm the Kingman incident. One asked, "Where is the object now?" the other became nervous when I mentioned Dr. Eric Wang's Office of Special Studies and asked me to leave him alone, as he wanted to live out his life in privacy. Atomic Energy Commission spokesmen in Washington and Nevada both confirmed the date and name of the tests and the name of the test director mentioned by Mr. Werner.

There were some inconsistencies associated with my investigation, but most of these appeared to be in the realm of memory lapses and exaggerations by the witness. Former employers and professional acquaintances held Werner in high esteem and all described him as a highly competent and moral individual. Documentation collected on him indicates that he has published a number of sophisticated technical papers; that he holds two bachelors degrees, in mathematics and physics, and a master's degree in engineering; and that he holds membership in professional organizations such as the American Association for the Advancement of Science.

In my final report evaluation, I discussed the pros and cons of his account's being a deliberate hoax, a joke that got out of hand, a prefabrication resulting from an emotionally disturbed mind, and the possibility of the account's being generally true. There seemed to be no motive for a hoax and no apparent evidence of a psychosis. One piece of evidence seemed to give a strong

element of truth to the bizarre account. In an attempt to
pin down the exact date of the alleged incident, Mr.
Werner agreed to search for a diary that he had kept
meticulously in those days. He found it, and I made an
appointment to examine its obviously aged pages. There
was no doubt in my mind as regards its authenticity. On
May 20, 1953, the page read:

"Well, pen's out of ink. Spent most of day on Frenchman's Flat surveying cubicals and supervising welding
of the plate girder bridge sensor which cracked after last
shot. Drank brew in eve. Read. Got funny call from Dr.
Doll at 1000. I'm going to go on a special job tomor-
row."

My eyes then skipped over to the entry on May 21st,
and a creepy feeling of awe swept over me as I read
what appeared to confirm his story, with all its stark implications.

"Up at 7:00. Worked most of day on Frenchman
with cubicals. Letter from Bet. She's feeling better now
—thank goodness. *Got picked up at Indian Springs
AFB at 4:30 P.M. for a job I can't write or talk about.*"
[Italics mine.]

I have talked with Ray Fowler several times by phone about the
Werner exposé. He told me on May 28, 1976, "My investigation
into this case continues; it's too important for research to leave
any of its ends unturned. Since the episode has been made public,
Werner has not changed his story. So far, he's been able to satis-
factorily answer all the challenging questions from people familiar
with his past work in atomic testing."

Because of the significance of the Werner disclosure, Fowler
has scrutinized every aspect of the affair.

"The negative issues also must be bared," he said. Basically, he
is concerned that Werner, in his original testimony given in the
privacy of his friends, was contradictory to the account he received later.

Comments Fowler, "Perhaps some of the discrepancies are just
memory lapses, but Werner did admit that he exaggerated about
the crash to children in the presence of their parents. Actually this

is how the story first slipped out: he was talking to the kids about the crashed spaceship."

Fowler, however, also questions the number of personnel (forty) involved in such a supersensitive project and why the investigators wore no protective clothing or masks to shield themselves against possible radiation or dangerous bacteria.

Summarily, Fowler believes it is a powerful case and, with more substantiation, it could blow the lid off secrecy!

I agree: The Werner disclosure is extraordinary. This one case alone could melt down official UFO secrecy like the fate of the Hawk missile pad in Binn, Korea!

Under the Pandora's lid of secrecy are hundreds of military cases of aircraft close encounters, and there are thousands more— all well documented—happening to citizens of the world, held back by the fear of ridicule, nourished by the media.

Under the same official secrecy lid, allegedly exists a 30-minute, 16 mm silent movie film in color, of early-1950 vintage, whose viewing was limited only to technical members of the military community. According to my informant, it shows a saucer-shaped craft fifteen to eighteen feet in diameter guarded by military personnel minus identifying unit insignia. The interior of the craft, exhibiting pastel colors, is equipped only with a simple panel with levers. I am told that, placed on a makeshift table next to the craft, are three dead bodies of humanoids four feet in height, lying side by side, wearing yellow, one-piece uniforms.

The informant relates that he witnessed the movie, which was shown in *secrecy* to a special group of eight military technical experts at Fort Monmouth, New Jersey, in April 1953.

Gordon Cooper, belonging to history as a pioneer in space for his Mercury and Gemini flights, told me on May 28, 1976, that he was convinced that the real UFO is an interplanetary vehicle using possibly antigravity propulsion. For the record, Cooper did *not* witness a UFO during his 1963 Mercury overflight of Australia, so popular in UFO literature, but stated that he did encounter a UFO in the early 1950s as an Air Force pilot on a scramble mission—with radar confirmation from the ground!

"UFOs are serious business," he said. "The Russians, in secrecy, view it seriously, and it's time we open our eyes to face the challenge, dispense with secrecy, and make it our priority to establish systems to communicate with other civilizations, in outer space."

Through my years of intensive research since 1950, I have hypothesized that the real unidentified flying object coursing our skies is of extraterrestrial origin. I further postulate that the occupants' apparent use of extraordinary powers, often reported by witnesses as strange psychic experiences during and after UFO encounters, should not pose, per se, a stumbling block to the extraterrestrial hypothesis. It is a reasonable assumption that a highly developed intelligence would resort to its great psychic skills as a means to achieve tactical advantage during surveillance, perhaps to study the human psyche or even manipulate the witness into a state of fantasy so as to hide its real purpose. I also believe that the UFO's ubiquity worldwide does not constitute a deterrent to the extraterrestrial hypothesis, and that their behavior, exhibited as evasive curiosity and sometimes as defensive belligerence, is perhaps no more unusual than our own. As to the UFO's vanguard, the humanoids and their seeming ludicrous acts, well, perhaps they are not as ludicrous in the universe as we, the viewers!

Time and its corollary, space, may someday reveal the truth. I hope we will be ready to understand it. But first we must face up to the UFO status quo, which is *SITUATION RED!*

X

Confrontation!

During the height of the '73 siege, serious UFO researchers gave priority only to close-encounter cases, and then only those cases in which reliable witnesses claimed physiological or electromagnetic effects or where physical traces were found in the area of the UFO's land contact. Hundreds of reports, many with these qualifying factors, were pouring into the major research groups such as the Mutual UFO Network, the Aerial Phenomena Research Organization, the National Investigations Committee on Aerial Phenomena, and the newly founded Center for UFO Studies.

Hard on the heels of the Pascagoula abduction case, the press, bulging with reports, broke at the seams. Many leading dailies presented a capsulated form of dateline reports from the nation's cities. Even John Chancellor, of NBC News, tailed his program for several nights with "more on the UFOs."

Then, on October 18, the press stunned the nation's readers with the Coyne case. This incident involved a military helicopter piloted by Captain Lawrence Coyne with three crew members, and a UFO. They were flying on a collision course, and by a feat of bizarre acrobatics, the helicopter was able to avoid disaster. The Coyne case, it seemed, like the Pascagoula abduction just days before, belonged to the realm of science fiction. Dr. Hynek, who promptly investigated the Coyne case, told me by phone that the case "seemed airtight." The Coyne case continues to stand up as one of the strongest cases for 1973. The initial report, filed with the commander of the 83rd USAR/COM, Columbus, Ohio, follows:

Commander, 83rd USAR/COM

1. On 18 October 1973 at 2305 hours in the vicinity of Mansfield, Ohio, Army Helicopter 68-15444, assigned to Cleveland USAR/FFAC experienced a near midair collision with an unidentified flying object. Four crew members assigned to the Cleveland USAR/FFAC for flying proficiency were on AFTP status when this incident occurred. The flight crew assigned was Capt. Lawrence J. Coyne, Pilot in Command; 1st Sgt. Arrigo Jezzi, Copilot; S. Sgt. Robert Yanacsek, Crew Chief; S. Sgt. John Healey, Flight Medic. All the above personnel are members of the 316th MED/DET (HEL/AMB), a tenant reserve unit of the Cleveland USAR/FFAC.

2. The reported incident happened as follows: Army Helicopter 68-15444 was returning from Columbus, Ohio, to Cleveland, Ohio, and at 2305 hours, east southeast of Mansfield Airport, in the vicinity of Mansfield, Ohio, while flying at an altitude of 2,500 feet and on a heading of 030 degrees, S. Sgt. Yanacsek observed a red light on the east horizon, 90 degrees to the flight path of the helicopter. Approximately 30 seconds later, S. Sgt. Yanacsek indicated the object was converging on the helicopter at the same altitude and at an air speed in excess of 600 knots and on a midair collision heading. Capt. Coyne observed the converging object, took over controls of the aircraft, and initiated a power descent from 2,500 feet to 1,700 feet to avoid impact with the object. A radio call was initiated to Mansfield Tower, who acknowledged the helicopter and was asked by Capt. Coyne if there were any high-performance aircraft flying in the vicinity of Mansfield Airport. However, there was no response received from the tower. The crew expected impact from the object; instead, the object was observed to hesitate momentarily over the helicopter and then slowly continue on a westerly course, accelerating to a high rate of speed to the west of Mansfield Airport, then turn 45 degrees to a

northwest heading. Capt. Coyne indicated the altimeter read a 1,000 fpm. climb and 3,500 feet with the collective in the full down position. The aircraft was returned to 2,500 feet by Capt. Coyne and flown back to Cleveland, Ohio. The flight plan was closed, and the FAA Flight Service Station was notified of the incident. The FSS told Capt. Coyne to report the incident to the FAA GADO office at Cleveland Hopkins Airport. Mr. Porter, 83rd USARCOM, was notified of the incident at 1530 hours on 19 October 1973.

An interesting point in the Coyne case is that, since the time the incident happened, the FAA has indicated that the Cleveland Hopkins Airport radar room confirmed contact with both the helicopter and the unidentified flying object.

Though there are hundreds of cases filed each year that provide strong evidence, as the Coyne case does, and many with radar confirmation from military and FAA sites, objective research still must contend with a few diehards who try to prove that all UFOs are either cases of mistaken identity or hoaxes. Philip Klass, senior avionics editor of *Aviation Week & Space Technology* and the nation's foremost debunker of the UFO, tried to pick the Coyne case apart in his recent book *UFOs Explained* (1975). After a scholarly attempt to juggle the testimony of Coyne and his three crewmen, he decided that they were all fooled by a giant Orionid fireball.

Comments Hynek, "Klass's theory is untenable. Meteors do not pace an object and then turn toward it. A bright meteor appears suddenly, follows a nearly straight but gently curving path and would *not* be in sight for well over a minute. We must take in account the length of the original pacing observation, the turn toward the helicopter, and the time it took Coyne to take the controls and bring the craft down from 2,500 feet to 1,700 feet. The helicopter then reportedly went up from 1,700 feet to 3,500 feet, which would mean that the meteor obligingly hung around for all that time. Meteors don't do that. They last for a few seconds."

Walter Andrus, Director of MUFON, told me that the Coyne case, in his judgment, was the most outstanding case for 1973, and will rank among the classics of all time.

While the Coyne case is an example of the effect that UFOs

have on man's machines, the Eddie Webb case is a sobering revelation of the UFO's direct effect on man.

Eddie Webb's encounter with a UFO nearly ended in disaster. He was instantly blinded by a "projectile" fired from a UFO while driving a tractor-trailer rig near Cape Girardeau, Missouri. As a result, Webb spent seven days in a hospital. The interesting part about the Webb case is the fact that it features an *unpublicized legal uniqueness*. Webb, denied workmen's compensation for his injury and time lost from his job—mainly because he could not prove the legal existence of the UFO—took his complaint to an attorney to plead his case.

Serving as public relations director for MUFON, I was provided by Walter Andrus the complete particulars of the Webb case in the event it should reach the courts, stir up the media, and require a formal statement. He also steered me to Webb's attorney, Edward O'Herin, of Malden, Missouri. When I discussed the case by telephone with O'Herin, in September 1975, he said it had been disposed of and obligingly sent me a copy of the question-and-answer statement he had taken from Webb for use in the case. Said O'Herin, "I hope to get the record straight on this case, and so does Webb."

O'Herin, because of an agreement with the lawyer for the insurance company, was unable to disclose the exact terms of the settlement. However, based on Webb's sworn testimony and the faith that O'Herin placed in Webb's plaintive honesty, I find that I must agree with Walt Andrus and other UFO researchers that the case stands up as another link of evidence suggesting that the UFO incursion of 1973 constituted a new posture—perhaps militant.

The incident occurred about 6:30 A.M. on October 3, when Eddie Webb, accompanied by his wife on a long trip from Parkersburg, West Virginia, was driving on I-55, headed for Sam Tanksley's Truck Stop, south of Cape Girardeau, near the Cape Girardeau Airport. Excerpts from Webb's taped statement with permission to publish in this book tell a harrowing story of his encounter with the UFO:

> . . . something was coming down the road without
> any headlights behind my truck . . . it was gaining on
> us rapidly. . . . The lights were beautiful, and they

were bright; they were the color of the rainbow but much brighter.

(During this period, his wife had awakened and was dressing in the over-cab bunk.)

I told my wife to look out her rearview mirror, because something was gaining on us at a very rapid speed. It was a foggy morning, and she made the remark that she couldn't see anything. By that time, in my mirror it had already caught up with me. There was a bright light, like a landing light or a spotlight, which shined on the rear wheel on the left end of my trailer. . . . I couldn't see what it was in the mirror, so I stuck my head out the window, which was already rolled down, to get a better look. What it was I don't know. I couldn't identify it any way except it was shaped like a turnip or top. It was silver and about thirty feet in diameter, maybe six or eight feet high, and had a rainbow of lights across the center of it. And it looked like the bottom half and top half of this machine might have been spinning.

I was seeing a little over half of the object sticking around on the left side of my trailer. We were on a four-lane drive, and it was taking up both lanes of our side of the highway. Almost half of. the object was behind my rig. At this time, when I stuck my head out the window I just got a glimpse of the object and something like a yellowish-red flash of fire hit me across the face and forehead. At that time, I didn't see any more, because I went blind. I put on my brake and set it down immediately, because I thought the lights and everything had gone out. The motor was dead on the truck, but I don't know whether the object killed the motor or whether my putting on the brakes so rapidly killed the motor, but I told the wife that the lights had gone out and I flickered my headlights on a time or two and she said that the lights were burning and that there was nothing wrong with them. She said it was me. So my eyes were burning and I was hurting with pain and she told me that I must have gone off my 'rocker,' and to get in the bunk and let her drive. So, that I did. When I pulled off my glasses I felt that one lens of my glasses was missing. I laid them on the 'dog-house' and crawled in the bunk with my shoes still on. I told the wife that my eyes were hurting, that I probably got glass in my eyes, but she told me that the lens wasn't busted, that they had just fallen out. Later they found the lens of my glasses on the floorboard of the truck.

I was driving a '73 Peterbilt with a 40-foot Dorsey trailer, refrigerated unit, but the refrigerator was not running, because we had on raw plastic. It was just a common load that we haul every few days.

I told my wife to get me to the hospital as soon as possible, but she told me she could not make those turns into the hospital at the Cape and it was only a short distance to the office, so she would continue out there and then take me into the hospital in our pickup, which was parked on the parking lot. Before we got to the yard, one of the other drivers, who had arrived earlier at the lot, came up to talk to the wife. He told me that he thought he should get hold of the dispatcher and have an ambulance called, because she was in no condition to drive me to the hospital. He called the ambulance, and they took me to the hospital in Cape Girardeau.

Unknown to me, somebody had reported it to the state police; the newspapers all showed up at the hospital to see what happened. What actually happened after that I don't know. I took treatments at the hospital and later saw a doctor in Cape Girardeau. Then they moved me from Cape Girardeau to St. Louis to another doctor, who was supposed to have been a specialist. He checked me out and admitted me at Barnes Hospital, in St. Louis. I spent about seven days in Barnes Hospital and was released.

At the close of the statement, attorney O'Herin asked his client if a sound had been heard as the silvery "turnip" followed his rig.

Said Webb, "The only thing I heard was a small humming, just like somebody humming a tune . . . just a very light noise . . . just a hum-m-m—like that, like a whizz or something."

Throughout the interview, O'Herin asked many questions, always maneuvering to find a terrestrial clue that might explain the "projectile" that hit Webb in the face, a clue that would conversely make it easier for Webb to win his workmen's compensation case. But Eddie Webb stuck to his story, case or not. He knew that he had encountered a UFO, and, workmen's compensation case or not, he was sticking to the facts as he knew them.

While some researchers tend to disbelieve Webb's story, medical testimony limitedly supports his complaint of vision disability. Five days following the incident, a St. Louis ophthalmologist found that Webb had only 20 per cent vision, and tests run for the entire week at the St. Louis Hospital showed that he had trouble seeing colors. A physicist who examined the glasses said that the frames appeared to have been internally heated, while an optical company said that an inconclusive analysis showed that the same heating effect could be produced by railroad flares.

A similar case to Webb's occurred on April 15, 1965, in Florida's Everglades. James Flynn, age forty-five, a rancher, of East Fort Myers, was on a hunting and camping trip in a swamp buggy.

While rounding up his dogs at 1:00 A.M., Flynn saw a huge light hovering above the cypress about a mile away. When the object descended, he drove his vehicle closer to investigate. Through binoculars he watched a large, cone-shaped object, which he later estimated to be about thirty feet tall and about sixty feet wide. The object had three rows of square windows that reflected a dull yellow light. The area under the object cast a reddish glow, and there was ample radiation to indicate that the surface was metallic.

Unafraid, and despite his dogs' protest, Flynn got within a few yards of the strange craft. He switched off the buggy's engine, doused his lights, and, walking to the edge of the UFO's red circle of light, he raised one arm and waved. In an instant, a beam of light shot out from under the bottom of a row of windows and struck him on the forehead. . . .

When Flynn awakened, he was alarmed to discover that he was blind in his right eye and had only partial vision in his left. Dimly, he could see a symmetrical circle of scorched ground where the object had been hovering. A number of cypress trees had been burned at their tops.

It was not until Flynn went into the office of Dr. Paul Brown that he realized that he had been unconscious for twenty-four hours. Dr. Brown was more concerned about his patient's loss of vision. Due to hemorrhaging in the anterior chamber, the right eye had the appearance of bright red marble. His forehead and the area around his eyes was inflamed and swollen.

Upon release from Lee Memorial Hospital, Flynn accompanied researchers to the site of the incident. The physical evidence of the scorched cypress and the burned circle of grass was still there.

The Coyne episode, well known in the annals of the 1973 flap, illustrates the UFO's total disregard for man's property; in this case, an aircraft. In the Webb case, we find that man himself was the direct target, with the vehicle he occupied only incidental in the action. Flynn's undoing was that he exhibited too much curiosity. Clearly, in these three instances man is a helpless victim.

By human standards or by man-made international laws, such aggressive assaults on man and his property constitute hostile acts.

But we are not dealing with an aggressor with a human mind and, therefore, must take a new and more abstract overview position to look at the history of the UFO performance as a whole, for both the long period before the 1973 flap and since. Here we find, with some assurance, that destruction and death-dealing cases are proportionately few in number, which, in turn, leaves us at best a borderline hypothesis that the Coyne-Webb-Flynn incidents were more random than programmed.

Whatever the reason, or non-reason, for the UFO actions against Coyne, Webb, and Flynn, and the many analogous cases recorded in the more than eighty thousand entries in Dr. David Saunders' UFOCAT data bank, it appears that humankind is at the mercy of a vanguard who, seemingly selfish in purpose, continue to *reconnoiter Earth, in chill contempt, to fulfill that purpose.*

Coyne and his crew were lucky that their helicopter remained airborne after its violent maneuver—a fate that I can luckily share when I reminisce my incident near Iwo Jima. There are many instances in which fate was not so kind to the pilot, his crew, or his passengers, who did not live to tell their story of a UFO encounter.

Many research buffs believe that the controversial Bermuda Triangle, or its counterpart, the Devil's Sea in the Pacific, lock in their watery depths or spatial heights the secrets of the strange happenings to man and his machines.[1] The facts, however, show that a far greater number of mysterious electromagnetic- and physiological-effect incidents occur over land masses.

Although not always as spectacular as the Coyne helicopter incident, there are numerous cases in the files of the major research groups that show UFO interference with man's power-driven machinery in the air, on the ground, and at sea. Well-documented records show that UFOs have caused power failures in many cities. The most celebrated was the blackout hitting New York in 1969. Qualified researchers, such as Ray Fowler, director of investigations for MUFON and author of *UFOs—Interplanetary Visitors* (1974), have dug deeply into this one incident and have unearthed some startling evidence to blame the UFO!

From NICAP files and reported also in Fowler's book is this electromagnetic eye opener from Nha Trang, Vietnam. The information came from Sergeant Wayne Dalrymple via a letter to his parents postmarked June 20, 1966:

> Last night about 9:45 P.M., this camp, which has about 40,000 men, went into a panic and, believe me, I was scared, too. We got a big generator in last week along with a movie projector and some movies, and we were outside watching one of them when a real bright light came from out of nowhere. At first we thought it was a flare which are going off all the time and then we found out that it wasn't. It came from the North and moving from real slow to real fast speeds. Some of the jet fighter pilots who were here said it looked to be about 25,000 feet, and then the panic broke loose. It dropped right toward us and stopped dead about 300 to 500 feet up.

[1] I am aware of electromagnetic disturbances to two naval vessels in the general Bermuda Triangle area never reported to the media or appearing in popular literature. One was witnessed by a high-ranking official in the Defense Department who was aboard the affected ship in the 1960s. I have been asked not to reveal the scant details entrusted to me.

It made this little valley and the mountains around look like it was the middle of the day. It lit up everything. Then it went up and I mean up. It went straight up completely out of sight in about 2–3 seconds. Everybody is still talking about it and everybody is going to be outside tonight. What really shook everyone is that it stopped, or maybe it didn't, but anyway our generator stopped and everything was black, and at the Air Force Base about ½ mile from here all generators stopped, and two planes that were on the runway ready to take off, their engines stopped. . . . There wasn't a car, truck, plane or anything, that ran for about 4 minutes. There are 8 big bulldozers that are cutting roads over the mountain and they stopped and their lights went out, too. A whole plane load of big shots from Washington got here this afternoon to investigate. It's on the radio over here. Is it at home? I swear, if somebody says they saw a little green man, I won't argue with them.

Fowler adds the following data: "Wayne estimated that the glowing object was about fifty feet in diameter, but no detail could be seen behind the round-shaped light. The aircraft that were affected were Skyraiders. The bulldozers were similar to civilian D-9s and were clearing an area to install Hawk missiles on Oak Hill. A total of six 100-kilowatt, independently operated, diesel-powered electric generators failed. All power and equipment functioned perfectly about four minutes after the UFO left the area. Wayne, in the course of his military duties, checked out each generator for defects. They were found to be in good order and experienced no further malfunctions. Fortunately, no aircraft were airborne in the area at the time of the incident! However, a Shell oil tanker anchored offshore experienced a complete power failure simultaneously with the blackout onshore!"

The most frequently reported UFO interference is that which affects the automobile, stopping the engine dead. Probably the most remembered incident on record and checked by competent researchers occurred at Levelland, Texas, in 1957. Ten vehicles were stopped within a short distance of each other, all independently, in a two-hour period during intense UFO activity, at zero altitude.

UFOs also affect TV reception, make telephones go dead, affect the delicate operation of heart pacemakers and non-electric clocks, and, in one report, a man claimed that everything in his car stopped, including the wristwatch he was wearing. Another case investigated by the late Dr. James McDonald, a professor of atmospherics, physics, and meteorology, found that several people reported fillings in their teeth hurting while a UFO was seen nearby. One of the strangest was a case investigated by Ted Phillips, MUFON and CUFOS specialist in research of physical traces. In a small town in Tennessee, he said, the proud owner of a collection of antique clocks, most of which were not electric, found them all stopped following a sighting of a UFO flying over their home!

Cases like Webb's, in which man suffers physical injury caused by a guided flare, are rare. Most do not make the news and the few that have surfaced to researchers have been kept confidential, on request of the victim, for fear of ridicule and public harassment. One of the few that surfaced for publication was reported to NICAP.

Young Gregory L. Wells, of Beallsville, Ohio, was returning from his grandmother's house to his own home, next door, when he saw an oval UFO hovering just over some trees. It was shortly after 8:30 P.M., March 19, 1968.

The large red object was so bright that it illuminated the road, according to Mrs. James E. Wells, the boy's mother. It had a band of dimmer red lights flashing around its center. "I stopped," Gregory recalled. "I wanted to run or scream, but suddenly a big tube came out of the bottom, which moved from side to side until it came to me, and a beam of light shot out." Gregory turned away as the light beam hit the upper part of his arm, knocking him to the ground. His jacket caught fire and the boy rolled around on the ground screaming with fright. Both his mother and grandmother responded. . . . Mrs. James Wells also reported seeing the UFO, which "just faded away."

During the sighting, a large night light on a nearby pole went out. This was confirmed later by Gregory Wells's father. There was also electromagnetic interference to a television set, and the grandmother's dog barked uncontrollably.

The witness was taken to Beallsville Hospital after the encounter and was treated for second-degree burns. Bruce Francis, who reported the incident to NICAP, confirmed the burns and said the scar was still visible three months later.

Sheriff F. L. Sulsberger, of Monroe County, investigated. He said he could find no explanation. The sheriff sent the burned jacket to the Ohio Bureau of Criminal Investigation (OBCI) in London for analysis. OBCI officials said they found no evidence of radioactivity. Civil Defense Director Ward Strikling, who combed the area with a Geiger counter, also found no radiation. He stated, however, there are types of radioactivity that leave no detectable traces.

"In the course of checking this case," wrote Dr. James E. McDonald, "I interviewed a number of persons in the Beallsville area, some of whom had seen a long, cylindrical object moving at very low altitude in the vicinity of the Wells property that night. . . . My conversations with persons who know the boy, including his teacher, suggest no reason to discount the story, despite its unusual content."

One of the most outstanding cases I have ever investigated happened to three women near Stanford, Kentucky, on January 6, 1976.

The incident, possibly the most fact-rooted abduction case on record, has all the attributes: highest witness credibility, professional investigation, and supporting witnesses to the UFO. The case also shows physiological and electromagnetic effects and animal reaction. Unaccountable in the first months of quiet investigation was an hour-and-a-half time lapse experienced by all three witnesses; strongly suspected was abduction.

I first got word of the incident when Jerry Black phoned me on February 20. A friend in Danville had sent him a clipping, describing its outlandish details, from the *Casey County News,* dated, belatedly, February 12.

Hoping to arrange a personal interview with the three women in their hometown of Liberty, Black ran into a block of resistance. He was told by one of the witnesses that they did not seek publicity, that what had been published had leaked out against their will, and that they were apprehensive of strangers coming into their homes. After several more phone calls, they finally agreed when Black suggested that Mrs. Peggy Schnell of Cincinnati would accompany Jim Miller of MUFON from Middletown, Ohio, and me to Liberty for the interview. Mrs. Schnell had had experience with a UFO during the 1973 flap, and she would provide the feminine "touch" in sharing the women's ordeal.

On February 29, the four of us drove to Liberty. We met in the tidy trailer of Mrs. Louise Smith, age forty-six, a trim, bespectacled county-extension-office assistant teaching food and nutrition. With her were witnesses: Mrs. Mona Stafford, a petite, soft-voiced owner of an arts-and-crafts shop, and a stoic and alert Mrs. Elaine Thomas. Within a few minutes the mood was cordial, and the three women, put at ease, began relating their experiences.

January 6 was Mona Stafford's thirty-sixth birthday. She and her two friends decided to dine out for the occasion at the Redwood Restaurant in Lancaster, about thirty miles northeast of Liberty. It was a happy, chatty dinner. Mona Stafford, a self-styled artist, even volunteered to pencil-sketch a gentleman near her table before they departed in Louise Smith's 1967 Chevy Nova to return home.

About 11:30 P.M., they were on Route 78 driving over a narrow, winding road under a cold, clear sky. There was a slight wind; tree limbs were seen stirring alongside the road. Near Stanford, while talking about the pleasantries of the evening, Mona Stafford, next to the driver, and Elaine Thomas, near the window, spotted a strange, intensely red glow high in the eastern sky. Suddenly the glow grew more intense and larger; then it rapidly descended at an angle to the right side of the car at tree-top level. There it seemed to stop, hover, and, to their shock, the large glow quickly formed into a disc. A row of rounded windows became sharply visible, each with blinking red lights rotating counterclockwise. Beneath these was a row of yellow lights; on top was a luminescent, bluish-white dome.

"The dome was blinding," said Mrs. Stafford, "and it reflected on a metallic surface which I'm sure was more than one hundred feet wide. It was much bigger than the biggest airliner I've ever seen—and it made no sound."

The giant object then glided toward the car, made a tight half circle, tilted, assuming a round shape, then moved in closer to a point slightly to the left side of the car. Suddenly three shafts of bluish-white light shot down on the middle of the road from the bottom of the craft. Then one flashed into the car.

"It lit up the inside of the car like daylight," said Mrs. Thomas, "and Louise stopped the car. I remember opening the door and putting my foot outside, but I don't remember what I did after that."

"She looked like she was petrified," volunteered Mrs. Stafford. "She couldn't move, so I pulled her back into the car. Then there was a dead silence. Even the wind stopped."

Enter limbo. . . . Recalls Mrs. Smith, "I had the strangest feeling of being deserted. We all felt like we were burning up and then our skin started to tingle, then we all got severe headaches."

All three remembered tears flowing from their eyes. Mona Stafford, not wearing glasses, suddenly felt as though she was blinded; the pain was severe. . . .

. . . Mrs. Smith resumed driving, but a glance at the speedometer showed eighty-five miles per hour. She removed her foot; the car remained at the same high speed. She tried to slow down, pressing her foot down on the brake . . . still no letup, the speed was constant—eighty-five miles per hour!

"I had no control of the car," she said, "and I pleaded with Mona to help me steer. Poor Mona tried, even though her eyes were in great pain. Neither one of us could keep the car under control. It felt like we were traveling over road hurdles or flying in air pockets on an airplane.

"Everything outside the car became dark and strange," continued Mrs. Smith. "All I could see was a long, straight road ahead, with no lights, no houses, nothing I could recognize. I'm not even sure if my headlights were on."

Said Mona Stafford, "I seem to remember the UFO's lights blinking out, first the dome, then the row of red lights around it. Then, I remember that our car seemed like it was being pulled and we were going over a long, straight road without any lights on either side, no divider line, and no cars passing by."

Mrs. Thomas nodded in agreement. "What's so strange about it is that the roads near Stanford and Hustonville *are not straight.*

They wind so much that for a car to go eighty-five miles per hour would be dangerous."

End of limbo. . . . Driving at normal speed, the trip home to Liberty was uneventful, trees were again swaying in the wind, cars passed, but their thoughts were numb and vague. Of greatest concern was the increasing pain from their burns and throbbing headaches. Mrs. Stafford's only thought was the unbearable pain in her eyes. Said Mrs. Smith, "All I could hear Mona saying was, 'We've got to get home.'"

All three women clearly remember piling into Louise Smith's trailer. All thirsting for a cold glass of water, they went into the kitchen. Mrs. Smith, looking at her electric clock, was stunned to see the time was 1:25. Her wristwatch read 6:00. Even more confounding, the minute hand was moving around the dial at the same speed as the second hand. Mrs. Stafford did not wear a wristwatch; Mrs. Thomas' had stopped! With apprehension, all three ran into the bedroom to check the alarm clock. It also read 1:25. Normally, said Mrs. Smith, and the others agreed, the trip from Lancaster would have taken about fifty minutes—thus, there was about one hour and a half that they could not account for. . . .

Refusing to believe her two clocks, Mrs. Smith bolted to her next door neighbors, arousing them from their sleep to get the *correct* time. But their clocks, like hers, ticking like sledge hammers, confirmed the awful truth!

As the hourless night wore on, the women's tensions increased and their burns became more agonizing. They tried to reconstruct that night's crazy events from the moment the UFO beamed its light into the car, but to them time had collapsed. Their only memory was the strange, straight "road" leading into silent oblivion. Finally, at some late hour, Mrs. Stafford decided to call the state police, but they offered no more than disbelief. Distraught, Mrs. Smith paced from room to room, stopping once to observe her pet parakeet, "Greensleeve," which had been skittish since her arrival. As she neared the cage, the bird went wild. Beating its wings, it bounced off the opposite end of the cage, spilling its food. Commented Mrs. Smith, "Normally, he comes to my finger . . . this was the last straw. I almost cried."

The next morning, the plight of the three women worsened. Mrs. Smith said her skin was red, swollen, and "looked like fish scales." When she bathed, she felt as if she were on fire. Everything seemed amiss: the parakeet fluttered every time she passed by his cage, she had no appetite, and her thirst for liquid was insatiable.

The next morning, Mona Stafford's eyes were like fireballs; the eyelids were puffed and painful. Her headache persisted without letup.

"My skin was red hot, feeling like it had been scraped," she said. "Even my skin under my rings was blistered." As the pain continued, she consulted her physician, Dr. G. S. She explained her UFO experience, which brought no comment, was treated for burns and was dismissed. No test was made for radiation.

"I was a nervous wreck," she said. "I became so frightened that I was afraid to be alone day or night."

The next morning for Mrs. Thomas was similar: headache, skin inflammation. "My skin was so raw I couldn't wash my face," she said.

Suffering from exhaustion following the incident, Mrs. Smith, on January 8, got into her car to report back to work. The engine stalled. A service station was called, and an attendant came to recharge the battery. On the way to the service station for gas, she was stopped by a police car. She had failed to signal a turn. To her dismay, she found that her signal and tail lights were dead! Coincidence? Or electromagnetic effects? For Mrs. Smith, life had become a nightmare.

During our interview on February 29, the effects of the close encounter were still plainly evident. Each of the three women, in separate interviews, stressed more concern about the health of the other two. The least complaintive was Mrs. Thomas, who tried to bolster morale, and the most troubled was Mrs. Stafford. Her emotional stress was obvious. Her eyes were still reddened and puffed; her headaches were intermittent, and since January 6 she had lost fourteen pounds. Also lost was her interest in art and the will and purpose to do anything. She said repeatedly, "I must know what happened to me that night. I can't go on this way."

I suggested regressive hypnosis by a psychiatrist. She agreed without hesitation.

Mrs. Smith had lost eleven pounds since the ordeal. "I know I should eat but I don't; all I want is liquid," she said. "I'm all tensed up, but I try not to show it when I'm on my job.

"Normally, I'm not a violent person," said Mrs. Smith. She went on to explain that since the night of the incident, her clock, after she had wound it, would stop at the slightest touch of her hand. "I put up with it for about a week and threw it as hard as I could on the ground."

Although we knew that the passage of time—fifty-four days since the incident—was probably too much to find skin-burn traces, we asked if any marks were still in evidence. Mrs. Smith quickly responded. Under strong sunlight, she lifted her hair covering the nape of her neck and showed us a reddish-gray blemish about the size of a half dollar.

Mrs. Thomas, who showed the greatest concern for her two friends, showed the least in physical-effect symptoms but admitted that her appetite had declined and that she, too, had an unusual desire for liquids. "I smoke more, too," she said.

I watched the faces, the eyes, of the women as they each related point after point of seemingly ridiculous happenings. I, too, felt moments of uneasiness, because before me were intelligent women emotionally distressed by anomalies they could not fit into their natural lives. Prior to their experience they had had no knowledge of UFOs.

To end the day's interview, Mrs. Smith put it on the line: "Mr. Stringfield, please tell me how my car could go eighty-five miles per hour with no foot on the accelerator over a straight road that doesn't exist?"

"Levitation," I said quizzically, and then smiled indicating that I did not know the answer. I was thinking of the Rhodesian case occurring in 1974 in which two people reported loss of their car's steering control and a mysterious aerial flight of the car over the distance of many miles as they watched strange scenery pass by.[2]

On March 7, in agreement with APRO, who had learned of the Stanford incident from publicity that leaped beyond Casey County into several Kentucky cities, Black, Miller, Mrs. Schnell, and I re-

[2] The Rhodesian experience was investigated by Carl Van Vlierden, MUFON representative in South Africa. The report was published in *Skylook*, the March 1975 issue.

turned to Liberty to be joined by Dr. Leo Sprinkle, psychologist at the University of Wyoming and APRO consultant, and UFO investigator Bill Terry of Louisville.

The news of the incident filtered throughout Kentucky as a result of Mrs. Stafford's call to the Navy Recruiting Office in Danville, the only local symbol of authority, after getting no satisfaction from the state police. In turn, the Navy Recruiting Office indiscreetly gave the story to a Lexington TV station, and it was later published by the *Casey County News,* on February 12.

By phone I discussed the nature of the case with Mr. and Mrs. Lorenzen, of APRO. We agreed to keep the continuing investigation low-key and out of the hands of the news media. I insisted that we must protect the three women, who were not emotionally able to cope with the pressures that would result from national publicity.

Dr. Sprinkle, capable, calm, and patient in his hypnotic technique, first put his subject, Mona Stafford, at ease. She was the lone volunteer of the three, anxious to have unlocked from her mind her great ordeal during the time lapse. Sprinkle's hypnosis first brought out the subject's sighting of the UFO, its close approach to the car, and then the light beam. Then hysteria! She could not go any further. Sprinkle tried again; more crying, and again the barrier. There was a third try, and the subject went into protracted silence.

Finally time ran out, as Sprinkle had to return to Louisville, where he was to catch a flight out to return to Laramie. Before departure, he suggested that I continue to probe, based on certain guidelines, as Mrs. Stafford was still in a state in which she might recall details.

While Black and Miller continued to question Mrs. Smith and Mrs. Thomas, I tried an experiment. I joined Mrs. Stafford sitting alone quietly at a large, round coffee table. I asked a few questions about the UFO's close approach and the light beam that came into the car, which produced the expected answers; then I withdrew from my briefcase a drawing I had made showing a number of humanoid types taken from known case histories and some I had created from composite reports. I put the drawing on the table directly in front of Mrs. Stafford. I said nothing.

The face of Mona Stafford changed dramatically. Her eyes

beamed down on the paper; then, with no hesitation, she pointed to one of the humanoid heads. "This is it," she said. "This one is the light I saw. It was shaped like that head."

Jim Miller drew closer and knelt down quietly by the table as Mrs. Stafford kept her finger on the one humanoid. After a few moments of silence, I asked, "Is this what you saw after you mentioned the light coming into the car?"

Said Mrs. Stafford, "Yes, I can see the face now, but it doesn't seem solid. It comes and goes, I mean, fades and reappears like in a fog. Its eyes are far apart and the bottom—the chin—is like that drawing."

She could recall no more about the apparitional head, nor could she see a body, arms, or legs. She tried to see more as Miller and I sat patiently. She could not.

Strengthening the UFO incident were a number of independent witnesses in Lincoln and Casey counties, who came forward following publicity.

Several hundred yards away from the site of the incident, Mr. and Mrs. O.T. watched an unusual light from the window of their home about 11:30 P.M. The object, traveling south, was shaped like a light bulb with a steady, glowing, "neon" light. Mr. T. was so concerned that his name might reach the newspapers that he was reluctant to reveal details about his sighting.

As I made more probes in the two-county area to discover people who had seen the UFO on January 6, each name acquired led to other names. Finally the names became endless and untrackable.

When I reached Randall Floyd, in Morgan Manor, near Stanford, he said, "The whole neighborhood saw it."

Mr. and Mrs. Floyd both saw the UFO early in the evening, about 8:00 P.M. Said Randall, "It was oval-shaped and large, with a brilliant circle of light of all colors. When I first saw it, it was standing still. I ran to get my binoculars, and, when I returned, it started to move slowly; then it shot away at great speed. It really moved fast."

Said Mrs. Floyd, "The object was round, with lights all around it in a row. It was terribly large and making no sound. I watched it for about three to five minutes hovering over one spot; then it moved away fast. It was no airplane."

About 8:00 P.M., Mike Fitzpatrick and a friend, David Irvin, his mother and father, and younger brother and sister, all watched the UFO from outdoors in Stanford. The object was hovering over the Angel Manufacturing Plant. Said Mike, age eighteen, "It then tilted on its right side, then straightened out and headed toward Danville. It was distinctly saucer-shaped, with an orange row of lights. Dave and I took off after it in my hot rod, but we lost it as it picked up speed. I reported the UFO to the Stanford Police, but they refused to accept the report."

During my investigations of the many sightings in and around a three-county area, I learned of one conflicting story. There was one report of a commercial aircraft flying near the Danville area sometime in January with a gaudy display of lights that read "Happy Birthday."

Although I was certain that an aircraft with "Happy Birthday" had no part in Mona Stafford's *unhappy* birthday, I checked out the story, calling all airports in central Kentucky. There was no record of such a flight on January 6. But the airport most suspect, because of its nearness to Stanford, is in Danville. There I was put in touch with a charter flying service and talked with Mrs. Ronald McDermitt, who, with her husband, manages the service. I explained the purpose of my investigation and she immediately cleared the confusion. Yes, they have an aircraft with "Happy Birthday" lights, composed of 360 bulbs, but its first flight was January 19. There were *no prior flights,* as their service did not own the aircraft in question until January 15. "Somebody got their UFO sighting reports mixed up," she said. "Your Stanford case still stands up solid."

From March 30 to April 4, Mrs. Smith had been hospitalized in Danville. Her illness was unknown. Mona Stafford, who called me, as they all had promised to do with any new developments, said she feared Mrs. Smith's illness might be related to the incident. Symptoms were loss of weight, fatigue, and vomiting. Various tests and X rays had been made to diagnose the cause. As of May 15, when I called Mrs. Smith, no cause had been found. She and the doctors remain puzzled. No mention was made to the doctors about her UFO experience. "They wouldn't understand," she said.

On March 31, the day following Mrs. Smith's admission to the hospital, her parakeet, "Greensleeve," which she had cherished and carefully trained for four years to sit on her lap and shoulders, was found dead in its cage by her neighbor, who was to care for it.

During my first visit, in February, when Mrs. Smith told me about the bird's strange reaction to her presence, I suggested that we make a test. I asked her to tempt her parakeet by putting her finger into the cage. As she predicted, "Greensleeve" frantically fluttered away. After a minute or so, I put my finger into the cage. Skittishly it retreated an inch; then it stopped and stood still on its perch without a quiver. Jim Miller also performed the test; the bird reacted similarly for him.

The known factor of time lapse reinforced by Mona Stafford's posthypnotic recall of a "head with eyes" emerging through a milieu of fog strengthened my suspicion that the three women had experienced abduction. Like the Sergeant Moody incident in Alamogordo and a score of other surfacing cases, the evidence was stacking up that alien craft, guided by a superior intelligence were abducting humankind for examination for reasons too abstract to understand.

When I reported Mrs. Stafford's revelation of seeing a head with eyes to Dr. Sprinkle, and he in turn to APRO, the case was given top priority for further hypnotic probes and hopefully other professional tests, including a polygraph. Mainly, the problem was funding.

While the Lorenzens and I discussed the next move, such as financing Sprinkle's return to the case or to bring in Dr. James Harder from the West Coast, a new development to elicit help came about unexpectedly. Jerry Black, on July 21, concerned about delays in securing adequate funds and out of concern for the women's health and the medical bills incurred since their experience, called Bob Pratt, UFO reporter for the *National Enquirer,* with a dramatic proposal. Unilaterally, Black negotiated terms for the *Enquirer*'s exclusive rights to publish the potentially big abduction story in exchange for the paper's funding the costs of a professional investigation plus remuneration for the three women. The women, living in a veritable state of terror since their incident and wanting to know more of what had happened to them, agreed to be hypnotized on the terms set out by Black and the *Enquirer.*

On Friday, July 23, at the Brown Motel, in Liberty, the probe began. Jerry Black, Jim Miller, Peggy Schnell, and I met Dr. Sprinkle, Bob Pratt, Bryan Moss, a photographer from the Louis-ville *Courier Journal,* and James C. Young, a professional poly-graph examiner and detective for the Lexington-Fayette County Police Department. The three women, although apprehensive, had braced themselves for the ordeal to come.

On Friday afternoon and into the evening, Young conducted closed-door polygraph examinations. It was a long, trying session for each of the women, but Young, at first skeptical of their claims, announced that all three women, without a doubt, were telling the truth. He added, "They even stood up under the stress of being insulted when I falsely accused them of conspiracy."

At dusk, Louise Smith was the first to undergo hypnosis by Dr. Sprinkle. Her orderly revelations took her to the scene of the inci-dent, an open driveway abutted at each end by a rustic, weathered fieldstone column and adjoining wall. Beyond the entranceway was a narrow dirt road flanked by tall trees and, beyond that, open pastureland.

At the wall, Mrs. Smith recalled her car going out of control, then felt a tug pulling the vehicle backward, toward the wall's en-trance. Then she could recall only a "strange darkness," wherein she relived the intense heat burning her exposed flesh and a severe dryness in her throat. Throughout her initial hypnosis, her most impassioned pleas were for Mona, who had vanished. "It's all so strange," she said repeatedly, while holding her throat. Then she explained tearfully that she could not move her arms.

None of the three women could explain under their first hypno-sis what had happened at the wall. Each saw darkness, each expe-rienced intense heat that was evinced by spasms of writhing and agonized cries. And each felt the fearful emptiness of being alone, separated from her companions. Mrs. Thomas went further. She told of being confined in a netted, cocoon-like device which at her neck formed a noose. When she tried to protest, speak, or even think, the noose tightened. She also recalled an instrument shaped like a bullet, jabbing above her left breast. "I wanted to say some-thing," she gasped, holding her throat, "but the pressure tightened around my throat." Crying, she uttered, "Why? Why?"

It was the first time I had seen Mrs. Thomas break down. Crying convulsively, she continued to pull at her throat as though trying to relieve the pressure causing her pain. It was during this period that Mrs. Thomas saw two eyes above her. Her face grimacing, she described one eye as large, round, and blue; the other, almost black. "The lids of the eyes looked like a turtle's," she said, "but the lids were blue, just like that one eye." Further questions about the eyes, a face, or a body led to the recall of shadowy figures, about four feet tall. She said, "They just drift by me." At this point she was shown the drawing of humanoid heads, one of which Mrs. Stafford had identified for me in February as her abductor. *Mrs. Thomas pointed to the same head!*

Mona Stafford's story under her initial hypnosis also revealed a more detailed "eye" before her as she recalled being forced down into a sitting position. Then, with a sudden jerk and an outburst of crying, she shouted, "I feel all closed in . . . there's something around me . . . someone breathing around me . . . there's something over my face, looking at me. It's got eyes!" The eye—now referring to only one—was purple, with a light, like lightning, radiating from a mechanism in its center.

Under Mrs. Smith's second hypnosis she reiterated her physical weakness and dryness and described the painful pressure being applied to her arms and legs while she was being held down on a table. During this ordeal, she recalls, she received a message that she was not to reveal her experience. At the close of her fitful hypnotic trance, obviously enduring excruciating pain, she finally described seeing a "strange form," then, obscurely, several more around her. Frightened, she said she closed her eyes, promising her examiners that she "wouldn't tell."

Sprinkle's final hypnotic session brought back Mona Stafford to the chair. Taking notes at the side of each subject, I could feel the agonizing events falling into sequence. Again we tried to get a clearer picture of the actual abduction process. During the beginning of this session Mrs. Stafford sat for a long time in deep silence. Suddenly she burst out crying, so severely she could not speak. Tears rolled down her face onto her blouse. When the crying subsided, she spoke almost murmurously: "I feel so hot; feel so burned. . . . It's like a volcano maybe. . . . My eyes! . . . Feels like they're being pulled out . . . like inside a volcano . . . it's all dark . . . just the eye. . . . Oh, no!"

Mona Stafford then clutched her face with both hands and went on, with tears continuing to stream down her face.

"I see a web in front of me. . . . Something is all over me like water, but it's not wet. It burns. . . . I feel all pressed in. . . . I don't know; it feels like my stomach is blowing up. I'm in a light. . . . It's high up, and it's shining on my stomach. . . . My head! . . . I see something white. . . . They're pulling me . . . [more writhing and crying] . . . Something is going over me like a liquid. It clings to me like cloth over my legs. . . . It's dark. I see glass; it's all around me. . . . I can't move. . . . Feet are stuck to the floor. I can't see Lou or Elaine. . . . I'm burning up . . . [more severe crying]. . . . Take this off me. . . . I can't take it any more. . . . Oh, no, no! Don't, don't, don't! [A long silence, then ecstatic laughter.] "They're coming back—Elaine and Lou. We're in the car!"

Question: "How did you get back into the car?"

Mona Stafford: "I don't know."

On Sunday, July 25, Mrs. Stafford went to church, Mrs. Thomas went home feeling ill, and Mrs. Smith, who was asked to undergo another hypnotic session, refused. "All the money in Fort Knox," she said, "could not make me go through another hypnosis!"

On Sunday, before departing, we decided to have a final meeting in the "hypnosis room" of the motel. Mrs. Stafford seemed refreshed, her eyes more alive than I had ever seen them before.

As a lead question I asked her if she could recall what she meant by "being in a volcano."

Her response was prompt, unhesitating: "It was a long tunnel, dark inside with an opening at the top. It's clear now; at the end I can see an operating room. Everything is white, a white, round light shining on a white table, and I can see four small beings around the table. They have a tube on somebody's stomach . . . it's a woman there on the table, but I can't tell who it is. Maybe it's me on that table being examined."

During our stay in Liberty, we all drove to the scene of the incident at night. I held Mrs. Smith's arm as we approached the rustic wall. It looked medieval, forbidding, in the car's headlights surrounded by quiet darkness. Suddenly Mrs. Smith withdrew. "I can't face that dreaded wall," she exclaimed, and returned to sit in the car.

On July 29, I called Mrs. Smith, as promised, to check on her well-being and inquire if she had any unusual experiences to relate. Frightened and crying, she said she was sitting on her bed, alone, too ill to return to her job. "I'm glad you called," she said tearfully. "Last night I had a terrible experience, one you will never believe."

Mrs. Smith had returned to the dreaded wall near Stanford! She said she got up from a sound sleep, urged by a strong message she had received, dressed in jeans, and drove there . . . alone! "I couldn't resist the voice or whatever it was," she said. "It told me to go to the wall."

She said she stood at the wall for a long time, shaking in fear but unable to turn away. She saw nothing unusual, she said, but she felt a tugging at her hands. Suddenly, at 3:00 A.M., she found herself running back to her car, got in, and started to drive to nearby Stanford. While driving along in fearful relief, she glanced at her hand and discovered that her two rings were missing. A look at the other hand showed a ring to be missing from it, too. Completely undone and in desperation, she stopped at an all-night service laundromat in Stanford and called Mrs. Thomas, asking her to drive up and be with her. Mrs. Thomas was unable to rescue her friend, as her car was almost out of gas and no station was open. "Somehow I made it home," said Mrs. Smith. "I tried to get back to sleep, but couldn't!"

There was no explanation for the three missing rings. I asked all the logical questions; her replies were all logical. The rings, difficult to loosen unless soap-moistened, had not been removed since she had been hospitalized a few months prior. At the hospital a nurse had to help her remove them. The next day, she called the police. Officer Mike Cooley joined her at the site and searched. No rings!

A reminder, perhaps, or a warning from the aliens? Mrs. Smith pleaded for an answer.

As prearranged, on the return trip to Cincinnati on July 25, Black, Miller, Schnell, and I stopped at Mitchellsburg, Kentucky, about twenty-five miles north of Liberty, to check into another reported UFO incident.

On July 18, 1976, Mr. and Mrs. Charles Gilpin, eight-year-old Charles, Jr., and the Gilpins' infant son, while driving in their pickup truck, witnessed a low-level, soundless, disc-shaped object pacing them on a lonely road at 11:45 P.M. As the UFO, about seventy-five feet in diameter, came within thirty feet above his truck, Charles Gilpin said he lost control of the wheel. His speedometer, he said, looking at me, puzzled, *showed that his vehicle was going eighty-five miles per hour, but he was positive that his speed was not in excess of fifteen miles per hour as indicated by the slowly passing scenery.*

Gilpin said he grabbed the steering wheel so tightly to keep the truck on the road that his arms later became swollen and sore. As they approached a lighted farmhouse, Mrs. Gilpin and the children ran to it for safety. As she stood near the farmhouse door, she said, the UFO moved over the house and she said she could hear its humming sound and could feel a sharp breeze. Charles Gilpin said he felt as though he was "frozen" in his truck and was temporarily unable to join his family.

When the UFO moved away from the farmhouse, the Gilpins started home again. Nearing Gravel Switch, Kentucky, they saw eighteen people standing outdoors watching the UFO. It moved across the farmlands at low level and finally disappeared into infinity.

A troubled Louise Smith wonders about the meaning of her missing rings; and I, as a researcher, look back over twenty-seven years to scan my own investigation of thousands of incredible cases, such as the Gilpins', and to ponder my own nearly disastrous incident near Iwo Jima. Surely there is an answer somewhere in the realm of space and time which man's mind cannot yet understand.

In a "Situation Red," the only certainty is the uncertainty of what may happen next.

Appendix I

MAJOR INTERNATIONAL UFO RESEARCH GROUPS

Walter Andrus, Director
Mutual UFO Network (MUFON)
103 Oldtowne Road
Sequin, Texas 78155

Dr. J. Allen Hynek, Director
Center for UFO Studies (CUFOS)
924 Chicago Avenue
Evanston, Illinois 60202

Dr. Dennis W. Hauck, Director
International UFO Registry (IUFOR)
P. O. Box 1004
Hammond, Indiana 46325

William Spaulding, Director
Ground Saucer Watch (GSW)
13238 North 7th Drive
Phoenix, Arizona 85029

Ray Stanford, Director
Project Starlight International (PSI)
P. O. Box 5310
Austin, Texas 78763

James Lorenzen, Director
Aerial Phenomena Research Organization (APRO)
3910 East Kleindale Road
Tucson, Arizona 85712

John Acuff, Director
National Investigations Committee on Aerial Phenomena (NICAP)
3535 University Blvd., West
Kensington, Maryland 20795

Appendix II

COMPUTER TESTING:
Image-enhancement Technology Applied to
Anomalous-phenomenon Photographs

Modern technology utilizes all types of pictures, or images, as sources of information for interpretation and analysis. These include portions of the earth's surface viewed from an orbiting satellite to chromosomes viewed through a microscope. The proliferation of these bases of pictorial data has created the need for a vision-based automation that can rapidly and accurately extract the useful information contained in these images. These requirements are being met with the new technology of image processing.

Image processing combines computer applications with modern image scanning techniques to perform various forms of image enhancement, distortion correction, pattern recognition, pixel (picture cell) analysis for distance factors, and object measurements.

UFO photographs are being evaluated with this new technology to determine the authenticity of the image and gain additional data that can verify the photographer's claims. Some of this data includes: a true display of the image's edges and surface(s), a pseudo-three-dimensional display of the image's shape, accurate digital densitometry, and the image's luminosity and factored distance measurements from all features in the photograph.

Finally, the original picture is computerized (digitized) to enhance the photo for any of the previous obscure details. Simply stated, the computerized end product will supply an enhanced reconstruction of the original image or a numeric/graphic report that relates all the specific data contained in the image.

WILLIAM H. SPAULDING, Director, Ground Saucer Watch, Inc.
Phoenix, Arizona
(Computerized Outputs by Spatial Data Systems)

Appendix III

Observations and Conclusions Regarding the Investigation of the UFO Experience of Ms. Smith, Ms. Stafford, and Ms. Thomas

BY R. LEO SPRINKLE, PH.D.

INTRODUCTION

The UFO experience of the witnesses, which occurred on January 6, 1976, came to my attention through the Aerial Phenomena Research Organization. I was asked to travel to Liberty, Kentucky, at APRO's expense, to learn if hypnotic regression procedures might be helpful to the witnesses in recalling the events of the loss-of-time experience following the UFO sighting.

It was agreed that I could serve as consultant to APRO and the Cincinnati group of investigators represented by Leonard Stringfield, director of public relations for MUFON. However, only a short time was possible for us to consider hypnotic investigation, and Ms. Mona Stafford found that the experience of regressing to the UFO sighting was unsettling to her.

Nevertheless, it was agreed by all who attended that initial session that more information probably would be obtained through hypnotic regression techniques, and discussion was initiated about how that might be accomplished.

It was with some surprise to me that it was decided that the women could now offer their story to the *National Enquirer*, since earlier discussions dealt with the wish that there should be little publicity; however, because of medical expenses, and concern about the anxiety stemming from the UFO experience, the women decided it was better to make sure that the investigation was complete. They agreed that the results of the complete investigation would be legally theirs to disseminate as they wish, assuming that the *National Enquirer* is willing to pay funds for the investigation and for releasing the story of the UFO experience.

I was asked, and I agreed, to serve as a consultant to the *National Enquirer* with the understanding that my report would be shared with APRO and the group of MUFON UFO investigators.

OBSERVATIONS

The results of the polygraph examination, by James C. Young, supported my initial impression that the women are truthful and that they are describing their experience in a sincere and open manner. The results of the hypnotic investigations are quite dramatic, although they are consistent with what we know about other UFO encounters, as well as consistent with the impressions we have about the women as individuals. I have asked the women to complete some personality inventories and a vocational-interest inventory; after they have had an opportunity to review my interpretation of results, I will ask them if they are willing to release the results of the inventories.

Ms. Louise Smith. Louise was willing to consider the use of hypnotic regression techniques; it was apparent in the early session that she was compliant in following the suggestions for relaxing deeply and for concentrating on each separate procedure. She appeared to experience a trance state which permitted deeper relaxation, although her anxiety about the UFO experience was great and she suffered much as she relived the experience. The behaviors, e.g. weeping, moaning, tossing her head, shuddering and shaking, etc., were evident to those of us who observed her, especially as she seemed to "relive" an experience of a fluid material covering her face. Her smile and evident relief in "seeing the street light" at the end of her hour-and-one-half loss-of-time experience was dramatic and indicated that she was "safe" in the car once again and returning home with her friends. Although she did not experience many impressions during the first session, it was apparent that she was beginning to recall more impressions of what appeared to be an abduction and examination; however, there is no impression that permits us to speculate on how she was removed from the car and how she was placed back into the car.

An interesting side issue is in regard to the behavior of her pet parakeet, which—according to Louise's claims and the claims of the MUFON group who observed the bird—refused to have anything to do with her after the UFO experience. Len Stringfield and Jim Miller indicated that they could come close to the bird and it would not react wildly; however, whenever Louise came close to the bird, it would flutter and move away from her. The bird died within weeks after the UFO experience; it is puzzling to speculate on the possible conditions that resulted in the bird's strange behavior and eventual death.

Ms. Mona Stafford. Mona had expressed trepidation about hypnotic techniques, but she also indicated that she had been experiencing a great deal of anxiety following the UFO sighting. Thus, she seemed to be willing to follow hypnotic procedures if there was some possibility that her symptoms would be alleviated. She had experienced skin sensitivity and redness around her eyes, according to her earlier description of the post-UFO experience. She said that she had gone to her family physician, who then suggested that she use eye drops for her eyes. She said that a red mark could be seen on the left side of her neck; she experienced some of the same symptoms as the other witnesses, including a feeling of fatigue, nausea, vomiting, and diarrhea.

She responded well to the hypnotic suggestions, and she was able to describe impressions that led her to believe that she was alone on a white table or bed. She saw a large "eye," which seemed to be observing her. She felt as though a bright white light was shining on her, and that there was "power" or energy that transfixed her and held her to the table or bed. She experienced a variety of physiological reactions, including the impressions that her right arm was pinned or fastened, her left leg forced back under her with pain to the ankle and foot, pressure on the fingers of the left hand as if they were forced or squeezed in some way, and a feeling of being examined by four or five short humanoids who sat around in "surgical masks" and "surgical garments" while observing her. At one point, she sensed that she was either experiencing out-of-the-body travel or else she was waiting outside of a large room in which she could view another person, probably a woman, lying on a white bed or observation table. She perceived a long tunnel or a view of the sky, as if she had been transported to an area inside a large mountain or volcano. Although she wept and moaned and experienced a great deal of fatigue as a result of the "reliving" of the experience, she felt better the next day; she expressed the belief to me that she now had a better understanding of what happened during the loss-of-time experience. She expressed appreciation for the assistance to her, because she now believes that—although she did not like the experience and regarded it as bothersome in many ways—she recognizes that she did go through the experience and was "returned." Thus, she believes that it is best that she release the repressed emotional material associated with the UFO experience.

Ms. Elaine Thomas. Ms. Thomas had been rather quiet during the initial interview, in February 1976, although it was obvious that she is perceptive and aware of other people's attitudes and feelings. Like the others, she has lost weight, but she also has experienced some personality changes. She dresses a bit more colorfully now, and she is much more willing to talk and to share her ideas with others. She, too, experienced a similar reaction during the hypnotic techniques: she apparently was responding well to suggestions to go deeper; when she "relived" the UFO experience, she experienced a great deal of emotional reaction. Her main impression was that she was taken away from her two friends and that she was placed in a "chamber" with a window on the side. She seemed to recall figures that moved back and forth in front of the window of the chamber, as if she were being observed. Her impression was that the observers were four-foot-tall humanoids with dark eyes and gray skin. One disturbing aspect of the experience was the memory that she had some kind of contraption or "covering" that was placed around her neck; whenever she tried to speak, or think, the contraption or covering was tightened and she experienced a choking sensation. At first, Ms. Thomas interpreted the memories as indication that she was being choked by hands or that she was being prevented from calling out to her friends; later, however, she came to the tentative conclusion that an experiment was being conducted, an experiment to learn more about her intellectual and emotional processes. She recalled a "bullet-shaped" object, about an inch and one half in diameter, being placed on her left chest; she had experienced pain and a red spot at that location.

SIMILARITIES AND DIFFERENCES OF IMPRESSIONS

During the polygraph examination and during the initial hypnotic sessions, each UFO witness was interviewed separately from the other witnesses. After the initial description of impressions, the women were invited to attend the additional hypnosis sessions, so that each woman could observe the reactions of the other two women. During these sessions, there was much emotional reaction, which seemed to arise from two conditions: the compassion of the witnesses for their friend who was "reliving" the experience and releasing emotional reactions to the experience; also, it seems as if the description by one witness would "trigger" a memory on the part of another witness, whether the experiences seemed to be "similar" or "different."

Certain similarities were observed: a feeling of anxiety on the part of each witness regarding a specific aspect of the experience. For Ms. Smith it was the "wall" and the "gate" beyond which she was afraid to "move" psychologically; for Ms. Stafford it was the "eye" she had observed and the impression that something "evil" or "bad" would be learned if she allowed the eye to "control" her; for Ms. Thomas it was the "blackness" that seemed to be the feared condition or cause for anxiety. Each woman seemed to experience the impression that she had been taken out of the car and placed elsewhere without her friends and without verbal communication. For Ms. Smith, the lack of verbal communication was most distressing, although she had the feeling of "mental communication" that she would be returned after the "experiment."

Differences were noted in that each woman seemed to have a somewhat different kind of "examination" and in a different "location." Ms. Smith did not have a clear impression of the location, although she did recall a feeling of lying down and being examined; Ms. Stafford had the impression of being in a "volcano or mountain," with a room in which a bright light was shining on a white table with white-clothed persons or humanoids sitting around and observing her; Ms. Thomas recalled impressions of being in the dark chamber with gray light permitting a view of the humanoids who were apparently observing her.

CONCLUSIONS

In my opinion, each woman is describing a "real" experience, and they are using their intelligence and perceptivity as accurately as possible in order to describe the impressions they obtained during the hypnotic regression session. Although there is uncertainty about their impressions, especially in regard to how each person could be transported out of the car and relocated in the car, the impressions during the "loss-of-time" experience are similar to those of other UFO witnesses who apparently have experienced an abduction and examination during their UFO sighting.

Although it is not possible to claim absolutely that a physical examination and abduction has taken place, I believe that the tentative hypothesis of abduction and examination is the best hypothesis to explain the apparent loss-of-time experience, the apparent physical and emotional reactions of the witnesses to the UFO sighting, and the anxiety and the reactions of the witnesses to their experiences which occurred after their UFO sighting. An interesting subsequent event is the concern of the women that they were "re-experiencing" the physical symptoms that had been experienced for several days following the January 1976 sightings.

In my opinion, the UFO experiences of these women are a good example of the type of apparent abduction and examination that seems to be occurring to more and more UFO witnesses. I believe that the investigation could be continued with the hopes of obtaining further information about their experiences. However, the present evidence suggests to me that the women have co-operated sincerely and openly in describing their reactions to their UFO sightings and loss-of-time experience, and the polygraph examination and hypnotic regression sessions have been useful in uncovering their impressions of the UFO sighting and subsequent events.

I believe the case is a good example of UFO experiences because of the number and character of the witnesses, because of the excellent primary investigation by the MUFON group, and because of the results of further investigation through polygraph examinations and hypnotic regression sessions.

Respectfully submitted,

R. Leo Sprinkle, Ph.D., Director
The Division of Counseling & Testing
Associate Professor of Psychology
The University of Wyoming

Appendix IV

DEPARTMENT OF THE AIR FORCE
WASHINGTON 20330

OFFICE OF THE SECRETARY   June 10, 1976

Dear Senator Goldwater:

This is in reply to your recent inquiry pertaining to the existence of "above Top Secret" information on unidentified flying objects (UFOs). Mr. Leonard H. Stringfield wrote to you concerning the matter.

Officials in Air Force Headquarters have reviewed Mr. Stringfield's request. No "above Top Secret" information pertaining to UFOs exists within the Air Force, including Wright-Patterson AFB, Ohio. Also, there is no code-named Air Force agency which holds any information concerning UFOs. We have no record or knowledge of any Air Force officer recently declaring any information pertaining to UFOs to be Top Secret or above in classification. Further, there is no involvement by the Air Force with NATO forces or other foreign governments concerning UFOs.

As you may recall, on December 17, 1969, the Secretary of the Air Force announced the termination of Project Blue Book, the Air Force program for the investigation of UFOs. With the termination of Project Blue Book, the Air Force regulation establishing and controlling the program for investigating and analyzing UFOs was rescinded. Since the termination of Project Blue Book, no evidence has been presented to indicate that further investigation of UFOs by the Air Force is warranted. In view of the considerable Air Force commitments of resources in the past, and the current extreme pressure on Air Force funds, there is no likelihood of renewed Air Force involvement in this area at this time. The entire collection of Project Blue Book is now unclassified and has been permanently transferred to the

Modern Military Branch, National Archives and Records Service, 8th and Pennsylvania Avenue, N.W., Washington, D.C. 20408, and is available for public review and analysis.

We appreciate your interest in this matter. However, since the Air Force is not involved in UFO studies, we are unable to be of assistance to Mr. Stringfield.

Sincerely,

Thomas S. Collins, Lt. Colonel, USAF
Congressional Inquiry Division
Office of Legislative Liaison

Attachment
Honorable Barry Goldwater
United States Senate

Appendix V

ARGENTINE AIR ATTACHÉ   WASHINGTON, D.C.

                                                      May 9th, 1955

Leonard H. Stringfield
Director
Civilian Research Interplanetary Flying Objects
7017 Britton Avenue
Cincinnati 27, Ohio

Dear Mr. Stringfield:

Reference is made to your letter dated February 1st, 1955.

Enclosed herewith you will find the information requested by you concerning Unidentified Flying Objects sighted in my country.

In return for this information I would like to have some of the ones you have collected.

                                    •   Sincerely yours,

                                              Saturnino G. Armenanzas
                                              Brigadier General
                                              Air Attaché

(This letter suggests international interest in the UFO puzzle. Attached to this letter was a report of a UFO seen over Córdoba Airport in 1954.)